Angel Meadow

Angel Meadow
Victorian Britain's Most Savage Slum

Dean Kirby

PEN & SWORD
HISTORY

First published in Great Britain in 2016 by
Pen & Sword History
an imprint of
Pen & Sword Books Ltd
47 Church Street
Barnsley
South Yorkshire
S70 2AS

Cover photograph of Mincing Street, Angel Meadow, courtesy of Manchester Libraries, Information and Archives, Manchester City Council. Map of Angel Meadow courtesy of the Digital Archives Association.

ISBN 9781783831524

Typeset in Ehrhardt by
Replika Press Pvt Ltd, India
Printed and bound in England by
CPI UK

Pen & Sword Books Ltd incorporates the imprints of Pen & Sword Archaeology, Atlas, Aviation, Battleground, Discovery, Family History, History, Maritime, Military, Naval, Politics, Railways, Select, Social History, Transport, True Crime and Claymore Press, Frontline Books, Leo Cooper, Praetorian Press, Remember When, Seaforth Publishing and Wharncliffe.

For a complete list of Pen & Sword titles please contact
PEN & SWORD BOOKS LIMITED
47 Church Street, Barnsley, South Yorkshire, S70 2AS, England
E-mail: enquiries@pen-and-sword.co.uk
Website: www.pen-and-sword.co.uk

And though it be long since the daisies grew,
Where Irk and Irwell flew,
If human love springs up anew
And angels come and go,
What matters it that the skies were blue
A hundred years ago.

(From *The Irwell and the Mersey* by Bessie Rayner Parkes, 1863.)

For my son, Thomas.

Author's note: Every story in this book is drawn from real events that took place in and around Manchester's Angel Meadow slum more than a century ago. The people in the book are real Mancunians – the ancestors of people who inhabit the city today – and their spoken words are printed here just as they were recorded by Victorian newspaper journalists, police officers, teachers, missionaries, magistrates and other social observers.

Contents

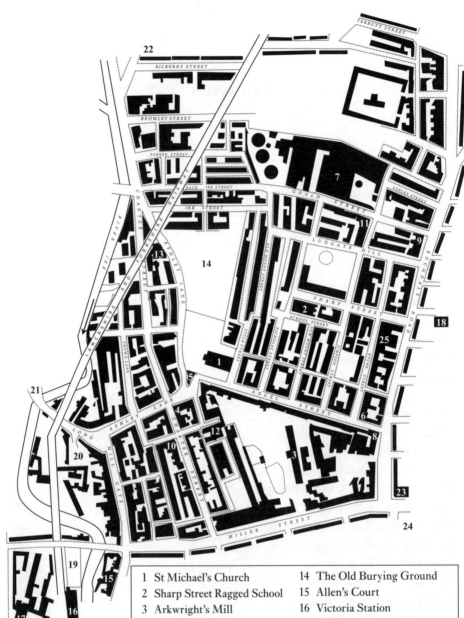

1 St Michael's Church	14 The Old Burying Ground
2 Sharp Street Ragged School	15 Allen's Court
3 Arkwright's Mill	16 Victoria Station
4 St Michael's Tavern	17 Manchester Workhouse
5 The Old Victory	18 Goulden Street Police Station
6 The Angel Tavern	19 Walker's Croft Cemetery
7 The Gas Works	20 Gibraltar
8 Kane's Lodging House	21 Red Bank
9 Downey's Arms Shop	22 Irish Town
10 Cabbage Ann's Den	23 Cholera Hospital
11 Bob Horridge's Hideout	24 Smithfield Market
12 The Rest Lodging House	25 Parker's Mill
13 Charter Street Ragged School	

Preface: Going underground

I became fascinated by Angel Meadow when I discovered that my Victorian forefather had been among the 30,000 souls who lived there. He was a farm labourer called William Kirby, who fled to Manchester from County Mayo on the rugged west coast of Ireland in the mid-1860s, after surviving the Great Famine.

As I trawled the city's archives for clues about William's life, I began to drift off to Angel Meadow in my imagination. I descended into damp cellars in search of him, stumbled through backyard pigsties and came face to face with scarred and tattooed scuttlers in the slum's smoke-filled beer houses. I learned that new arrivals to Angel Meadow were forced to sleep naked with strangers in dingy lodging houses, cockroaches were welcomed because they ate the bed bugs and skulls were kicked around during games of football in a graveyard packed with the bodies of 40,000 paupers.

The more I read, the more astonished I became by my ancestor's battle for survival which led, more than a century later, to my own existence in the city that his blood, sweat and tears helped to create. I eventually stumbled upon the location of his house in Charter Street, one of the slum's forgotten thoroughfares, using old maps and rent books.

Then, in February 2012, archaeologists searching for evidence of the slum at the site of the Co-operative's new headquarters off Miller Street made an astonishing discovery – my ancestor's home. They gave me permission to visit the site during the filming of a TV series on British history. On a rain-soaked Saturday morning, I clambered down a metal ladder like a time traveller and reached out to touch the bricks of William Kirby's fireplace. Peering into the gloom, I could see that the walls of his 10ft square house were only half a brick thick. The archaeologists had found metal hinges, fragments of wooden door frames, broken bottles and, amazingly, a door key. They also found the privy William had shared with 100 other people.

Sadness swept over me as I stood in the bowels of the earth and thought about my ancestors. Only three of William's seven children survived to adulthood. The departed included his fifth child, who died in that same house in February 1877. The baby, named William after his father, was just two weeks old and his death was caused by convulsions brought on by a fever. By coincidence, the archaeological dig began on the anniversary of his birth and lasted only slightly longer than his short life.

The bricks and mortar could tell me nothing of the grief that would have filled that house all those years ago. William, who could not write, signed his mark on his son's death certificate in a shaky hand.

I left the dig with a brick from William's fireplace – still covered in soot from the fire that had kept him warm on a similarly wintry day. I knew then that the story of Angel Meadow had to be told.

Dean Kirby,
Manchester, 2016.

Prologue: Firestorm

On Saturday, 6 May 1893, the sun blazed in the heavens and the backstreets of Manchester were hotter than the boulevards of Paris. Spring had arrived early with an unflinching spell of dry weather – the start of Britain's longest drought. Crops would fail, cattle would starve and Manchester Corporation would take the frightening step of shutting off the city's water taps to conserve supplies and prevent a famine.

But at dusk that day, the sun turned pale as it slipped from the slate roofs and chimney stacks of Angel Meadow and the heat of the day was replaced by a deepening chill. Thomas Matthews, 28, buttoned up his waistcoat and jacket as he stepped heavily out of the Exile of Erin beer house in Nicholas Street. Two layers of tweed, a billycock hat, some facial hair and a bellyful of ale would help keep out the chill as he staggered home. They were comforts of sorts to a man whose lungs were scarred by bronchitis. At least the cool night air had diluted the cocktail of smells from Angel Meadow's gasworks, tanneries, boneyards and privies, which had been overwhelming in the midday heat.

Matthews sniffed the air and set off. Lodging houses gaped from all sides as he turned down the slope of Angel Street, one of the slum's main inroads. Their patrons glided like ghosts out of alleyways and disappeared into the cavernous doorways. The gaunt bell tower of St Michael's Church loomed above them in silhouette. In the Old Burying Ground next to the church, the flagstones covering the mass graves of thousands of paupers were pewter grey. The slum's factories, back-to-back houses and smoke-blackened railway arches stood silent and in shadow. Angel Street's four gas lanterns gave off a jaundiced light.

It was almost 11pm. Soon the landlords of the gin palaces would be calling last orders. When the gasworks clock struck midnight, it would herald the start of Matthews' day of rest.

He would have one cherished day of respite until Monday, when he would rise before the sun and trudge back up Angel Street towards the teeming passageways of Smithfield Market, where he worked as a porter. Competition for work among the stalls piled with fish, rabbits, turnips, cabbages and other produce was fierce and often turned violent – a tough job for hard men. Soon Matthews would be climbing the three stone steps to the front door of his rented tenement in Old Mount Street and then up the wooden staircase to lie with his wife, Mary Ann. Their five-year-old daughter, Margaret, would hopefully be asleep.

Matthews heard the women's screams before he spied them in the darkness as he rounded the corner. Ellen Philbin and Kate Lyons, two factory hands dressed in clogs and shawls, were causing an uproar in the street. Lyons, 28, had been banging on Matthews' door for ten minutes, shouting that he had savagely beaten her brother. Tommy Lyons, 27, worked in a cotton mill. He and Kate came from a large and troublesome family in Nicholas Street, near the Exile of Erin. Tommy Lyons had threatened to 'do' Thomas Matthews after they had come to blows the previous weekend. Now their simmering feud was being turned into a vendetta by Kate Lyons.

Mary Ann Matthews finally threw open the door and screamed that her husband was out and she had nothing to do with it. "Oh no," shouted Lyons. "He had a _____ cheek to take advantage of our Tommy."

Matthews' brother, Patrick, who lived around the corner, had heard the commotion and was now on the doorstep defending Mary Ann. He warned Lyons and Philbin to 'drop it' and let the men settle their differences in the proper way – with a fair fight in the Old Burying Ground. But Lyons stood her ground. "When I get hold of him," she shouted, "I'll knock off his big-headed pig's head for hitting my brother."

Lyons and Philbin were still arguing with Patrick and Mary Ann when they saw Thomas Matthews coming down the street. Lyons flew at him like a banshee. She punched him in the face with such force that he was sent spinning to the ground. Philbin, 30, gave Matthews a huge 'clout' with her fist and then slipped off one of her clogs and smashed it on the right side of his head.

Patrick Matthews pushed the two women away. He lifted his brother from the cobbles and began to drag him home. It was then that Philbin cried out the fateful order: "Get Henry!" Lyons disappeared into the shadows as she went in search of Ellen Philbin's brother Henry Burgess – the most feared man in Angel Meadow.

Aged just 21 and only 5ft tall, Henry Burgess was 'one of the worst characters in Manchester', according to a senior police inspector. He possessed distinctive piercing, steel-coloured eyes and wore his brown hair closely shaved. He worked as a labourer and flitted between the slum's lodging houses. Burgess was also a notorious street fighter or 'scuttler' and in just three years had amassed 15 convictions for crimes including assault, theft, burglary, shop-breaking, and rioting. Eleven of his convictions were for assaults on police officers.

Thomas Matthews sat down heavily on the top step outside his house and waited, trying to recover his breath. He had grown up in Angel Meadow and had lived in the same street now for more than 20 years. The slum he knew was a strange and disorderly world governed by thieves and beggars, where 'tommy' shops sold ribs and pea soup at a penny a pint, where druggists gave opium to mothers to quiet their crying babies, and where pawnbrokers loaned money to the poor so they could buy drink.

Beer houses such as the Exile of Erin, named after a mournful ballad of Irish emigration, were dens for gangs of conmen and pickpockets who slipped back into the Meadow at night after a day spent thieving in the city. They were the rendezvous, one Victorian writer claimed, of the elder thieves, the fighting men, the swindlers and the mutilated beggars.

But the slum was Matthews' home. He could stand up for himself and had fought for his place in the pecking order. Before earning his market porter's licence, he had worked as a blacksmith's striker. His Irish-born wife Mary Ann, 29, was a seamstress. Together they earned just enough to cover the weekly rent of three shillings and nine pence for the three-room house they shared with another family. The houses in Old Mount Street were situated higher up than those down the hill in neighbouring Style Street and were built almost on top of them. According to one writer: 'These houses of two tiers hold an enormous quantity of food for fever. Each room is let out as a separate tenement and each holds a family – sometimes even two.'

Matthews had no time to recover as he sat on the steps. Three men suddenly ran into Old Mount Street from a covered passageway leading to Nicholas Street. Henry Burgess, known as Harry to his relatives, was with two of Ellen Philbin's neighbours, Peter Ford and James Brady, who were both in their thirties. Philbin pointed a bony finger at Matthews and cried: "That's him!"

Burgess wasted no time. He ran up to Matthews and punched him on the side of his face. Matthews went inside and removed his jacket and waistcoat, ready for a fight. When he rushed back into the street, he was surprised to find that Burgess and his accomplices had disappeared back through the arch that marked the entrance to the passage. Patrick grabbed him by the arm and dragged him to the nearest place of safety, their mother's house a few doors away.

It must have only seemed like seconds before Burgess and his thugs returned. They were marching in a torch-lit procession down the passageway – their clogs echoing like the sound of marching soldiers. Burgess was at the front, carrying a large paraffin lantern he had grabbed from his sister's parlour.

Matthews eyed them from his mother's doorway. A mob of about 40 people had now gathered in the street. A quick-thinking woman named Elizabeth Mulholland realised what was about to happen and tried to snatch the lantern from Burgess' hands, but Ellen Philbin pulled her back by the hair and punched her in the mouth. Mary Bourke, a mother with a baby in her arms, tried to snuff out the lantern flame with her shawl, but the mob ripped the shawl from her grasp and she never saw it again. Burgess called her a cow and shouted: "I'll do for you as well as them!" Philbin, now armed with a brass candlestick, grabbed Bourke's hair and pulled her to the ground.

Then Burgess walked up to the house. He planted his feet on the ground, shook the lantern to make it burn brighter – and launched it. The globe-shaped glass bowl of the lantern smashed into the brickwork at the side of the doorway and burst into pieces, raining burning paraffin down on Thomas Matthews. In seconds, Matthews became a human fireball. He rolled down the steps as Patrick fought to put out the flames with his coat. His screams echoed across the slum as his clothes melted to his skin.

Burgess and the rest of the mob fled into the darkness. Jim Healy, 31, who lodged with Matthews' mother, and a bystander named Margaret Gilmore were also splashed with burning paraffin and suffered burns. Patrick wrapped his brother in his mother's bedspread and ran for the constables.

Matthews was taken to the infirmary in a horse-drawn ambulance shortly before midnight. He died from shock and burns at 6.40am – one hour after sunrise on what should have been his day of rest. His widow Mary Ann had to identify her husband's charred remains.

The inquest began at 11am the next day. Burgess was arrested by the great Manchester detective Jerome Caminada, but claimed he had only meant to 'frighten' Thomas Matthews. Brady, Ford, Philbin and Lyons were also caught. Newspaper journalists lapped up every morsel of detail from the court case – a fresh outrage in Angel Meadow. After examining the blackened remains of the lantern, the jury returned a verdict of manslaughter against Burgess, Lyons and Philbin, but the women were later acquitted because there was too little evidence to convict them. Philbin denied everything, claiming: "I don't remember being there or seeing the lamp." Ford was jailed for a month. Brady was discharged.

Henry Burgess admitted manslaughter and was jailed for just 12 months with hard labour for his 'reckless' behaviour. Burgess told the court: "The lamp didn't hit him. I knew where I was throwing it. If I'd wanted to hit him, I could've done. I've nothing else to say except that I was stupid drunk." The prison sentence failed to teach Burgess a lesson. Just days after being released from prison, he ambushed a police officer named William Corns in the same passageway off Old Mount Street where he had attacked Matthews. He smashed Corns on the head with a poker and tried to evade capture by removing his clogs so he could run silently though the streets of Angel Meadow. He warned Corns: "Your time has come. I'm going to settle you."

There was one remaining voice in the story, that of Thomas Matthews. Hugh Wilson Clarke, the infirmary surgeon, said that he 'rapidly sank' before he died, but was able to give a statement despite the burns to his lips and tongue. Matthews' words were immortalised in black newspaper ink: "I am burnt very much. Burgess is a young man. I don't know where he lives – he lives anywhere – in lodging houses." Matthews ended his statement by making a terrible prophesy as he lay in his hospital bed waiting for the sunrise: "I am very ill, and I believe I am going to die."

Violence was so commonplace in Angel Meadow that the chief constable had already doubled patrols in the slum after 10pm, but the extra officers had failed to prevent Matthews' death. Several policemen had passed Old Mount Street in the ten minutes before and after the attack, but had seen 'nothing unusual'. They kept such a regular beat that Burgess would have known when they were due to pass, giving him a 20-minute window in which to kill Matthews.

An anonymous writer who dubbed himself 'The Scout' described the slum during that hot summer of 1893:

> The dreary wastes of Angel Meadow. Down Angel Street, with its pestiferous lodging houses, with its bawds and bullies, its thieves and beggars, one had need to visit such a place when the sun is high in the heavens. When night falls I had rather enter an enemy's camp during the time of war than venture near such dens of infamy and wretchedness. But the poor live here and die here.

There would be no break in the hot weather for ten days after Thomas Matthews' death. But on Tuesday, 16 May, a soft, warm rain finally fell on the back streets of Manchester. The raindrops washed down the faces of the lodging houses, the factories, the yards and the smoke-blackened railway arches of Angel Meadow. They washed over the gaunt tower of St Michael's Church and over the grey flagstones covering the unmarked graves in the slum's old cemetery.

The raindrops also washed over the newly-scorched cobblestones outside a rented tenement in Old Mount Street, where a young widow was quietly weeping.

Chapter 1

Savages

A ngel Meadow's reputation as Victorian Britain's most savage slum was forged by Henry Burgess and an army of thugs like him, who terrorised their neighbours and even the police. By the spring of 1893, violence and poverty had become ingrained in the bricks and mortar of the slum's lodging houses, factories and beer shops.

A journalist from the *Manchester Guardian* revealed the extent of the violence during a visit to Angel Meadow:

> Doors are torn from their hinges – evidence of the fierce struggles they once shut in or shut out. Now they are powerless to do either and are simply propped up against their frames, and offer no shelter or protection from violence. It is all free fighting here. Even some of the windows do not open, so it is useless to cry for help. Dampness and misery, violence and wrong, have left their handwriting in perfectly legible characters on the walls.

Readers of the *Guardian* may have given an involuntary shudder when they read about Burgess and Matthews, perhaps as they cracked open boiled eggs in the breakfast parlours of Manchester's genteel suburbs. Angel Meadow was more alien to them than the jungles of uncharted Africa, but the ill-named slum was part of a world that they had created – a heart of darkness in the world's first industrial city.

Victorian Manchester was the marvel of its age – celebrated for its ingenuity, guts and swagger. The city's factory owners made astonishing riches by turning a small textile town into 'Cottonopolis' – the powerhouse of the Industrial Revolution. Soon Manchester's wares were being shipped to distant shores across the British Empire. It was said that cloth produced in Manchester was worn in Siberia, Africa and China, and even clothed the Indian squaw in Canada's Rocky Mountains. Yet, the rain-soaked city of mills, warehouses, furnaces and chimney stacks was stinking, noisy and dangerous for the 300,000 souls who fed its machines – a Jekyll and Hyde city of blinding wealth and binding poverty.

The French writer Alexis de Tocqueville explained to Parisians in 1832 that Manchester was a 'watery land of palaces and hovels', where 'pure gold flowed from a raw sewer' and civilised man was 'turned back almost into a savage'. He marvelled at the shrieking boilers, beating cotton looms, crunching machinery and the streets strewn with necklaces of stagnant puddles.

Manchester was a place in which crowds were constantly in a hurry – their faces sombre and harsh. 'A sort of black smoke covers the city,' de Tocqueville wrote. 'Under this half daylight, 300,000 human beings are ceaselessly at work. A thousand noises disturb this damp, dark labyrinth, but they are not at all the ordinary sounds one hears in great cities.' Another writer, German visitor Johanna Schopenhauer, felt that Manchester resembled a huge forge or workshop and was permanently dark and smoky from coal vapours: 'Work, profit and greed seem to be the only thoughts here. The clatter of the mills and the looms can be heard everywhere.'

Manchester's middle classes saw themselves as separate from the workers, who faced a daily fight for survival as the cotton empire was built upon their backs. The well-off lived far beyond the city gates, leaving Manchester in the hands of an overstretched police force at night and fleeing in their horse-drawn carriages to villas in the suburbs far beyond the curtain of acid rain and smoke.

By day, the rich paraded their wealth in the stock exchange, banks, chambers and brilliantly-lit shops of Manchester's grand commercial district, beyond which stood their cavernous warehouses and mills with their cinder-paved yards and chimneys. The slums stretched like a girdle around the edge of this gilded inner city. An Angel Meadow ragged school teacher said that the slums formed a 'dark tide of misery and wretchedness' stretching around the 'centre of wealth'. An investigative journalist, Angus Reach, said they were home to the 'great mass of smoky, dingy, sweltering and toiling Manchester' and noted that their inmates lived in wretched, damp and filthy cottages – mere dens and caves. There were streets so narrow that daylight could not penetrate them unless the sun was directly overhead.

Angel Meadow was the worst slum of all. A wild and brutal borderland at the northern edge of the city, it was home to more than 30,000 souls, many of them Irish immigrants, who were sucked into a rabbit warren of streets covering an area of less than a square mile. Like Whitechapel in London and the Five Points in New York, Angel Meadow's reputation was born in its damp lodging houses, airless cellars and back alleys. But the narrow streets and courts of the Meadow were far more terrifying, filthier and deadlier than the worst rookeries of the East End or Lower Manhattan.

In 1888, the death rate in Whitechapel was 21.8 per 1,000 people, while in Manhattan it was was 25.1. In the same year, Angel Meadow had the worst death rate in England, at 31.9. Rescue workers from Whitechapel were shocked when they travelled to Angel Meadow. *The Manchester Guardian* said the slum was more dangerous than St Giles and a tough New York police officer was robbed and badly beaten when he spent a terrifying night in the slum in 1898.

The men who lived in Angel Meadow were malnourished and short, squat and sallow. They wore heavy cotton clothes that soaked up the rain and stiffened like sheets of armour in the cold. The women were stunted and pale, and clad in dingy dresses and dark shawls flaked with specks of cotton. Their outfits were made from 'devil's dust' – cheap cloth which grew threadbare in a fortnight. The slum's Irish inmates mended their clothes with so many patches that the original colours could not be detected and they also had the dubious distinction of having introduced the custom of going barefoot.

One writer described how life passed in the slum: 'Born in misery, the inhabitant of the slum passes on uncared for, the record of his life being written chiefly in previous convictions and the last official notice taken of him is with a piece of blue paper inscribed with his name, pinned to his breast, as with a white sheet over him, he lies on a stone slab in the dead house of the workhouse.'

Wanderers stepped off steam trains at the nearby Victoria Station and made the short walk to an unsafe harbour in the slum's gaudily-painted lodging houses. There they laid down their heads for a fearful first night in beds shared with strangers – some sleeping naked because removing their clothes and hiding them under the pillow was the only way to keep them free from bed bugs. Those who survived those first few nights burrowed underground into hot, airless cellars or paid extortionate rents for ramshackle back-to-backs, where damp soaked into their bones and tuberculosis scarred their lungs. Armies of rats roamed the streets at night, following their leader from one factory to the next.

The slum stood on a low hillside leading down to a sluggish, black and sewage-filled river, the Irk, which bubbled with sulphurous gasses. Fog seemed to have a peculiar affection for Angel Meadow. It was blamed for the high rate of bronchitis and was sometimes so green and thick like pea soup that the city corporation kept the gas lights burning until the afternoon. The slum's two main inroads, Angel Street and Charter Street, were hinged at St Michael's Square. The slope leading down from Angel Street to Charter Street was so steep that a pub landlord warned in the winter of 1854 that horses were 'daily and at times hourly' being lamed.

Only the brave, the stupid and the helpless entered Angel Meadow. The brave included journalists, ragged school teachers, priests and doctors. Among them was Friedrich Engels, who toured the deepest realms of the inferno and brought it to the world's attention in a provocative book, *The Condition of the*

Working Class in England, in 1845. He said Angel Meadow was 'hell upon earth' and the houses were nothing more than 'cattle sheds for human beings'.

Engels wrote: 'If anyone wishes to see in how little space a human being can move, how little air – and *such* air – he can breathe, how little civilisation he may share and yet live, it is only necessary to travel hither.' Journalist Angus Reach also told readers of the *Morning Chronicle* that Angel Meadow was the 'lowest, most filthy, most unhealthy and most wicked locality in Manchester'. He said it was 'full of cellars' and inhabited by 'bullies, thieves, cadgers, vagrants, tramps and in the very worst states of filth and darkness'.

The streets Engels and Reach visited were crammed with lodging houses, pubs and marine stores or 'putty shops', where thieves fenced stolen goods. Italian barrel organists played in the streets and vendors sold mussels, pigs' trotters, herbal tonics and tripe. Backyard slaughter houses, breweries, gasworks, boneyards, catgut factories and piles of dung tainted the air with a cocktail of aromas. In narrow alleys stood privies with urine-soaked floors and ash-pits overflowing with rotten vegetables. The stench, even in a hard frost, was sickening.

Towards the end of the nineteenth century, a tobacco factory also filled the streets with a sickly-sweet and toxic odour. The whole scene was overlooked by the bell tower of St Michael's Church, which stood next to the Old Burying Ground, a dumping ground for rotten oysters and straw from fever beds. The high walls of Manchester's Strangeways Prison and Manchester Workhouse watched over the slum like sentinels from a short distance – quietly waiting for those who would pass through their doors.

Strangers entering Angel Meadow had to make their way past a gang of youths who threw stones, cabbage stalks and mud at anyone who ventured near. In winter they hurled stones disguised as snowballs and it was said that no-one who came within range could 'avoid a cold salute about his ears and collar'. An unlucky few had their hats knocked off by another kind of missile – a dead cat. One Manchester vicar lamented the loss of his new hat, which 'was sent to an early grave by a dead kitten'.

Dozens of stray cats lived on waste ground near the entrance to Charter Street and spent their days being chased by feral children or 'street arabs'. The cats were attracted to a huge fish-gutting works in a half-demolished warehouse with its rafters and uneven bricks exposed to the sky. The pavement outside the factory became a favourite pitch for card sharps and swindlers, whose scouts climbed into the rafters and kept watch for policemen. Those who evaded their prying eyes found themselves heading deeper into a strange world of conjurers, tipsters, lurkers, mouchers, jugglers and beggars who inhabited the gin palaces, rookeries and dens of Angel Meadow.

Victorian essayist Benjamin Redfern wrote in 1875 that Charter Street was home to an assortment of hawkers, umbrella menders, bell hangers, knife grinders, ballad singers, criers of murder and prize-fight broadsheets, and tinkers. 'There are German bandsmen and foreign musicians of every grade, Highland pipers from Dublin, dog and bird fanciers, beggars, mountebanks, street jugglers, itinerant preachers, Lancashire bell ringers, Tyrolese minstrels and Negro serenaders from Birmingham, and to sum up a general *olla podrida* of odd and paradoxical characters.'

Prostitutes also worked Angel Meadow's streets and the Reverend John Mercer, the vicar of St Michael's Church, estimated in 1897 that only one in four houses in Charter Street were free from vice. In the middle of the day, between 50 and 100 thieves could be seen loitering outside the slum's beer houses and at street corners, lying in wait for the unwary. They had a listless and heavy look that lent the appearance of mental and bodily depression. If a policeman stepped around the corner, they would disappear down alleys and over walls and the streets would be left deserted.

Most savage of all Angel Meadow's inmates were the scuttlers – tribes of young street fighters who went around town wearing punchers' caps and flared trousers and attacking rival gangs with knives and belt buckles. One case involving scuttlers from Angel Meadow sparked national outrage. It began with a drunken row outside a beer house just outside the slum.

At 11pm on Saturday, 5 February 1887, Charles Burns, 17, a militia man in uniform and a notorious scuttler from Angel Meadow, got into a row with Joseph Brady, an 18-year-old dyer. After Burns punched him in the face, Brady fled to his lodgings nearby. Burns and his scuttling gang, led by a teenage thug named Owen Callaghan, followed and were soon hammering at the kitchen door. Burns shouted: "Come outside and face this!" The gang were on the steps armed with knives. Two drunken women in the house, Anne Marie Collins and Martha Judge, began launching pots at them from the upper windows. Burns and four other scuttlers then crashed through the door. Brady shouted: "I'm stabbed!" before he fell in the doorway, with his feet outside the house and his head and body resting on the floor. He died instantly – stabbed in the heart.

The women found a blood-stained knife in the folds of Brady's shirt and went to the slum's fortress-like Goulden Street police station to report the murder, taking the knife with them. They were attacked on the way by Charles Burns' brother, Sonny Burns, 20, and Callaghan, 19. The men tore off Judge's jacket, knocked her down and kicked her. When she screamed, they ran off. Judge returned to Brady's house, put on his coat as a disguise and arrived safely at the police station with the murder weapon.

Charles Burns was arrested nearby. A knife was found in his pocket. Callaghan and another lad from Angel Meadow, John Brannan, were also charged. Brannan, 18, a labourer, was arrested in Style Street. He told police: "I was never there, if I was to drop dead." Callaghan, a moulder from Dyche Street, fled to Yorkshire and was dragged back to Manchester in chains. Others arrested included Joseph Ryan, 21, an umbrella maker, Sonny Burns, a brush maker, and two women, Kate McTighe and Martha Gray, who were seen outside the house during the incident shouting: "Go on!"

Joseph Collier, the infirmary's medical officer, said Brady's wound was inflicted by a clasp knife with a blunt edge. The blade had cut through the cartilage of his fourth rib before entering his heart. Brady's mother, Margaret, identified his body, still clad in his slashed waistcoat and shirt.

All the prisoners were acquitted except Owen Callaghan, who was found guilty of manslaughter and jailed for 20 years. The prosecutor said Manchester's scuttlers behaved 'like tribes of wild Indians' and had no motive other than a 'ferocious love of fighting'. Witnesses told the trial that Callaghan struck the fatal blow after shouting: "Draw knives. Let's finish him!" The judge, Mr Justice Wills, said: "Life in parts of Manchester is as unsafe and uncertain as it is amongst a race of savages."

Chapter 2

The Meadow

The only safe way to see Angel Meadow was from the carriage of a steam train speeding a few feet above the slum's rooftops, on the Lancashire and Yorkshire Railway. The railway line's brick viaduct had been built straight through the slum in 1844, leaving the lowest streets in permanent shadow. Smoke from the engines billowed into the houses and stained the walls and ceilings with soot. Passengers approaching Manchester on the railway first became aware of a distant grey canopy encroaching on the blue sky. The rivers began to run murky and thick with pollution. Tall chimneys rose up around the train, the grass turned brown, the trees grew stunted and the paths were blackened with coal dust.

As they entered the city, passengers were whirled along the rooftops above the labyrinth of Angel Meadow's mean streets and between the black monoliths of the mills. One Victorian passenger, Edwin Waugh, described the view as he travelled back out of Manchester over this 'moral desert' and 'swarming hive of ignorance, toil and squalor' in 1855: 'In a few minutes, we were darting over the tops of that miserable human jungle known by the inappropriate name of Angel Meadow. Here all is mental and moral malaria, and the wild revelry of the place sounds like a forlorn cry for help.' He added:

Up rose a grove of tall chimneys from the dusky streets lining the banks of that little slutchy stream, creeping though the hollow, slow and slab, towards its confluence with the Irwell. By the time we had taken a few reluctant sniffs of the curiously compounded air of that melancholy waste, we began to ascend the incline and lost sight of the Irk, with its factories, dye houses, brickfields, tan pits and gasworks, and the unhappy mixture of stench, squalor, smoke, hard work, ignorance and sin, which makes up the landscape of its borders.

Waugh's train finally slipped out of Manchester and passed through real meadows crowned with buttercups, wild violets and primroses – the black city far behind him. 'The throstle sang loud and clear in the trees and little dells near the line as we rolled along,' he wrote. This rural paradise was a reminder of what Angel Meadow had once been.

For hundreds of years, long before Angel Meadow became a slum, the hillside that formed the steep slope of Angel Street was once a lush grazing pasture. Before the clanking of mill machinery filled the air with thunder, the only sound that could be heard was the sweet melody of skylarks.

Until the late eighteenth century, anyone standing at the top of Angel Meadow would have gazed down upon fields, tree-lined lanes and the dusky-coloured River Irk, which teemed with trout and eels. Ancient hedgerows, including one that marked the future track of Angel Street, provided a haven for wildlife. The view across the river was unobstructed by back-to-back houses or factory chimneys, or the railway. The essayist Benjamin Redfern lamented the loss of this 'heavenly landscape', which he said had been 'one of the most beautiful views of vale and river, hill and woodland'.

The common myth is that Angel Meadow took its name from this vision of angelic beauty, but it was actually named after a pub. The *Manchester Courier* noted in 1827:

Some persons may suppose that the term Angel Meadow has been ironically given to a part of the town now inhabited by characters of both sexes of the very worst description. The fact is it was formerly a pasture field, usually held by the occupiers of a public house called the Angel, situated in the present Angel Court in the Market Place, and much frequented by drovers, who put their cattle in this field.

The first bridge across the Irk was recorded in 1381. The river, which may have been named after the Anglo-Saxon word for roebuck because of its swiftness, was known for its destructive floods. In 1480 a deluge was said to have worn out the riverside path. One of the few men to pass beneath the meadow in the sixteenth century was the swineherd Thomas Ranshawe. At 8am each morning he blew a hunting horn to round up Manchester's pigs and led them along Ashley Lane to a grazing pasture upstream. The pigs spent the day snuffling for acorns until Ranshawe turned them back towards town just before nightfall.

The same tree-lined lane also led to a quarry, where purple-red sandstone rocks formed 280 million years earlier by desert sand dunes were carved by the stonemasons responsible for creating some of Manchester's most prestigious buildings. The sandy earth around the quarry also proved useful for burying bodies quickly. Victorian road builders discovered the lead coffins of plague victims who had been isolated in huts in the fields north of Angel Meadow in 1666.

A corn mill, a bake house and a row of woollen mills were the first permanent structures to be erected on a path near the Irk that became known as Long Millgate. More bridges would soon be built, including one named Scotland Bridge. The fast-flowing river, which would eventually turn coal black and sluggish with sewage and pollution, gave the Lord of the Manor Oswald Mosley a plentiful supply of fish, although he banned the local peasants from fishing it.

Elizabethan anglers said the grease from the woollen mills fattened the Irk's eels so much that they were the largest in the whole of England. James Chetham marvelled in 1681 at the 'goodness and deliciousness' of these 'very excellent' eels, but his friend, Dr Charles Leigh, warned: 'They are to that degree of fatness that they almost nauseate.'

The first detailed plan of Manchester, made in 1741, showed how the meadow had been divided into three hedge-lined fields. Within 20 years, a generation of merchants and artisans would turn those fields into a luxury playground. Two wealthy men, Roger Bradshaw and John Smith, erected palatial houses with formal gardens and an apple orchard. This was the start of a 40-year golden age that would see Angel Meadow become a gentrified suburb at the edge of the rapidly expanding town. New streets were laid out across the fields and dozens of smart houses were built with views over the river. The names of two of these earliest streets, Style Street and Old Mount Street, hinted at the area's rural origins.

The merchants' houses were spacious three-storey buildings with cavernous fireplaces and architectural flourishes, such as curved sandstone steps and door frames decorated with classical columns. Some had cellars beneath. Others had attics with long, gallery windows that allowed in extra light for artisan handloom weavers. One house even had an underground wine cellar and a private well.

The Reverend Mercer later looked back with envy on these comparatively untroubled days from his vantage point in 1897:

Angel Meadow, neglected, forgotten as it now is, has seen better days, of which there are relics still remaining. In Old Mount Street there are pillars and dignified flights of steps at the main entrances to the houses, showing that they were built for members of the well-to-do classes. In Long Millgate there are some half-timbered houses in good preservation, which evidently once overlooked the river, when the valley below was yet a pretty sight, and when the walks along it were among the pleasantest around Manchester.

Angel Meadow's first residents included professionals and tradesmen: flour dealers, bakers, shuttle-makers, hatters and dress designers. Schoolmaster John Abbott and midwife Mary Hadfield were neighbours in Angel Street, while William Holdsworth, a butcher, and Matthew Brougham, a tax inspector, lived in Blackley Street (the original name for Charter Street). Thomas Hanson, a commissioner, owned one of the large houses in Old Mount Street. The area's wealthy merchants entertained guests with gingerbread and home-made wines. Cows still grazed in the few remaining undeveloped fields and milk was sold from nearby dairies or 'milk houses'.

But even in those halcyon days, Angel Meadow was earning a dubious reputation. Two teenage handkerchief weavers from Angel Meadow named John Wilson and John Davies were arrested at a ferry house in Flint, North Wales, and charged with belonging to a gang accused of having 'infested the country'. Wilson sported a bottle-green coat and a black waistcoat, while Davies, whose face was marked by smallpox, wore a drab greatcoat and a cape. A thief named Benjamin Hilton, alias Big Ben, was also arrested in Sheffield for croft-breaking in Angel Meadow. Police searched his house near the Meadow and found 50 picklock keys secreted in a hole near the chimney.

It was unsurprising that thieves were drawn like moths to Angel Meadow, when the area's inhabitants had every luxury and amenity. Towards the end of the eighteenth century, the local residents even had their own pleasure ground, in the form of Robert Tinker's grandly-named Grape and Compass Coffee House and Tea Gardens. The gardens stood between Angel Meadow and the quarry to the north. Tinker later re-named them the Elysian Gardens, after the place in Greek mythology in which the souls of the virtuous were laid to rest. Finally, he called them Vauxhall Gardens after the more famous pleasure ground in London. The locals knew them simply as 'Tinker's Gardens' and the nearby quarry became known as 'Tinker's Hollow'.

The wealthy flocked to the gardens, dressed in their finest clothes, and paid one shilling and sixpence to dance on lawns and sip tea beneath trees lit by 3,000 coloured lanterns. The gardens were famous for their cucumbers, which flourished in the sandy soil. One, reported to be more than 7ft 8in long, was sent to the Prince Regent for inspection. Some of the world's first balloon ascents took place in the gardens, including one that drew a crowd of 50,000 people. The entertainment at Tinker's was said to be 'intellectual, rural and delightful'. There were wild beasts in cages, rabbits, guinea pigs and even a fish pond. A poet, Alexander Wilson, said Tinker's was 'the grandest place in the nation'.

The tea-drinking residents of Angel Meadow soon had their own church in the shape of St Michael's and All Angels. The church, ironically named after the archangel who cast Satan from paradise, was built at the junction of Style Street and Angel Street by the prominent citizen Humphrey Owen and consecrated by Bishop William Cleaver of Chester on 23 July 1789. St Michael's was known as a 'carriage church' because wealthy churchgoers could trot there in their horse-drawn carriages on Sunday mornings.

The church was built of brick in a 'classic style', with a chancel and side chapels, and a nave with high windows. It could seat 1,000 people on a raised wooden gallery supported by iron pillars, which ran around three sides of the interior. It eventually gained a tower on its western side with a pyramid-shaped roof and a 'fine' bell. A huge, three-deck pulpit stood in front of the communion table.

Deep inside the church's communion recess stood some oversized paintings of saints. Joseph Aston, in his 1816 guidebook *A Picture of Manchester*, was less than complimentary about the church and its paintings: 'It is a brick building... nothing remarkable in any point, either on the outside or the inside, except for some colossal saints, which outraged nature.' The *Manchester Guardian* went even further in 1888:

> Why one of the ugliest-looking churches in Manchester situated in one of the most crowded and notorious parts of the city should so long have enjoyed the pleasant-sounding name of St Michael's, Angel Meadow, is beyond all understanding. Of course, when good Humphrey Owen built his church, one could have understood the fitness of the description. Scarcely any stretch of the imagination can realise the fact that the site of the church was as pretty then as it is repellent now.

In the last quarter of the eighteenth century, Angel Meadow seemed to provide its wealthy residents with every comfort, but its popularity faded overnight. As Manchester grew, the areas closest to the town centre became dominated by industry. The merchants and artisans fled to new areas, such as Ardwick Green to the east, which was now within trotting distance of their carriages. Angel Meadow quickly became a slum. The large old merchants' houses were let out to lodgers as Manchester's population doubled to 100,000 within just 25 years. The architectural flourishes remained – giving the slum an air of faded grandeur – while builders, operating without planning restrictions, threw up new houses in every spare nook. The pastures that once rolled down to Irk were ripped up and the trees growing along the lanes were cut down and turned into rafters.

A new area opened along the bank of the river, at the foot of Tinker's Gardens. It became known as New Town and was soon home to a flood of Irish immigrants. Near the Irk now also stood a new slum enclave called Gibraltar, which was so low that parts of it were below the level of the river. The sloppy building work resulted in several houses and a soap factory plunging into the Irk after their foundations were undermined by the water.

Angus Reach later wrote that these old districts of Manchester had become the worst in the city: 'They contain the largest proportion of cellar dwellings, of close, filthy courts, undrained lanes, and rows of houses built back-to-back, without any provision for ventilation, and with very little for cleanliness.' He derided the builders as 'utterly unheeding, or perhaps profoundly ignorant of, the sanitary and social guilt of their doings'.

Friedrich Engels, who toured the slum in 1844, found the ghosts of fashionable Angel Meadow when he came across some of the old merchants' houses in Long Millgate: 'These are remnants of the old pre-manufacturing Manchester, whose former inhabitants have removed with their descendants into better-built districts, and have left the houses, which were not good enough for them, to a population strongly mixed with Irish blood.'

Unscrupulous landlords stopped carrying out repairs and their occupants began using the houses' wooden frames as firewood, leaving them in a permanent state of ruin. Covered passages soon led from the streets to inner courts where no two human beings could pass at the same time. The courts were soon ankle-deep in the filth, with heaps of ashes and offal lying where they were thrown. Engels found that cottages were built by the dozen, with walls the width of just half a brick. He wrote: 'Of the irregular cramming together of dwellings in ways which defy all rational plan, of the tangle in which they are crowded literally one upon the other, it is impossible to convey an idea.'

The death knell for Angel Meadow was the building of a paupers' cemetery next to St Michael's Church. In 1787, the local overseers of the poor seized a large plot of land next to the church's private, walled graveyard. In just 30 years, they filled it with the bodies of an estimated 40,000 paupers. The cemetery, which became known as the Old Burying Ground, had to be closed and another opened in a field across the Irk named Walker's Croft, which had a small chapel, gateposts guarded by stone lions, and a bed of fine, dry sand which made it a 'most eligible burying place'.

Joseph Aston, whose guidebook to Manchester was published during the year the Old Burying Ground closed, told his shocked readers how 'many thousands' of bodies lay buried in Angel Meadow's 'depot' of the dead: 'A very large pit is dug and covered with planks, which are locked down in the night, until the hole is filled up with coffins piled beside and upon one another. The cavern of death is then closed, and covered up with earth, and another pit is prepared, and filled in the same manner.'

In 1876, local author Isabella Banks penned her famous novel *The Manchester Man*. She opened the story in 1799 with a great flood on the River Irk which carried her protagonist Jabez Clegg, then only a baby, downstream in his cradle. A violent thunderstorm devastated the valley. The river 'surged and roared' and turned the 'pleasant meadows' into a 'turbulent sea'. Soon the water was beating against the tanning yards on the river bank 'with frothy tongue and lip, like a hungry giant, greedy for food'. Banks painted a vivid picture of the symbols of country life being thrown down the river in the strong current: 'Hay bales, bushes, beehives, chicken coops and more than one squealing pig.'

Banks' description of the 'green and undulating uplands' and 'luxuriant hedgerows' swirling in the flood showed how Victorian writers looked back fondly at a time when the northern edge of Manchester had been a rural idyll. But the truth was that, by 1799, the great tidal wave of the Industrial Revolution was already sweeping over Angel Meadow. The once-fashionable suburb was now being swamped by a flood of migrant workers who rapidly turned the lush pastures into a slum.

Chapter 3

Killing Fields

A great crowd of handloom weavers watched in silence as the dragoons formed their horses into a long line on the far side of the field in the early evening light. They could hear the dragoon captain shouting orders before the line finally jolted forward. The horses came on slowly at first, but in seconds the ground was trembling beneath their pounding hooves as they kicked up a cloud of dust. When the weavers saw the glint of the riders' sabres, they started to flee in all directions, but they had nowhere to hide in the wide expanse of the field.

Then one of the weavers did the unthinkable: he stood his ground. As the dragoons galloped towards him, he picked up a brick and launched it towards one of the horses, hitting its head. The rider levelled his pistol and fired. The weaver fell down dead. Then the dragoons swarmed through the fleeing crowd, hacking at everyone in their path. It was 25 May 1808, and the place was St George's Fields on the outskirts of Angel Meadow.

Handloom weavers had stayed in Angel Meadow when other artisans and merchants packed up their belongings and fled to the city's outskirts. They had been making a good living and the 'knick-knack' of their looms could be heard constantly in Angel Street and Blackley Street. But within the space of just a few years, the once-prized work of their nimble hands was being snatched away by giant weaving machines.

In 1780, the manufacturer and inventor Richard Arkwright answered an advert in the *Manchester Mercury* offering the lease of a field off Miller Street, at the edge of Angel Meadow. The field, the location of the original meadow, had been used as a brickyard by builders erecting new houses and included a 'fine breast of clay' two yards high. Here, Arkwright and his business partners erected the world's first steam-powered cotton factory.

The colossal, five-storey building was 200ft long and each floor was connected by an external wooden staircase. The rooms were a marvel of their age – they contained no partitions and stretched the entire length of the building. The beams in the floor were made from pine and oak baulks fixed with iron pins and were designed to spring against their own weight to resist the pressure from above. Crowds of awestruck onlookers stood gazing skywards as the chimney, the tallest structure in Manchester, was being built.

Arkwright also dug out two large ponds above and below the mill to help power his machinery. John Aiken wrote at the time that the mill's machines were as accurate as clockwork and were 'most wonderful to behold'. Arkwright's son, also named Richard, later took over operations and brought in two brothers, Samuel and John Simpson, as partners and managers. By 1791, they were running 4,000 cotton spindles and preparing to add 1,000 more. They leased homes in nearby Angel Street for a new army of mill workers, whose heavy clogs matched the rhythm of the mill machinery.

The mill's success sparked the building of more than 60 others over the next 40 years as the cotton magnates competed in a technological race. The Reverend Richard Warner, a vicar who toured the North of England, described one of the new Manchester mills in 1802:

> It is scarcely possible to conceive a more animated or curious scene than this work where 1,500 people, young and old, are busily employed under one roof, directing the operations of machines of the most beautiful contrivance, which move with a rapidity that prevents the eye from detecting the rotations.

Workshops, a dye works, two iron foundries and a rope works opened in Angel Meadow to service the new cotton industry. Within a few years, the Irk had more mills along its banks than any other river of the same length in England. The French journalist Eugène Buret said the Irk presented 'the most disgusting view possible', with houses 'rotting in humidity' hanging over the water. He claimed France's notorious Bièvre, a river that flowed into the Seine outside Paris, was 'like a stream in Arcadia' compared with the 'muddy waters of the Irk'.

By May, 1808, the artisan handloom weavers of Angel Meadow were in uproar. They were unable to compete with the new cotton factories and many were now unemployed and starving, while those still working had seen a huge drop in their income. Then they were hit by the economic downturn caused by the Napoleonic Wars. Up to 8,000 weavers walked away from their looms and gathered on St George's Fields in protest. The final straw was Parliament's rejection of a bill that could have provided them with a minimum wage.

St George's Fields stood to the north-east of Angel Meadow and was named after a large brick church dedicated to the patron saint of England. When the church was built, Rochdale Road was just a narrow country footpath named

Back Lane, which for a time became known as St George's Road. Speculators had built the church in an isolated position as a rival to St Michael's in the mistaken hope of making a profit. The church finally opened its doors on 1 April 1798, after being shut up half-finished for several years.

Magistrates learned of the weavers' protest and ordered special constables and yeomen to muster. They also called in a detachment of the 4th Light Dragoons, one of the regiments later decimated as they galloped towards Russian canons during the ill-fated charge of the Light Brigade in the Crimean War. A former lieutenant-colonel named Joseph Hanson was on the weavers' side. Hanson, a cotton magnate, was a self-made man who had started out as a handloom weaver. He had helped the weavers apply to Parliament for a minimum wage. He was now 35 and described as wavy-haired and 'Byron-browed'. It was said that although he had 'wealth and ease', Hanson possessed 'no torturing meanness of spirit writhing with ambition'.

Hanson galloped to St George's Fields and urged the weavers to go home. Newspaper reports said they 'swayed in a passion of admiration' around his horse as he told them: "You must disperse. Give no cause for retaliation or the cavalry will ride over you." He offered them £3,000 of his own money to leave the fields. They were getting ready to depart when the dragoons suddenly charged. The *Morning Post*, described the scene that unfolded:

> In a moment a general consternation took place, by the cavalry galloping through the ground in all directions. Some were rode over and a few that were obstinate in dispersing wounded with the cavalry's swords. One of the people threw a brick and hit one of the horses' heads. His rider immediately levelled his pistol and shot him dead on the spot.

About 40 people were arrested, including Hanson, who was jailed for six months and fined £1,000 – worth more than £60,000 today. Mr Justice Goose, the judge at his trial, commented: "It is necessary that the workers should receive a fair living profit. If they receive more than is equal, it very often promotes intemperance and idleness." But Hanson's sacrifice had touched the weavers so greatly that 40,000 of them paid a penny each to buy him a set of presentation silver.

The *Manchester Mercury* reported that the dragoons who shot the unnamed protestor were also planning a grand gesture. They each paid a day's wages into a fund for the dead man's widow. The newspaper claimed that this 'act of generosity' showed they were motived by 'the most benevolent feelings of humanity while acting out their painful though necessary duty'. A coroner concluded that the man's death was 'justifiable homicide'.

At the end of May, the cotton manufacturers finally agreed to increase the weavers' wages by a fifth. But this was only a brief respite in hostilities. Manchester was now wallowing in an economic depression. The lack of a popular vote led to calls for political reform. The whole of Lancashire elected only two members of parliament and voting was restricted to adult male landowners with a freehold of 40 shillings or more.

Events were now leading up to the Peterloo Massacre, named in mock irony after Wellington's victory over Napoleon in the Battle of Waterloo. Seventeen Angel Meadow slum dwellers ended up on the list of casualties on that fateful day, 16 August 1819, along with eight from New Town, which was now dominated by immigrant Irish weavers.

Radicals, men who wanted radical reform of the electoral system, called for a public meeting in St Peter's Fields on the far side of Manchester. The orator Henry Hunt, who was due to chair the meeting, arrived in Manchester in an open-top carriage days before. He was greeted with a fanfare as he turned through Angel Meadow en route to the outlying village of Smedley, where he was staying with fellow radical Joseph Johnson, the founder of *The Observer* newspaper. Johnson had sent Hunt a letter saying: 'Nothing but ruin and starvation stare one in the face. The state of the district is truly dreadful, and I believe nothing but the greatest exertions can prevent an insurrection.'

Hunt halted his carriage as he passed beneath St Michael's Church and stood up to address a crowd of 1,000 people. Angel Meadow resident Samuel Morton later told how Hunt waved his white hat and the weavers greeted him with a loud 'huzzah'. A reporter from *The Times* wrote that Hunt appeared 'elated' with his 'daring enterprise' and gave a signal for three cheers. He wrote: 'The whole group had the most wretched and shabby appearance possible to conceive, and were it not for the crowd they assembled, would almost be too contemptible to be noticed.'

The sky was bright, sunny and cloudless on the morning of the Peterloo Massacre. Across town at Hulme Barracks, the yeomen under the command of Colonel L'Estrange sharpened their sabres and received a new magazine of musket balls. By sunrise, thousands of men, women and children began marching towards Manchester from towns across the region. A party of 6,000 men and women led by the radical poet Samuel Bamford was heading to Manchester along St George's Road. As they neared town, orders arrived from Hunt to meet him at Smedley and to follow the low road to Manchester through New Town and Angel Meadow. The marchers gave a cry of 'New Town, New Town', as Bamford called out an order of 'left shoulders forward' and wheeled them down the hill. Bamford later wrote in his memoirs:

At New Town we were welcomed with open arms by the poor Irish weavers, who came in their best drapery and uttered blessings and words of endearment, many of which were not understood by our rural patriots. Some of them danced, and others stood with clasped hands and tearful eyes, adoring almost, that banner whose colour was their national one, and the emblem of their green island home. We thanked them by the band striking up 'St Patrick's Day in the Morning' – they were electrified – and we passed on, leaving those warm-hearted suburbans capering and whooping like mad.

Samuel Morton described how 'many thousands of people' followed the procession through Angel Meadow, marching six abreast 'like soldiers'. It took them nearly half an hour to pass through the tight gully below St Michael's Church. Morton said later in a witness statement: 'I had lived in the town 40 years, and never saw anything so tumultuous there before. I was afraid. There were so many running up and down, it was hardly safe.'

Up to 80,000 men, women and children were packed so closely together in St Peter's Fields that their hats seemed to touch. Many were wearing their best clothes. Hunt was on the hustings when some yeomen pushed into the field to try to arrest him. They became stuck in the tightly-packed crowd and began to hack about them with their sabres. Their horses reared and plunged as people tried to get out of the way. The soldiers lost 'all command of temper' as they began to destroy the protest banners and flags. The hussars then formed their horses into a line to the east and charged into the crowd. Other yeomen charged from the south, cutting at everyone in reach. Constables and soldiers armed with truncheons and bayonets stopped people escaping.

At least 15 people died and up to 700 were injured. They were trampled by charging horses, slashed with sabres, bayoneted, clubbed with musket butts, shot and hit with truncheons. Injured weavers from Angel Meadow who had followed Hunt's carriage limped home bloodied and badly bruised. They included a tailor named Peter Wood, of Blackley Street, who was trampled by the cavalry and received a sabre cut to his right elbow. Wood, 32, was an old artillery man who had been disabled while serving his country in the Napoleonic Wars. Mary McKenna, 14, from Nicholas Street, and Owen McCabe, 62, from Old Mount Street, were among the youngest and oldest injured. McKenna, described in casualty lists as an 'interesting girl', spent a month in hospital with a head injury after she was trampled by a horse. McCabe spent the rest of his life on crutches after his ribs were crushed and his hip smashed in the cavalry charge.

Eight of the injured were neighbours from the four streets that formed the heart of New Town. James McConnell, 50, from Portland Street, was unable to dress himself for a month after his groin was crushed when special constables threw him into a cellar. For ten weeks following the massacre, he was only able to earn 10 shillings in wages. Charles Harper, 20, of Dixon Street, was shot, sabred and hit with a truncheon. Three neighbours in Dimity Street were also hurt, including Patrick Reynolds, 24, whose legs were burned when he was driven into a lime pit by the cavalry.

Riots broke out that night in New Cross, an open area marked by an old market cross a five-minute walk from the centre of Angel Meadow. A mob began attacking anyone they feared was on the side of the authorities. The windows of a provision shop owned by a man named Fletcher were smashed and hussars galloped to the scene and opened fire – shooting dead two women and a teenager named Joshua Whitworth.

A mob of 1,000 people gathered outside the home of a special constable named Robert Campbell in Miller Street as dawn broke the next day. They believed he had killed a child at Peterloo. "The villain," they shouted, "Kill him!" Campbell fired a pistol from an upstairs window – giving him just enough time to slip out of the house and run up Miller Street with the mob in hot pursuit. He somehow found the strength to rip a door from its hinges, which he used to protect his back from a volley of stones. But the mob dragged him out into the middle of the street and swarmed around him. When the kicking started, he must have known he was a dead man.

Chapter 4

Anarchy

L iving conditions in Angel Meadow deteriorated further in the 1820s, as an economic depression hit Britain following the end of the Napoleonic Wars. Many weavers were by now so poor that they resorted to begging. Five 'miserable looking' weavers were hauled before the magistrates' court and subsequently discharged when they promised never to beg again. Another was jailed for a month after he was found begging in circumstances that 'made it dangerous to refuse to give'. Weavers' wives also fell into begging and prostitution.

A doctor named James Phillips Kay criticised the 'squalid and loathsome wretchedness' of houses in the slum: 'That mass of cottages filling the insalubrious valley through which the Irk flows.' He said the inhabitants were 'gross, ill-fed and ill-clothed' and wallowed in the 'unrestrained licence of animal appetite'.

One incident above all signalled Angel Meadow's downfall. On a dark night, three men slipped out of a house in Dyche Street and crept downhill through the slum towards St Michael's Church. Two carried spades and took care not to clang the metal blades on the cobbles, while the third held a small wooden box wrapped in cloth. They were heading to the paupers' graveyard to carry out a grim and secretive task: the burial of a baby girl born dead two days earlier. The men clambered over the cemetery wall and were already digging when they realised they were being watched from the shadows. They were spooked and fled into the night, leaving the baby's body to be found on the cold ground the next morning.

Manchester coroner John Milne later scolded the baby's mother, Eliza Leather, and warned that she could be charged with murder. She was saved by the coroner's surgeon, who proved through a post-mortem that the baby had been stillborn. Milne claimed she could have given the baby a proper burial for just sixpence, if she had only asked the church's sexton for help. But sixpence was more than poor Eliza Leather, like many of her contemporaries in the slum, could afford.

Tempers soon flared in response to the increasing poverty. In 1820, John Dunn was rattled by three prostitutes who lodged next to his home in New

Mount Street. Every night, the three 'frail unfortunates' kept him awake with their nocturnal revelry. Dunn, a weaver with a wife and 13 children, went to the window and fired a pistol, shooting dead one of the women, Margaret Grimes. He was found guilty of murder and jailed after a jury heard he was 'labouring under temporary insanity'.

As the slum descended deeper into chaos, the inmates reserved their most deep-seated hatred for figures of authority. Special constables and watchmen, remembering the murder of Robert Campbell, armed themselves with pistols when they patrolled the streets. At 2am on 8 September 1822, three men who had been drinking heavily in New Town made their way into the Meadow, which had earned a reputation for 'abounding with loose women of the lowest description'. One of the men, William Atkinson, began taking liberties with a woman who was standing at the end of an alley and then 'jawed' her (punched her in the face). A notorious thief named Philip Clarke, who lived with the woman, and his accomplice James Lusherbrand, chased Atkinson up the street.

When Atkinson slipped and fell, Clarke began kicking him in the head. Atkinson started shouting: "Murder! Watchman!" Clarke and his companions fled, only to run straight towards an officer named Haslam, who heard Atkinson's cries and now loomed out of the darkness.

Haslam grabbed hold of Lusherbrand. As they wrestled, Lusherbrand stabbed Haslam in the hand with a large clasp-knife before getting to his feet. Removing his pistol from his breast pocket, Haslam shouted: "Stand or I'll blow your brains out!" He shot Lusherbrand in the chest. People were woken by Lusherbrand's cries. He asked for some water and drank two gulps before dying on the steps of a nearby house. His bloody knife, with a blunt end, was found close to his body. Haslam was cleared of the murder by an inquest jury who found that the killing was justified.

The weavers of Angel Meadow might not have forgiven Haslam, but other police officers won their hard-earned respect. Henry Bailey was a fine, upstanding officer. Born in 1793, he worked as a baker and confectioner before joining the force. The married father-of-six rose to become the Deputy Constable of Cheetham, the district across the Irk from Angel Meadow.

Bailey's bravery in battle was legendary. He was on duty when he learned that around 70 of 'the worst characters in town' had gathered in a field to watch a pitched battle between two men named John Dean and Joseph Fagan. Bailey picked up a thick stick, marched into the ring and seized hold of Dean. The thugs watching the fight tried to rescue Dean and threw missiles at Bailey – a brick caused him to suffer a severe head wound. Dean escaped but Bailey recaptured him after another battle and other officers arrested Fagan.

It emerged that Dean had only recently been released from prison, after being jailed for killing a man in an earlier fight.

Bailey suffered a black eye while separating two men in another fracas. John Connah was on the ground holding down his victim, whose face was black and his nose spurting with blood. Bailey arrested Connah, but he tried to escape and punched Bailey in the face. He was ordered by a judge to buy Bailey a new hat.

Bailey's other job was to keep watch over the river bank. His office had a window overlooking the water near the junction of the Irk and the larger River Irwell. It was a deadly spot, with the Irwell turning almost upstream at the point where it met the Irk, which caused dangerous currents. Despite being unable to swim, Bailey frequently rescued drowning children.

At 5pm one day, the swollen Irk and Irwell were just starting to subside after the worst flood in recent memory, caused by heavy rain and meltwater from snow storms which had battered Manchester for seven days. Bailey, then 40, had just finished his shift and was at home when he heard people screaming that a five-year-old boy named Trees had fallen into the water.

Bailey handed his pocket watch to a boy, rushed down the steep bank and plunged into the murky Irwell. He grabbed hold of Trees and, with one hand stretched out for the bank, shouted: "My God, save me!" He battled the raging river and managed to hold the boy above the surface as he grabbed hold of a bystander's outstretched finger. But then his own hand slipped free as the current dragged him and the boy to oblivion. Bailey's head smashed against some rocks and he sank beneath the water. Only his hat could be seen floating downstream.

The *Manchester Guardian* praised Bailey as 'a man of extraordinary courage and resolution' and a 'very mild and forbearing temper', which 'admirably fitted him for the office he held'. Local people were so struck by Bailey's bravery that they raised more than £1,600 in subscriptions for his widow and children. The river was dredged, but his body could not be found.

A service was held in Bailey's memory at St Michael's Church, where the Reverend E D Jackson preached a sermon on the 'omnipotence of death'. He said Bailey's death would 'disturb whole neighbourhoods' and 'carry terror and grief into the bosom of afflicted families'. He added: 'It may be that his mouldering remains lie in some secret recess, never more to be discovered till the end of all material things. But let not this cost us a superfluous tear. There is a mind that knows and an eye that beholds the place of repose.'

It would be six months before Bailey's badly decomposed body was discovered at Sticking's Island, several miles downstream. Two girls who lived on a barge were picking mushrooms for breakfast when they found Bailey's body half buried in a sandbank. He was wearing a pair of newly-soled shoes, the remnants of a linen shirt, a flannel waistcoat and a belt. His head was bald, save for a lock of black hair. He was identified by his shoes, which were recognised by a cobbler named James Moore as his own handiwork.

Bailey's body was moved to an outhouse behind the Ducie Arms near Manchester Workhouse and his funeral was held the next day. It was said an 'immense concourse' of people watched the funeral procession pass through the cemetery gates at Walker's Croft.

The death of another policeman highlighted the extent to which conditions in Angel Meadow had deteriorated. Sandy-haired Eliza Moorhouse was in bed when a weaver named Robert Lattimer knocked loudly on the front door of the brothel in Simpson Street where she lived, early on a Saturday morning in 1829. The young prostitute heard his heavy clogs coming up the wooden stairs before he burst through the bedroom door. He stood swaying by the bed, fumbled in his pocket and tossed a shilling and nine pence on the counterpane.

Moorhouse and Lattimer, a Scotsman, had been drinking in the cellar of a beer house near Smithfield Market earlier that evening. Now Lattimer was demanding to share her bed. Eliza refused and threw the coins on the floor. "He told me to give it him and I would not, and he struck me and cut my lip," she said in a witness statement. "He then went away, and said he'd fetch someone that would make me give it."

Lattimer returned alone two hours later. Now he wanted more than the girl – he wanted revenge. Finding the door of the house locked, he began waking the neighbours. "Damn her," he cried. "I'll have her life." Mary Johnson, who ran the house, shouted that there were men inside and she would send them out. "If you have any men in there," Lattimer warned, "turn them out now and they shall not be men for long." He waited a few moments before staggering to a police station near Smithfield Market. There he found an officer named George Howarth and reported that Eliza had robbed him of three shillings.

Howarth, who had a reputation for being a 'very steady' watchman, already knew the ways of Angel Meadow. He grabbed Lattimer by the collar and swung him back through the door, before hitting him twice with his stick. Then he threw him into the night and warned him: "Go about your business." Just three hours later, Howarth was dead. He was found in a side street off St George's Road after being stabbed with a large carving knife. The blade had ruptured his intestines and diaphragm.

Another watchman, John Boller, found Howarth lying in a pool of blood and holding a fist-sized lump of his own bowels in his hand. Howarth told Boller: "Dear me. I'm stuck." He explained that Robert Lattimer had pulled out a carving knife from under his coat and stabbed him in the stomach after shouting: "You shall die." A manhunt was launched with a £20 reward offered for Lattimer's capture.

Well before dawn, Lattimer wrote to his wife saying that he was heading home to Scotland. Then he slipped out of his lodging house and set off northwards through the streets of Manchester. He was just nine miles from the Scottish border when he was caught days later and hauled back to Manchester. By the time Lattimer's case reached court, the main prosecution witness Eliza Moorhouse had fallen ill and died. The brothelkeeper Mary Johnson said Moorhouse had been with no other men that night. Two others had been to see a girl named Fanny and they had slipped out of the back door when Lattimer arrived.

The prosecutor showed the jury the murder weapon. It was stated that Howarth had told a nurse at the infirmary that he was stabbed by a man who had been with a 'bad girl' and had lost his money. The court heard that Lattimer, 32, a father-of-four, had travelled to Manchester six weeks earlier to find work as a weaver. His Friday night attire included a hat and an old pair of trousers with a patch on one knee. In his pocket he carried a colourful handkerchief, which he sold to a fiddler on the night of the murder, in return for some extra beer money.

Charlotte Hindley, who lived at the same lodging house as Lattimer, said she had heard him return home that night. She slept in a room above the front door, which made such a loud noise when it scraped across the flags that Lattimer could not have slipped back out to kill Howarth without being heard. She saw their kitchen knife resting on the table at 8am and believed it had been there all night. James McCormick, who also lived in the same house, said he had left Lattimer smoking his pipe by the fire in the early hours. Lattimer's brothers, who travelled south for the trial, swore he was a 'quiet, peaceable and humane man'.

Newspaper journalists described how 'tears dropped from his cheeks' in court and noted that he had a medium build and a 'pleasing countenance' – not the 'ferocious, forbidding look generally associated with a murderer'. The jury cleared him. The judge, Mr Justice Bayley, said: "If I had been upon the jury, I should have given the same verdict on the evidence. Where the truth may be, God knows."

The same year in which Lattimer was cleared, Manchester's oppressed weavers rose up again. On Sunday, 3 May 1829, hundreds of them gathered once more at St George's Fields. They were angry because local mill owners were making them pay for their own 'pickers', pieces of animal cartilage used for striking the end of a cotton shuttle to send it zipping across the machines. The pickers cost more than a penny a pair. Mill owners argued that pickers were being frequently broken or stolen and charging the workers was the only way to make them more careful.

A crowd now marched on the cotton factories. In one mill they demolished 53 power looms with lump hammers. In a second mill, they destroyed 46 looms and smashed scores of windows. Police arrived armed with cutlasses and pistols, but were forced to take shelter in a pub. One officer was hit on the head by a large stone which smashed into the pub's doorpost. Another only managed to stop a brick from striking his skull by slashing it in two with his cutlass.

The mob arrived at a large, seven-storey cotton factory in Dyche Street at about 1pm. The owners, John and Joseph Parker, were inside with their night watchman and two servants. The mob poured a volley of stones through the upper windows. Three men then smashed their way inside with an axe. They dragged out a long beam and used it as a battering ram to force open the doors. The mob smashed up the looms and threw the cloth into the street before setting the building on fire using turpentine to ignite the flames.

The Parkers had barricaded themselves in a room on the second floor armed with pistols, but had little ammunition. When flames licked the stairs they had no choice but to flee. They leaped through flames at the bottom of the stairs, dashed outside and found a new hiding place in the foreman's house near the factory gates. The fire spread quickly through the building's wooden floors. Flames burst through the windows and the roof collapsed to the ground. A counting house and a warehouse were also destroyed.

Nearly 30 dragoons and a troop of marines were sent to the scene by the authorities. Flames were towering above the low houses that surrounded the burning factory when they arrived. Shouts rang out as bystanders saw that the hungry fire, fed by a strong wind rolling in over the Irk, had begun to lick at their own rooftops. Soon a row of shops and houses on three sides of the factory were alight. Weavers now risked all to save their scant possessions. They disappeared into smoke-filled lodging houses and cellars before emerging with blackened faces clutching their prizes.

A reporter from the *Manchester Guardian* described the shocking scene as 'sublime and terrific':

The white ashes fell as thick and dazzling as a heavy shower of snow and, nearer to the factory, many persons were slightly scorched in the hands and face by the fall of glowing embers. The alarm of the inhabitants, the shrieks of the women and children, and the removal of the aged and infirm, together with the terrific glare of the flames, formed a scene which while it lasted was affecting in the highest degree.

Manchester descended deeper into chaos over the next few days. Shops stayed closed and police and cavalry patrolled the streets. They hunted the arsonists without success. At 9am the next morning, a large gang of thieves began heading up St George's Road and plundered every provision shop. They swarmed around a baker's cart and stole his bread. Some shopkeepers threw loaves and money from their windows in a bid to stop the mob from smashing their way inside their shops. John Sykes, a provision dealer in St George's Road, fired a pistol into the air, hoping to scare off the mob, but they threw stones through his upper window and tore down the shutters. After gaining entry, they stole everything they could find inside, including brushes and pumice stones, and trampled cheese, loaves and ham underfoot.

Four out of five rioters were reported to be teenagers. Newspapers claimed that women also took an 'active part' and had been seen 'instructing the lads to proceed with their work of destruction'. One newspaper speculated: 'The plans were no doubt laid by older heads who made their escape as soon as the work began.' Another suggested that the riots were more likely being led by professional thieves rather than weavers.

Dragoons fought constant skirmishes as they tried to clear the streets. The rioters escaped down narrow lanes and then re-emerged in even larger numbers. They threw stones from alleyways and the dragoons were constantly exposed to a shower of missiles. They charged down passageways armed with cutlasses and made arrests.

A group of weavers held a final meeting in St George's Fields – their true cause lost amid the rioting. They had just arrived when they saw a large troop of dragoons coming along St George's Road. The dragoons were reinforcements arriving in Manchester from Rochdale, but the crowd feared they had been sent to break up their meeting and would charge across the fields just as they had in 1808.

They were seized with a great panic and began to flee back to their homes in Angel Meadow. Their struggle for better conditions was over and the slum, for now at least, was quiet.

Chapter 5

The Cholera Riot

C holera arrived in Manchester in May 1832, after sweeping through
cities unknown to the poor weavers of Angel Meadow: Cairo, Shiraz,
and Tabriz. The disease, known as the 'blue death' because it turned
the skin of its victims blue-grey, came ashore at Sunderland when a ship
carrying stricken sailors docked in port. It wreaked havoc in London, Glasgow
and Belfast before it reached Manchester.

The town's Board of Health placed two watchmen on the River Irwell, but
kept no vigil over the rail passengers arriving from Liverpool on the world's
first intercity train line, which had opened in 1830. Doctors said the board's
bid to stop the disease reaching Manchester resembled a country gentleman
nailing shut his gates to keep out the crows. No one knew that the deadly germ
was already in the city's water supply.

At the time of the outbreak, none of Angel Meadow's streets were paved.
The slum's muddy lanes were rutted with cart tracks and the courtyards had
become dumping grounds for offal and animal dung. Whole families lived
below ground in cellars and in attic garrets. Gangs of scavengers were deployed
by the authorities to clean the courts and letters were sent to landlords urging
them to whitewash their houses in a last minute bid to avoid disaster. Friedrich
Engels later wrote: 'People remembered the unwholesome dwellings of the
poor and trembled before the certainty that each of these slums would become
a centre for the plague.'

Cholera's first victim in Manchester lived outside Angel Meadow in another
slum off Deansgate. He was 29-year-old coach painter James Palfreyman – a
stout, well-proportioned man and an occasional drunkard. Palfreyman began
vomiting a milky liquid and suffering from diarrhoea – cholera's calling cards
– after a Friday night dinner of lamb's head, heart and liver. He died at 2pm
on 10 May in Coronation Street, Salford. The epidemic had arrived.

Cholera attacked Angel Meadow with extraordinary venom in early June.
It arrived first at the door of a lodging house at 12 Blackley Street, where a
stinking, overflowing privy stood next to the back door. Eight out of the 18
lodgers were killed in quick succession on a fateful Saturday night. They
were tramps, vagabonds and travelling circus hands. Their deaths were

carefully noted by Henry Gaulter, a doctor who recorded details of 300 Manchester cholera victims. He painted a shocking picture of the slum and its inhabitants.

The first victim in the house was a hawker named Martha Hope, who had the unusual distinction of being described as 'sober'. Martha and her husband, noted by Gaulter as a 'black man who exhibited at country fairs as a juggler', were followed to their deaths by a juggler named Jim Mills, who slept next to Hope in a garret of seven beds. Mills, known as 'Long Jim' because of his above average height, was a 'dissolute and drunken fellow' who could swallow a sword nearly a yard long. The next to die was Sailor Jack, a 'deformed profligate little man' who went about on crutches and had lost his jacket in a drunken fight the previous night. Jane Lewis, who was six months pregnant and married to a tramp, also died that day along with her unborn child. The remaining lodgers fled like fugitives and the house was shut down. Mrs McAllister, the landlady, was struck down by cholera but survived after fleeing to the countryside.

Panic spread through every part of Manchester. A gardener named Alexander Whirk was murdered by his wife with a poker in a violent row after he suffered diarrhoea for a week, because she feared he had cholera. A bone-boiler seen throwing several tonnes of rotten salmon into the River Irk was accused of spreading the disease and attacked as a result.

At New Bailey Prison, a huge gaol on the bank of the Irwell at Salford, prisoners were scrubbed down and kept in quarantine. Warders even stopped the treadmill for the duration of the epidemic. Nonetheless, cholera found its way under the cell doors and 19 inmates died. Six men also died in just one room at Manchester Workhouse.

The most alarming outbreak, however, took place alongside the River Irk. Allen's Court was a foul place – a row of houses built 40ft below street level. It was entered via a steep, dark passage from Long Millgate. Dr Gaulter wrote of the court: 'You descend through a passage to the row of houses on the river's edge by interrupted flights of steep steps and you find yourself at the bottom in a kind of well or pit, suffocated for want of air and half poisoned by the effluvia arising from two conveniences which stand in the centre of the well-like area.' Eighteen people contracted the disease there in 48 hours during a 'frightful explosion' of the disease and only four survived. A tripe-boiling works stood on one side of the court, opposite a cat gut factory. It was piled high with cow hooves and pig offal. The Walker's Croft cemetery, which became the main burial ground for Manchester's cholera victims, also overlooked the court from beyond a tannery and backed on to the workhouse garden. The Irk ran almost under the houses and was described by Dr Gaulter as 'dyed and defiled by impurities of every kind'.

The first man to die in Allen's Court was an old soldier named William Bostock, who shared his filthy, ground-floor room with three other people. Bostock, a match seller with a winter cough, was a hard drinker. Gaulter said a 'pint of rum was nothing to him', but he was never seen drunk except on the days when he collected his pension. Bostock had believed the 'enchanted ring' he always wore protected him from diarrhoea and drink-induced cramps. He died from cholera two days after he lost it during a drinking binge.

Against the authorities' advice, Bostock's wife kept his body at home for two days instead of sending it across the river to the cemetery. Dr Gaulter wrote: 'The impression of the people of Allen's Court that Bostock's dead body had bred the infection was so strong that they could hardly be restrained from laying violent hands on his widow.' Some people in the court did try to help – and suffered for it. Anne Godwin, the sober and respectable wife of an impoverished silk weaver, was so poor she lived mainly on cups of tea. She died after she was seen to recoil at the foul smell of Bostock's corpse while delivering a note to his wife.

Unluckiest of all was William Turner, 53, a singer from Dublin, who had had to abandon a career on the stage after his teeth fell out. He learned to weave silk, but was forced to flee to Manchester when cholera arrived in Dublin. The disease arrived in Manchester just before him, however, and Turner died at Allen's Court in a room he shared with another family and two dogs. The death toll was so high in Allen's Court that it became known as 'Cholera Court'. It was finally evacuated, fumigated and whitewashed by the Board of Health.

By 14 July there had been 74 cases of cholera, including 49 deaths. The *Manchester Guardian* reported: 'We believe the whole of the new cases are from New Town, Angel Meadow, Back Irk Street, and their immediate neighbourhoods.' Cholera spread deeper into Angel Meadow during the ensuing weeks, with 23 cases in Angel Street alone. Patrick McBride, a shoemaker, had been drunk on rum for four days before he became ill and it took him 12 hours to die. Two sisters, Anne and Margaret Hannah, aged three and eight, died in Back Irk Street, down the middle of which ran an open sewer.

Thomas Nobel, aged seven, lived in a 'very loathsome court' with his mother, a destitute Irish widow. The street was covered with mud and ashes and was considered one of the filthiest in Manchester. Their house stood next to a large pool full of excrement and rotten vegetables. Nobel died after trying to eat a red herring for dinner. Phoebe Drew, 45, and her husband James, a 50-year-old weaver, lived in filthy house in No.1 Court off Blackley Street with six children and no furniture. Phoebe recovered, but James and two of their children died.

William Johnson, aged five, lived in a narrow passage with an open cesspool. His father Edward, 45, was a powerfully built joiner. Before William died, Edward picked him up and kissed him several times. He then began to make his son's coffin with his own tools, but became so distressed that he was found lying next to the body in a drunken heap.

Angel Meadow's inmates lived in mortal fear of being sent to the cholera hospital, because so few returned home. More than 200 people died there, after spending their final hours enduring experimental treatments, such as having their blood drained or being given stimulants including brandy, ammonia, castor oil, turpentine and opium. Doctors forced patients to vomit non-stop, while others had their heads shaved and were made to sit in bed with leeches sucking their scalps.

Cholera victims' neighbours gave anonymous tip-offs to medical officers and the horse-drawn cholera van soon trundled towards their homes. Gaulter said the hearse-like van was greeted by the 'most distressing scenes'. Victims who refused to leave their homes were thrown in the van overcome with fear. Others were carried to the hospital by their families in slings made from bed sheets. The next journey for many was in a 'dead van' carrying them to Walker's Croft, the resting place, according to Friedrich Engels, of 'the outcast and the superfluous'.

Five nurses and a porter at the cholera hospital died within a month. The staff drank to forget the horrors they witnessed. One nurse, Ruth Coe, 74, was short, bent and shrunken with old age. She ate nothing but slops and gin for days, and died after a final meal of sour gooseberries. Jane MacBride, 34, a drunken nurse who sucked lemons when she was thirsty, survived, while her colleague Mary Waddington, 43, a stout woman with a taste for ale, died after carrying a patient's body to the dead house. Jane Buckley, 35, binged on gin and ate a potato pie supper before cholera took her.

Hospital porter William Rydyard, 47, was a recovering alcoholic. He lived in the hospital lodge and only went to the wards to deliver messages. He concealed his diarrhoea for a fortnight but the end came on 29 July, when he was ordered to put some of the bodies from Allen's Court into coffins. He became 'powerfully agitated' before he died. Other victims at the hospital included Elizabeth Isaacs, a visitor who spent a long time removing a ring from the hand of her daughter Mary Barlow – eventually snapping the corpse's finger to retrieve it.

Fears were heightened that summer when the Anatomy Act was passed by Parliament, allowing unclaimed corpses at hospitals or workhouses to be dissected. People feared the sick would be whisked off by bodysnatchers or 'Burkers' – named after Burke and Hare, the two notorious Edinburgh murderers executed in 1828 for selling corpses to doctors for dissection. Medical students carrying out dissections on Manchester cholera victims had a plentiful supply of fresh bodies. The death toll reached its peak in August, with 650 new cases. Just a month later, the growing panic exploded into a riot. The boiling point came after a pensioner named John Hayes discovered that a medical student, 19-year-old Robert Oldham, had cut off the head of his three-year-old grandson, John Brogan.

John Brogan, the son of a weaver, took ill from cholera on Friday, 31 August and died four hours after he arrived at the hospital. At 8.30am the following Sunday, his body was being buried at the cemetery when his grandfather John Hayes noticed that no name was chalked on the lid. He grew suspicious and asked for the coffin to be opened, saying he wanted a lock of his grandson's hair. The sexton, growing angry, said Hayes could open the coffin if he kept quiet until the end of the service.

Hayes found to his horror that his grandson's head was missing and had been replaced with a brick wrapped in straw. He quietly closed the lid and helped cover the coffin with earth. Afterwards he went to find Father Daniel Hearne, the parish priest of St Patrick's Catholic Church – a large redbrick building which had opened at the northern edge of St George's Fields just six months earlier, on 29 February.

Hearne, a tough Irishman from Waterford, lived in a house next to the church in Livesey Street with a Wesleyan minister, the Reverend John Smith. They had agreed to drop their religious differences and worked together to visit the sick and relieve the poor. During the cholera outbreak, Hearne did more than anyone to help victims of the disease.

Hayes and Hearne went to the cholera hospital to investigate Hayes' claims and they were told that the old man's suspicions were true. Hayes then returned to the cemetery with a crowd of men, women and children, who rushed into the gates behind the dead van. Hayes began clawing at the wet clay until he reached the only coffin with no name chalked on the lid. He then lifted the headless body of his grandson into the daylight and cradled him in his arms.

The screams of the women broke the silence. A newspaper report later described the scene: 'The groans and howls of the men, the shrieks of the women and the screams and crying of the children were quite appalling.' Hayes had shown them proof of what he already knew to be true. "To the hospital," the crowd shouted. "Pull it to the ground!" It was 5.15pm on 2 September 1832. Moments later, the streets around Angel Meadow were engulfed in a vicious riot that dwarfed all those that had gone before.

John Brogan's body was perfectly white and appeared to have been drained of blood, which led the crowd to believe he had been murdered. Three men named Joseph Pugh, Thomas Gibson and John Burke seized the coffin and began carrying it up Miller Street towards the hospital, telling everyone they met that the child's head had been stolen by the cholera doctors. Rumours spread like wildfire through Angel Meadow. Soon the mob had swelled to 3,000 angry people. When they reached the hospital, they smashed their way inside as the doctors and nurses tried tò flee. Some patients were taken home by their families in a state of collapse and later died.

One nurse jumped into bed and began writhing in fake agony to make the rioters believe she was a patient. The doctors climbed a ladder and escaped over the back wall, but the mob found the 'dead van' driver in the stables. Hayes shouted: "Give me my child's head!" The driver fled over the wall as the mob pulled the van into the street and set it on fire. They dragged beds, tables and chairs outside and threw them onto the blaze. The hospital was only saved because the mob was too afraid to remove some of the inmates and they spared the windows in the wards where the patients lay.

Stephen Lavender, the deputy constable, arrived with 15 police officers and special constables armed with cutlasses. They arrested two people, but the mob launched a desperate rescue. One officer, William Booth, was knocked down three times and lost his hat. Another, Samuel Clough, was hit with a large paving stone which smashed his elbow. Benjamin Braidley, the borough reeve, arrived with reinforcements at 7.20pm. As they began hitting the rioters on their backs with the flat sides of their cutlasses, Father Hearne climbed on a barrel outside the hospital gates and begged the mob to go home.

They began to disperse just in time. Horses' hooves echoed through the streets as four troops of hussars galloped to the hospital. They were the same regiment that 16 years earlier had charged on the crowd at Peterloo. Some injured rioters fell as they fled back to Angel Meadow and those captured were taken to New Bailey Prison, while the hussars patrolled the streets on horseback until the early hours. They ordered the pubs and beer shops to close. The riot was over.

The mutilation of John Brogan's body sparked national outrage. It emerged that 19-year-old medical student Robert Oldham had severed the boy's head after bribing a nurse to keep quiet. He fled Manchester as magistrates issued a warrant for his arrest and managed to escape justice. Mr Lynch, who ran the hospital, was cleared of any blame.

Shocking details emerged of what the mob had done with John Brogan's body. Thomas Gibson, John Burke and Joseph Pugh had left the hospital while the riot was still raging and carried John's coffin through the streets, showing it to everyone they passed and demanding money 'for the parents'. They even stopped a stagecoach and forced the passengers to pay 'contributions'. A surgeon named Robert Sharpe was ordered to climb down from his carriage and inspect the body. The court heard Burke in particular had been 'very busy' pulling off the coffin lid and showing people the corpse in return for money. He wore a rough-skin cap and held it out to collect pennies. When police arrived, he rushed forward and tried to escape. Burke and Gibson were jailed. Only Pugh was discharged, as the court found he was 'not of a very sound mind'.

Father Hearne went looking for John's head. He found it in Robert Oldham's lodgings. He wrapped it carefully in his handkerchief and carried it to Manchester Town Hall, where it was sewn back on to John's body. Hearne then went to see John's family and also secured a promise from the authorities that all Catholics who died from cholera in the coming weeks could be buried in the cemetery at St Patrick's Church.

By the time the cholera epidemic finally subsided, more than 2,100 people in Manchester had contracted the disease and 920 had died – many of them in Angel Meadow. Cholera would return to the town in 1849, 1854 and 1866. The Victorian historian Thomas Swindells later wrote: 'During those terrible months, no one in the town was more assiduous in his endeavours to relieve the sufferings of the victims of the disease than Father Hearne. He was to many a sufferer a ministering angel.'

John Brogan's second funeral took place at St Patrick's at 5pm on 3 September. Hundreds of people flooded through the church gates. After the funeral, Hearne walked down the altar steps and pleaded with the crowd to go quietly to their homes. The priest blamed the riot on the 'imprudent youth' Robert Oldham and denied rumours that he had raised a cholera victim from the dead. He wrote a note in the burial register that evening: 'This child whose corpse was mutilated in the cholera hospital by R Oldham, who was obliged to fly on this act to appease the populace. The body, after the head had been attached to it, was re-interred in St Patrick's burial ground in a lead coffin.'

Only a few more cholera cases were reported that day and by the next week the epidemic appeared to be in decline. The sound of hammering echoed through the streets as workmen began repairing the cholera hospital.

Chapter 6

Irish Town

It was just after 3pm when the fight broke out in Angel Street. An Irishman, fresh out of a beer house named the Red Bull, was arguing with a prostitute when a Mancunian interfered and punched him in the face. Now the prostitute entered the fray, swinging wild punches at the Irishman. If the rector of St Michael's had been watching from the bell tower, the woman and the two men scuffling below would have appeared small and insignificant. It was a Sunday afternoon and drunken fights on the Sabbath were nothing unusual.

Then some of the Irishman's friends rushed to his defence, while Englishmen joined the side of his opponent. Within seconds, the whole neighbourhood was in uproar. The argument that sparked the fracas had little to do with the nationalities or faiths of the two men, but the battle lines were now clearly drawn: Irishman against Englishman, Catholic against Protestant. The Irish were driven back, but returned with reinforcements and began charging through the streets attacking every Mancunian they could find. Rumours spread through the streets that the Catholics were about to murder all the Protestants. An Irishman, Joseph Kittrick, added fuel to the fire when he shouted: "Kill the heretics!"

The Irish mob cornered a bystander named Booth in Nicholas Street and knocked him down some cellar steps. An Irishman named Andrew Cosgrove jumped down the steps and stamped on Booth's head. Joshua Stubbs, a neighbour who witnessed the attack, tried to flee but was knocked down and beaten by 20 men. The Irish took as good a beating as they gave – Edward Kittrick, the brother of Joseph Kittrick, was so badly beaten that his face was unrecognisable.

Police officers arrived and tried to make arrests. Two constables named William Kilby and Joseph Coyle grabbed hold of Cosgrove outside the Red Bull as the Irish pelted them with bricks. The badly-bloodied Edward Kittrick picked up a heavy piece of iron from outside a foundry and launched it at a third constable named Johnson, missing his head by inches and hitting Kilby in the groin. Joseph Kittrick then threw a brick at Kilby – striking him in the neck and causing blood to spurt from his ears. The constables were forced to retreat but other officers armed with cutlasses and pistols arrived and finally managed to restore order.

Cosgrove, the two Kittricks and another Irishman named James Glennan were arrested and charged with leading a desperate riot. The magistrate, Mr Norris, said it was one of the most 'outrageous and disgraceful' cases he had ever seen. He warned Cosgrove that he could face jail for the 'unmanly barbarity of his conduct'. Cosgrove and the Kittricks denied being involved and Glennan claimed that he had remained at his lodgings all day. They were ordered to pay bonds to keep the peace. Newspapers reporting the incident blamed the Irish for the riot.

Irish migrants had been travelling to Manchester since ships had begun crossing the Irish Sea. Most would scrape some money from seasonal farm work before returning to their rented plots for the potato harvest. But during the Industrial Revolution large numbers decided to stay. Whole families sailed by steamer from Dublin to Liverpool – the journey taking three hours and costing just a few pence. The poorest travelled for free as human ballast on empty coal ships. One overcrowded vessel arrived at the mouth of the Mersey carrying 72 dead, after the captain battened down the hatches in a storm. At Liverpool docks the Irish had to avoid robbers known as 'man catchers' before setting off inland to Manchester.

New arrivals gathered in two areas of the city: Chorlton Row to the south and Angel Meadow to the north. Chorlton Row, which became known as Little Ireland, was an area of low swampy ground cupped by a bend in the River Medlock. The chimney pots stood only a little above the level of the road, and during heavy rain the Medlock would burst its banks and flood the houses. Water rose up through holes in the floors and the Irish would spend days bailing out their parlours.

Those who went north to Angel Meadow took over a group of densely-packed houses in New Town, which was soon re-christened Irish Town. Friedrich Engels wrote: 'Here all the features of a city are lost. Single rows of houses or groups of streets stand, here and there, like little villages on the naked, not even grass-grown, clay soil.' According to Engels, the houses were filthy, damp and unclean, and colonies of pigs were kept penned in small sties or yards, or left wandering through the neighbourhood. He said: 'The mud in the streets is so deep that there is never a chance, except in the driest weather, of walking without sinking into it ankle deep at every step.'

A journalist from the *Manchester Guardian* later described how the pigs took over every open space in New Town. Behind Dimity Street, he found 16 pigs crowded in a pen without any drainage to 'carry away the filth'. 'It soaks through and runs amongst the soil till the place is offensive in the extreme for yards away,' he wrote. 'Dimity Street itself is a wretched and most squalid place. The roadway is full of filthy puddles, and the houses in disrepair, and no one seems to care.' In Olive Street, a dozen houses shared a privy without a door. The street had a high wall shutting it out from an open space in front, which contained yet more pigsties. In a shed, the journalist found hundreds of cow hooves and bones waiting to be boiled.

Pump Yard, a court with an open gutter running down its centre, held four privies and an ash-pit. 'As the rain washes over them the liquid filth runs down the yard, till the grid at the bottom is choked,' the journalist wrote, 'after this it overflows and drops into the back yards of some houses at a lower level, where we leave it fulfilling its mission of death.'

Silver Street was said by sanitary inspectors to be 'most abominable and disgusting' and a source of 'plague and pestilence'. Dead dogs floated in a pool of stagnant water behind the starch works in Back Buckley Street. In Flag Row, the privies were so bad that the occupants of four houses used the railway line as a toilet instead.

In 1828, there were more than 1,500 Irish in New Town. Three years later there were more than 4,000. The new arrivals fanned out across Angel Meadow. The Irish community was so large and their living conditions so poor that they became scapegoats for the worst horrors of the Industrial Revolution, occupying the cheapest, dampest, dirtiest homes. A brother and sister named Hudson collapsed and died in the 'tainted atmosphere' of a damp and filthy cellar, which they shared with four other people. They were starving and had been suffering from fever for 14 days, but they were so afraid of being sent back to Ireland that they delayed going to the workhouse. Newspapers blamed them for their own demise and expressed astonishment at the 'miserable' conditions Irish families would endure to 'drag on existence'.

Dr James Phillips Kay did more than anyone to damage the reputation of the Irish. He argued that the rapid expansion of Manchester's cotton industry had caused Ireland to 'pour forth the most destitute of her hordes'. Kay claimed the Irish had taught their English neighbours the 'fatal secret' of how to live 'like a savage'. He wrote: 'I consider that the buildings erected in Irish Town, and in some other of the worst parts of Manchester, almost entirely owe their existence to the immigration of the Irish. If it had not been for the Irish, there would have been no class of persons on whose willingness to put up with so small an amount of convenience it would have been prudent to speculate.'

Another doctor, Peter Gaskell, claimed the habits of the Irish were 'vile in the extreme' as they lived alongside their pigs – an early form of central heating – in cellars that were 'disgusting receptacles of every species of vermin which can infest the human body'. After touring New Town and Angel Meadow, even

Friedrich Engels wrote: 'The Irishman loves his pig as the Arab his horse, with the difference that he sells it when it is fat enough to kill. Otherwise, he eats and sleeps with it, his children play with it, ride upon it, roll in the dirt with it.'

Engels said the Irish were unaccustomed to furniture and made their beds from heaps of straw, sacking and a few rags. A broken chair, a tea-kettle, a few pots and dishes were all the furniture they needed. When they ran out of firewood, they burned chairs, door-posts and even floorboards. 'Drink is the only thing which makes the Irishman's life worth having,' he said. 'So he revels in drink to the point of the most bestial drunkenness.' Engels felt their 'brutal habits' placed the Irish 'but little above the savage'.

One mill owner, Mr Potter, sacked all his Irish weavers because he claimed they were 'slovenly and mutinous'. Others encouraged Irish immigration. Mr Taylor, who owned a Manchester silk mill, regularly applied to Connaught for workers when his English hands went on strike. He explained:

> The whole family comes – father, mother, and children. I provide them with no money. I suppose they sell up what they have, walk to Dublin, pay their own passage to Liverpool, and come to Manchester by the railway, or walk it. I should think that more than 400 have come over to me from Ireland, many of whom left me after they had learnt their trade.

Many Irish took up work as labourers. A report on the state of the Irish poor in England in 1835 stated that they were employed in the 'roughest, coarsest, and most repulsive' work. But Irish priests, including Angel Meadow's own Daniel Hearne, felt the Irish faced discrimination in the workplace. Hearne said: 'There are instances where the Irish are prevented from advancing in the world by feelings of jealousy. A manufacturer would prefer employing English to Irish simply on the ground of their being Irish, and not of their being worse workmen.'

Irish workers began bypassing the labour market by taking up stalls on Smithfield Market – a vast emporium to the south-east of the slum. It was home to thousands of merchants dealing in butter, tea, groceries, cheese, ham, spices, fish and other provisions. Hungry lads gaped at the shellfish on display. Stalls, booths and barrows lined the pavement. Flaming naphtha lamps threw out a lurid glare on to customers' faces and lit up the stock exposed for sale. Within the space of a few years, the Irish controlled three-quarters of the market and a report claimed they were driving out English stallholders. The Irish succeeded because they were content with less profit. They were the lucky ones. Many of their countrymen fell into poverty and had to beg or go hawking to survive.

Some streets in Angel Meadow were three-quarters Irish. Dr Gaskell said the sight of the Irish emerging from their 'loathsome' dwellings and setting off in search of work was 'truly astonishing':

All are ragged, all are filthy, all are squalid. They separate to pursue various callings, either shutting up their dens till night, or leaving a child as the sole occupant. A great portion of these wander the town and its suburbs, begging or stealing. Others hawk little matters, such as pins, matches and oranges, and bring back with them any fragment of meat or bread they have been able to procure.

Superintendent Edward Davies of the Manchester Watch claimed two-thirds of people arrested in the city were Irish and they accounted for a 'greater proportion of the youthful thieves'. He said: 'We believe that we have here the worst part of the Irish population – persons who leave their own country in order to fly from justice.' But the Irish were also victims of crime. One Monday night, an unnamed Irishman was talking to a woman named Sarah Mills when he was attacked by four men and robbed of his watch, hat and snuff box.

The Irish were notoriously fond of fighting and carried out 'terrible outrages' on their own countrymen during drunken brawls. William Sims was charged with stabbing Henry Dorvill in Angel Street on the day he became godfather to Dorvill's child. After the baptism, Sims had a drunken argument with Dorvill's wife and threatened to 'kick out her brains'. Dorvill attacked Sims, who pulled out a knife and stabbed him seven times in the arm. Dorvill, a strong and powerful man, collapsed. When Sims was later arrested, his shirt sleeves were dyed red with his friend's blood.

Newspapers told how three 'natives of the Emerald Isle' named Flanagan, Brannan and Walsh, were also charged with murdering a countryman named O'Brien with a poker, and threatening to stab his wife. The *Manchester Courier* reported: 'After hearing from many witnesses, some of them very hard swearing, and after several different versions of the row, the magistrates decided that O'Brien had certainly been beaten if he had not been murdered and he fined the three prisoners each 20 shillings, or one month's imprisonment.'

Street battles between Irish factions were common in Angel Meadow and Irish Town. It was said that, if a fight broke out, a crowd of 1,000 men and women could appear in just five minutes. They fought with pokers, sticks and clubs. Dr Gaskell wrote: 'Often the whole population of a court, street, or entire district, forms a faction in opposition to that of some other in the neighbourhood and the cries of O'Flanagan and McCarthy are as rife as in the heart of Connaught.' One fight only came to an end when Father Hearne called a peace summit. John Redman, New Town's overseer, explained:

> Some of the Irish in this neighbourhood are from the north, but the chief part are from County Leitrim and County Roscommon. A fight between these two counties lasted more or less for a fortnight the summer before last. Both men and women joined in it. They fought with weapons and fists. It was at last put down by the interference of the priest, who called a meeting in the Sunday school. The police interfere sometimes, but not much.

Hearne was a fearless champion of Irish causes. One parishioner said the priest was 'exceedingly popular' and bore a 'wonderful resemblance' to the Irish politician Daniel O'Connell. A parishioner named Joseph Johnson remembered walking along St George's Road with Hearne as a boy when they saw a great crowd forming a ring around two Irishmen, who were fighting in the middle of the street. Johnson later wrote:

> The good father quickly placed me in a doorway, telling me not to move until he returned, and then sprang into the crowd, wielding a mahogany stick, which he let fall upon the shoulders of all indiscriminately. A thunderbolt could not have cleared the street quicker or more completely. No-one attempted to retaliate. Notwithstanding this rough method of reproving the members of his church, he was greatly beloved and by the poor he was almost worshipped.

The fighting Irish were quick to defend their kinsmen against outsiders and, when police tried to make an arrest, hundreds of people would pour out of their homes to stop the perpetrators being taken to the cells. Superintendent Edward Davies said a force of up to 20 officers had to be deployed each time the police needed to arrest one Irishman in Irish Town. He warned: 'The whole neighbourhood turn out with weapons – even women, half-naked, carrying brickbats and stones for the men to throw.'

An Irishman would try to fight arrest to buy enough time for his friends to muster a rescue. When he was finally taken kicking and screaming to the police station, he would have barely a stitch of clothing left on his body. The streets had weapons of their own and many people kept a supply of stones in their homes, which they used 'with great effect' – leaving the street littered with them. One writer claimed: 'Before a disturbance, not half a dozen could have been found on the roadway, but when all was over they could be counted by the hundred. Many a hard fight was waged with the police, who did not always come off without serious hurt.'

Superintendent Edward Davies added: 'Scenes of this kind happen more particularly on a Saturday night. It rarely happens that the Irish think of going to bed for the whole of that night. There is not one in 20 of the inhabitants of the Irish quarters of the town who would dare to appear against an Irishman if he was assaulted or his property damaged. He would expect to have his life taken.'

Joseph Sadler Thomas, the Deputy Constable of Manchester and a former superintendent of Covent Garden in London, observed that it was 'extremely dangerous' to make an arrest at a factory where Irishmen were employed: 'They will throw bricks and stones on the officers' heads as they are coming up stairs, and frequently succeed in driving them off.'

On 1 January 1829, a crowd of up to 400 Irishmen began fighting outside a pub in St George's Road. The pub's windows were smashed. The rioters went to a house in Angel Meadow, where they armed themselves with fire irons and bludgeons. Two police officers named Cook and Williamson were sent restore order, but they came under fire from a volley of stones and were knocked down and beaten. Williamson escaped. Cook was forced into a dark alley and attacked by men who jumped on his head and smashed his nose with a poker. His left eyelid was hanging loose and he went blind in his right eye for nine days. His jaw was so badly bruised that he could eat no solid food for a fortnight. Two men, Thomas Kelly and Thomas Dillon, were jailed for six months for the attack.

Deputy Constable Thomas blamed the violence on a large number of Irish-owned beer shops selling home-made whiskey or poteen, an illicit spirit made by distilling fermented potatoes. Superintendent Davies said these shops were 'crammed with Irish the whole of Saturday night': 'Parties of men come mad drunk out of these places, armed with pokers and staves, and patrol the streets in order to assault any person they may meet, but especially Irish from other provinces. Very few English mix in these rows, or drink with the Irish.'

The *Manchester Guardian* claimed the area around St George's Road was now 'as bad or worse than St Giles in London', which was famed in the capital for its violent rookeries and gin palaces:

If there were any effectual means of discovering and putting down the illicit whiskey distilleries which abound thereabouts, and from which, after drinking there all night, the Irishmen turn out on the Sunday mornings, more like infuriated wild beasts than anything human, the neighbourhood would become, comparatively speaking, as quiet as any other.

On Easter Monday in 1829, a landlord named Arrowsmith who ran the Gas Tavern in Gould Street, stepped out of his parlour for a few minutes and returned to find his brewer lying flat on the floor with a large Irishman jumping on his head – his face now shockingly mangled. The rest of the customers were fighting in the packed front room. They were driven out but soon returned and smashed the window panes and shutters in an attack lasting a full hour. They only went home to their beds when Arrowsmith fired a pistol over their heads. One man named Loftus Burns, a 'newly imported Irishman', was arrested.

Arrowsmith offered a reward for the capture of Burns' accomplices, but no-one in Angel Meadow or New Town was brave or stupid enough to give evidence against them. The Irish now dominated the slum.

Chapter 7

Hell on Earth

Police constables Joseph Dugmore and Benjamin Pollitt were on duty during a foggy January night in 1838 when a roof slater named Peter Lea banged on the door of their police station and begged them to follow him to New Mount Street. Lea, who lived in the street with his wife and four children, had discovered an old couple named John and Elizabeth Hatton in a 'deplorable state' in a garret. The officers found the house in darkness. Dugmore took a candle, climbed the stairs and pushed open the door. As he waved the flame into the shadows, he found John Hatton sitting on the hearthstone of an empty fireplace. His shirt was unbuttoned, exposing his chest.

Dugmore recalled later: 'He appeared not in his proper senses, as he first pulled his hair, then thrust his hand into his breast and seized a rug lying near him.' Elizabeth Hatton was on her hands and knees moaning with pain. 'The stench in the room was dreadful,' Dugmore reported. 'There were two old chairs, one table at one end of the room and another at the side. Some old pictures were in the room and about three quarters of a pound of old bread, quite hard, and a little bit of coffee wrapped in a paper.'

A thick fog was rising from the Irk as the officers ordered a horse drawn coach and prepared to take the couple to Manchester Workhouse. As they crossed Ducie Bridge over the river, the coachman crashed into the kerb and was thrown into the air. His tired horse stood completely still and Dugmore was able to get him back into his seat. But when they finally reached the workhouse, the gatehouse keeper refused to admit the Hattons because they had been taken from a house and had not been found on the street.

The officers were enraged. Dugmore seized the reins and drove the coach across town to the home of Deputy Constable Joshua Thomas, who immediately gave Benjamin Pollitt two shillings and ordered him to get the couple some brandy and hot water from the nearest beer house. Pollitt said later: 'It was warm but weak. I gave it to them, holding the glass, and they drank it very freely and eagerly.' Mr Thomas then handed Pollitt a letter for the workhouse governor. It stated: 'Sir, I send you, herewith, two poor old persons, as I think in a famishing state, and very ill, and I have to request that you will not refuse them admission into the workhouse.'

Pollitt returned to the workhouse and banged on the door, but the gatehouse keeper now refused to give the letter to the governor. Pollitt had no choice but to drive two miles to New Bailey Prison, where he carried the Hattons through the prison yard to the hospital wing. John, 55, and Elizabeth, 65, were too weak to stand. Mrs Walker, the wife of the prison gatekeeper, prepared some gruel and put them into bed. By the time the fog had cleared in the morning, they were dead.

Henry Ollier, the prison surgeon, carried out a post-mortem, which revealed that John had died from fever and diseased lungs. Elizabeth was very thin, her lungs were also diseased and her stomach badly ulcerated. They could have survived, he said, with prompt medical attention at the workhouse.

But John Redman, the overseer of the poor, claimed that the proper procedure was for him to visit the poor at home and decide whether they should be admitted. William Robinson, the workhouse governor, said he would have refused the couple even if the gatehouse keeper had handed him the deputy constable's letter. The workhouse had been hit by an outbreak of fever and he was cautious about admitting new arrivals. The coroner absolved Robinson of criminal negligence and the gatehouse keeper faced no charges. The jury found that Mr Thomas had acted with 'great humanity', but he told the inquest he was motivated only by 'the desire of doing his duty to his fellow creatures'.

Fever, bronchitis, tuberculosis and typhus were the biggest killers in Angel Meadow throughout the 1840s. The slum had become a giant fever nest, with more than 900 cases recorded in one year alone. The worst outbreaks were in winter, when people bolted their doors and stayed huddled around fires in airless, overcrowded rooms. Two-thirds of houses in the slum were reported at any one time to contain sick inmates and the death rate was said to be 'alarming'. The *Manchester Courier* blamed the 'unclean people' drifting into Manchester in search of work, who would have no access to bathing facilities when they arrived.

Doctors at the time believed fever was caused by human waste, overcrowding and intemperance, and that typhus was incubated in the slum's cesspools. Dr John Leigh said that fever 'prevailed' in the Meadow. He deduced that smoke from the slum's factories was causing bronchitis and found streets where gas seeped from grids and settled in people's homes. According to Leigh, the slum's privies were 'disgusting' and the houses badly overcrowded. He felt the conditions were exacerbated by the ignorance of the inhabitants: 'Sometimes, the people make the matter worse by their own habits.'

Scrofula, a disease that disfigured people's necks and faces, was also common in Angel Meadow. Investigators found that 97 out of 317 men, women and children at Manchester Workhouse had some form of scrofula, while 45 were suffering from tuberculosis.

Old maps show how conditions had deteriorated in the years since the 1832 cholera outbreak. Victoria Station opened below the workhouse in 1844 and the Lancashire and Yorkshire Railway viaduct soon curved over Angel Meadow and New Town. The line crossed the Irk three times and trains had to be pulled up the hill using a wire rope. Careless engineers building the viaduct sank wooden piles into the graves in the Walker's Croft cholera cemetery, causing putrefying liquids to ooze from the swampy ground and fill the neighbourhood with 'revolting gasses'. They also opened some of the old hidden courtyards beside the river, leaving their private horrors on public display. Builders covered the Irk's tributaries and created a cavernous brick tunnel connecting the Irk to the Irwell beneath Victoria Station. Map makers mistakenly coloured the Irk a vibrant blue.

A huge gasworks was also built at the northern edge of Gould Street, with three gas towers adding a new layer of toxicity to the stinking atmosphere. The gasworks produced six million cubic feet of gas per day and was a huge powder keg, with its cellars holding 25,000 tons of coal, 6,000 tons of coke and 300,000 gallons of tar and ammonia water. It was prone to explosions and, at 7am one Saturday, a number of men were blown up and the slum rocked by a huge explosion. The men were knocked down by the blast and covered by a sheet of flames and badly burned. The poor could be seen hanging around the gasworks every day, scavenging pieces of coke for their fires.

Inspectors from the Manchester and Salford Sanitary Association reported that the enclave of Gibraltar had become 'abominable', as the houses there were 'excessively overcrowded' with up to 30 men and women living together in a single cellar. Strangers here were watched with suspicion and on every side could be heard the sound of the axe or knife. Around 20 pigs were kept in the only patch of open space. There were no water taps in Gibraltar. The inspectors called for the area to be wiped from the map and for the Irk to be completely sealed over.

In Back Simpson Street, the inspectors found a huge hole filled with offal being used as a public toilet. Beard's Court, off Simpson Street, contained a backstreet slaughter house. In Welsh's Court, off Angel Street, human waste was causing 'the most noxious smell'. Flag Alley, off Ludgate Street, had no drainage and was in a 'sad, dilapidated and neglected state'. The alley was 14ft wide and 96 people lived in its eight houses. The street's water taps had been stolen, whereas in other streets the taps were only switched on for one hour each day.

The inspectors found men, women and children sleeping naked in a double bed and others lying on wood shavings on the floor beneath an old blanket. 'In one house,' they observed in their report, 'the floor of the upstairs room was literally covered with human beings.' In every house, the windows were sealed shut and the ceilings were so low that it was impossible to stand upright. The privies were overflowing and the passages leading to them were full of faeces. One inspector said: 'The possession of a privy by the inhabitants of each separate house is a luxury I have rarely discovered.'

The fever epidemic's epicentre was the Old Burying Ground next to St Michael's Church, which had closed to burials in 1816. Neighbours used it as a dump for ashes, offal, dead cats and rotten shellfish. They tore up the old headstones and used them to fill holes in their floors and walls. Children played in piles of straw from slum dwellers' fever beds. They set the straw on fire and took part in games of football with the skulls that emerged from the uneven ground. Some bodies were buried just 14 inches below the surface.

Bodysnatchers had long been creeping into the cemetery at night to dig up bones, which they would sell to Manchester's glue factories. This had been happening since 1800, when the *Manchester Mercury* reported an attempt to dig up a pauper who had died in the workhouse. A candle was found in the grave and a coffin lid had been forced open, but one side of the burial chamber had collapsed, which had caused the body snatchers to flee. Hawkers also removed cartloads of soil from the cemetery and sold it for compost. Benjamin Redfern revealed:

> Skulls, arms and leg bones very often come to the surface, for there are many thousands of bodies interred here, yet no care is taken to enclose the ground and prevent the fearful desecrations which its levelled walls and open character entails. The mere sight of it is enough to cause nausea to any but angelic stomachs.

Mr Cliffe, the Meadow's oldest resident, had known the cemetery since 1817 when it was covered with a 'pleasant carpet of grass' and was 'duly respected by the inhabitants'. It had now become a 'serious disgrace' to Manchester. He recalled: 'About 1830, the wall began to give way, and ultimately it disappeared altogether, after which deposits of various kinds were made upon the ground. Beds were emptied upon it and, not infrequently, large quantities of mussels were thrown there, the stench from which was dreadful.'

The district's medical officer Dr Edward Meacham wrote to Whitehall urging government ministers to intervene. His wish was granted and an inspector visited the cemetery with the Earl of Shaftesbury, who was attending a social science congress in Manchester. After the visit they retired to a wooden shed in Angel Meadow to listen to Meacham's concerns. He told them that the cemetery had become a 'disgrace to any civilised community'. Meacham called for the ground to be paved over – a wish that was later granted on the orders of Queen Victoria.

By 1847, the Irish were being blamed for Manchester's high death rate. A huge influx of immigrants had arrived during the devastating potato famine in Ireland. While many sailed to America in unseaworthy vessels known as coffin ships, others, by accident or design, settled in Britain. Around 1,500 arrived in Manchester every few weeks and soon the town's Irish population hit more than 52,000. They were blamed for the spread of typhus, measles and 'famine fever'. The registrar of the district that included Angel Meadow wrote:

> It is not unknown to find 20 or 30 persons living in one house, when there is not accommodation for one-third of that number. During the last two or three months, large numbers of the poor from Ireland have crowded themselves in the district – droves of them rambling about the streets seeking lodgings and no doubt being exposed to the severe and inclement weather. Many of the poor creatures have died from cold-producing fever and other diseases.

The registrar made inquiries and found that most of the dead had only been in England a few weeks. 'The poverty and destitution of the district at the present time is very great,' he wrote. 'The houses are very badly ventilated and the unhealthy odour arising from so many persons huddled together in a confined apartment must have a very injurious effect. It cannot be surprising, that while such a state of things exists, the mortality should be so great.'

Officials were finally accepting that the shocking living conditions, and not the Irish themselves, were to blame for Angel Meadow's notorious reputation. The *Manchester Guardian* said the high death rate could not be 'ascribed in any great extent to the influx of Irish'. Instead, the newspaper blamed the high price of food, depression of trade and a cold winter for the deaths.

Living conditions in the Meadow were now about to reach worldwide attention through a provocative book. Friedrich Engels, the son of a German cotton manufacturer, was sent to Manchester by his father to work at the family's mill in Salford. He arrived in December 1842 from London, then met and fell in love with the daughter of Irish immigrants named Mary Burns, who took him on a tour of Manchester's underworld in 1844. Burns was a factory girl and a fierce Irish patriot. Engels was 22, tall and slender, with brown hair and piercing blue eyes.

When Engels first arrived he stayed in lodgings in Strangeways, just a short walk from the slum. He wrote in a letter home that Manchester was a town that 'changed water into stinking slops'. In his book, *The Condition of the Working Class in England*, he described the slum as 'hell upon earth'.

Engels peered over a high parapet on Ducie Bridge at the narrow stairs that led down over heaps of rubbish to Allen's Court, opposite the workhouse. He wrote of the view:

> At the bottom flows, or rather stagnates, the Irk, a narrow, coal-black, foul-smelling stream, full of debris and refuse, which it deposits on the shallower right bank. In dry weather, a long string of the most disgusting, blackish-green, slime pools are left standing on this bank, from the depths of which bubbles of miasmatic gas constantly arise and give forth a stench unendurable even on the bridge 40 or 50 feet above the surface of the stream. But besides this, the stream itself is checked every few paces by high weirs, behind which slime and refuse accumulate and rot in thick masses.

To the north, Engels saw the gasworks, bone mills and tanneries. The houses in the railway viaduct's shadow were 'black, smoky, crumbling and ancient'. The sky was blocked out by barrack-like factory buildings. In a row of houses and mills that stood squashed on the right bank, the second house was a ruin, its roof collapsed and the interior piled with debris.

Engels descended from the bridge into a labyrinth of covered passages leading from Long Millgate. He found himself wading through filth and grime. At the entrance to one passage he discovered a privy with no door, which could only be reached by venturing through pools of urine and excrement. Onwards he went into the courts of Angel Meadow, where he found pigs imprisoned in small pens rented out by small-time gangsters known as 'pork raisers'. The neighbours dumped offal in the pens and the pigs grew fat. 'The atmosphere is utterly corrupted by putrefying animal and vegetable substances,' Engels wrote.

The houses grew worse as he ventured north along the river. He turned countless corners into narrow, filthy nooks, until he was again completely lost. He described the scene:

> Everywhere half or wholly ruined buildings, some of them actually uninhabited, which means a great deal here – rarely a wooden or stone

floor to be seen in the houses, almost uniformly broken, ill-fitting windows and doors, and a state of filth. Everywhere heaps of debris, refuse, and offal, standing pools for gutters, and a stench which alone would make it impossible for a human being in any degree civilised to live in such a district.

Engels passed beneath the railway viaduct, through a web of washing lines and entered 'a chaos of small one-roomed huts'. The inhabitants watched him in silence, leaning heavily against their doors – a 'physically degenerate race, robbed of all humanity'. He wrote of the area: 'This whole collection of cattle-sheds for human beings was surrounded on two sides by houses and a factory and on the third by the river, and besides the narrow stair up the bank, a narrow doorway alone led out into another almost equally ill-built, ill-kept labyrinth of dwellings.'

He finally left the Irk and penetrated north-east up the hill towards St George's Road and became lost once again in a labyrinth of streets, going up a blind alley and turning a corner, only to end up where he started. Safely back at his lodgings, Engels later reviewed his notes. 'If any one wishes to see in how little space a human being can move, how little air — and *such* air — he can breathe, how little of civilisation he may share and yet live, it is only necessary to travel hither,' he concluded.

Manchester's sanitary inspectors finally took action three years after Engels' book was first published in Germany in 1845. They sent an army of 100 night-soil men across the city with 50 carts. In just 12 days they cleaned 1,900 ash pits and cleared 3,600 tons of human waste and 1,800 tons of rubbish. It was said that their work in the Meadow required 'great labour'. They found tons of human waste which hardened like concrete and had to be smashed with pickaxes. Their report revealed: 'One ash-pit occupied four men during six nights to empty it, and there were taken from its 36 cart loads of night-soil and rubbish. It was stated by the night-soil men that it had not been emptied to the bottom for the last 17 years.'

Within a year, the men had emptied two-thirds of Manchester's 30,000 ash-pits. But their efforts failed to prevent cholera from returning in 1849 and killing 700 people in the town.

The first victim of the new outbreak was James Robinson, 21, a prize-fighter from Angel Meadow. Robinson, whose grandfather was from North Africa, had followed his father, Matt Robinson, into the ring. Known as 'Jemmy the Black' and 'Young Phenomenon', he had fought a series of pitched battles and by 1849 was Champion of the Lightweights. Robinson married the daughter of a pub landlord, but, shortly before he died, he quarrelled with his family and moved to a room above a beer house off Miller Street, the Bird in Hand, where he led an 'irregular life' under the guidance of the drunken owner, Hartley.

On 1 June 1849, Robinson joined Hartley on a four-day drinking binge in Liverpool, which was already wracked by cholera. He downed vast quantities of ale, stayed in a filthy lodging house packed with sailors on the docks and took a swim in the Mersey. He returned to Manchester on 7 June to sober up and sweat down for his next fight, but was suddenly attacked by diarrhoea. By Sunday he was writhing restlessly in bed – his legs badly cramped. Rumours spread that he had eaten some putrid oysters, which were thought by some to be a cause of cholera.

Robinson's wife and mother refused to call a doctor and he suffered for six hours. They tried a series of useless remedies: beer, cayenne pepper and a tincture of rhubarb. When a doctor named Isaac Franklin finally arrived, he prescribed opium pills and mercury chloride. He rubbed hot turpentine on Robinson's stomach, coated his legs in an oatmeal poultice and cooked bricks in the fire and placed them on the soles of his feet. The boxer fought death for 21 hours, but his skin gradually turned cold and his pulse faltered. Dr Franklin noted a hard lump in his stomach the size of a fist. Finally, Robinson's fingernails turned blue. He sucked in his cheeks and died at 7am. The *Manchester Guardian* criticised the 'neglect, delay and foolish quacking' of his 'ignorant friends', who should have summoned the doctor sooner.

Just weeks after Robinson's death, an overseer of the poor was called to the home of an Irishman named Bernard Burns in Back New Mount Street. Burns had applied at the workhouse for a coffin for his wife, Bridget, who had died hours earlier. Their back-to-back house, owned by a shoemaker named William Finnerow, was 'exceedingly filthy' and 'crowded to excess with inmates'. Five families, totalling 26 people, lived in just two rooms, one upstairs and one downstairs. There were no beds and the inmates slept on litters made from wood shavings.

Burns, 55, and his wife had left County Cavan three weeks earlier with their four children. They were sent to England by an Irish poor law union which paid their five-shilling steamer fare. Mrs Burns died at the house on 21 June after being sick for 15 hours. Burns had feared they would be sent back to Ireland so he kept her illness secret. When a surgeon named Daniel Noble finally saw her blue-tinged body, he realised she had died from cholera. A police inspector had the house shut down and the straw from Mrs Burns' bedding was burned in the Old Burying Ground.

Burns, described as a sober man, was seized by cholera three days later as he was heading home from church. Two priests arrived at the house and found

Burns being violently sick. He was taken to a new cholera hospital across town in Canal Street, where Dr Franklin made 'vigorous' attempts to revive him with doses of opium before he died at 11am the next day.

By the end of July, 1849, cholera was spreading like wildfire through Angel Meadow. One man who was no longer there to help the slum's cholera victims was Father Daniel Hearne, who had been forced out of St Patrick's in controversial circumstances.

A rival vicar claimed he had seen one of Hearne's parishioners crawling about on his hands and knees while performing a penance. The poor man was found to have mental health issues and Hearne successfully sued for libel. But more trouble lay ahead when Hearne had a disagreement with his curate Father McCormick. At Sunday Mass, McCormick climbed into the pulpit and denounced Hearne. Members of the congregation were reduced to tears and the choristers were so shocked that they refused to sing any more hymns during the service.

Although angry parishioners made deputations to the bishop, he gave Hearne his marching orders in June 1846. They were so annoyed that they booed his replacement during Mass and showed their appreciation by presenting Hearne with a green silk purse containing 270 sovereigns, a large gold crucifix, a gold watch and a silver breakfast service. Hearne went to Rome, where he narrowly escaped an assassination attempt by an Italian revolutionary. He then moved to New York, where he died when some scaffolding collapsed while he was overseeing the building of a new church.

Back in Manchester, cholera was rampaging through the streets. By September 1849, it had killed 108 people in Angel Meadow. Police inspector William Gifford found two stagnant pools, a dirty slaughterhouse and six houses where pigs were kept by their owners for warmth. He instructed 38 landlords to whitewash their buildings. It was too little, too late.

Chapter 8

Family Life

Rachel Atkinson was 18 and heavily pregnant when she arrived at Bridget Barrow's lodging house in Angel Meadow late one January night in 1837. She had no money, but Bridget took pity and let her stay. Barrow cared for Rachel for five weeks by giving her scraps of leftover food and even helped deliver her baby girl, but Rachel knew she could not take advantage of Barrow's kindness for much longer. Soon, she would have to leave. Rachel was unmarried and the baby's father had disappeared. She earned a little money by wandering the streets selling ribbons and pins, but the goods in her basket were worth just sixpence and she was known to go five days without a wholesome meal.

It was 5pm when Rachel stepped out of the lodging house for the last time. She told Barrow she was taking the baby to be nursed by an old woman. John Corless was walking along a canal north east of the Meadow an hour later, when he saw her on the far bank in the gloom. He watched as Rachel knelt on the towpath and slipped a small bundle into the black water – her baby daughter. The baby floated so far across the canal that Corless was able to reach out and grab her tiny leg. She had already stopped breathing. Corless put the girl face down on his knee and slapped her back until she finally began to cry. He looked around, but Rachel had fled.

Corless took the baby to Ellen Scholes, the wife of an overseer of the poor, who wrapped her in warm flannels. Men began searching for Rachel and eventually found her wandering along the canal in the darkness, with her hair hanging down her face. A man named John Brown put a firm hand on her shoulder. "We want you," he said. "I know what you want me for," she told him. "I have put the child in the water and I'm not ashamed to say it." She handed Brown a small package containing the girl's frock and pinafore. "Here are the child's clothes," she said. "I was going to sell them."

A jury later found Rachel guilty of 'attempting to destroy' her daughter and, in light of her circumstances, they begged the judge to show Rachel mercy. Her sentencing went unrecorded and her fate remains unknown. One newspaper wrote: 'She had been seduced and abandoned by the seducer. Since then she had endured the utmost distress and in a state of misery and despair had thrown the child into the water.'

A stable family life was a rare thing in Angel Meadow, where troops of boys and girls became parents of rickety children before they were out of their teens. A boy would begin to throw off the shackles of parental control at 14 and start hanging around the slum's beer houses in the hope of cadging a glass of ale. By 21, he was likely to be married and to have set up a home of his own in a house lacking in comforts. Dr James Phillips Kay, who investigated living conditions in Angel Meadow, said: 'Home has no other relation to him than that of shelter – few pleasures are there – it chiefly presents to him a scene of physical exhaustion, from which he is glad to escape.'

Hardly any houses in Angel Meadow had a back yard. Almost all of them were built back-to-back – stopping air from circulating inside. They stood no higher than 14ft to the eaves and contained two 10ft square rooms, one above the other. The lower room served as sitting room, kitchen and bedroom, with steps leading from the front door straight down into the street. Wooden stairs led to the upper floor, which was sometimes split into two smaller bedrooms. If they were lucky, a family might have a cupboard for plates and cups, a table and a couple of chairs. A smoke-browned china ornament often sat on a shelf above the fire, while further luxuries included a painted tea tray and a clock – essential for mill workers who needed to get up for work. Those who had no clock relied on the 'knocker-uppers' – men who could be trusted to tap at the bedroom shutters with a long stick in the early hours for a small charge.

The poorest could only afford cellar dwellings, which were never well furnished and often had just a bed made from orange boxes in a dark and airless corner. The fire would smoulder among unswept ashes. The floors of many cellars were constantly wet with water draining in from the street and some were so damp that their ceilings were permanently shrouded in fog.

A writer named George Shore described how a married man from the slum would soon begin to spend more time with his old drinking friends, staying away from his miserable home: 'His week nights will for the most part are spent in the beer shop. Saturday afternoon will possess the attraction of foot races, rabbit coursing, cock fighting and secret prize-fighting. He will finish Sunday by getting drunk.'

Domestic violence was common within marriages and women in the slum were often seen with two black eyes. A couple named Patrick and Ann Doherty were charged with fighting in a 'most brutal manner' in Dyche Street. Ann's face was left horribly disfigured, but she begged the magistrates to discharge her husband and added: "All the baiting I got, I richly deserved."

One spring morning, Manchester's coroner held an inquest at the slum's Victory Tavern following the death of a woman named Lee. Her husband James Lee was hauled there from the New Bailey Prison on foot, followed by a great crowd who hooted and shouted 'murderer'. Charles McGuire, who lived in the couple's house in Angel Street, had found Mrs Lee dead on the floor of their room the previous Sunday, her mouth clogged with blood. Lee told him: "We had a few words. She awoke me in the morning and started calling me names. I gave her a bit of a kick and she fell off the stool."

McGuire roused the other people in the house and they put Mrs Lee's body on the bed. The inquest heard she was in the habit of getting drunk and often squabbled with her husband. James Looney, a shopkeeper who owned the house, said he had heard her screaming 'murder'. He said: "I didn't think it worthwhile to interfere. It's such a common occurrence." The couple had been drinking heavily the previous night. Lee was said to be a steady, hard-working man and the inquest was told that it was unlikely he had intended to harm his wife. A surgeon found she had died from a fit caused by drinking and the jury took just a few minutes to clear Lee of murder. He had to leave the pub by the back entrance to escape the mob who intended to kill him when he stepped outside.

Men could be victims too. One couple, Mary Hartley and Robert Todd, appeared in court together with their heads swathed in bandages. She had been arrested on a Sunday morning in Charter Street – the new name for Blackley Street. She had thrown a beer bottle at Todd's head during a row in the early hours. The answers Todd gave to the magistrate, later reported in the Manchester newspapers, provoked laughter in court:

Magistrate: How did this happen?
Todd: I don't know whether I hit her first or not, but you know, sir, it was all a pure accident.
Magistrate: Were you both drunk?
Todd: It was four o'clock in the morning.
Magistrate: Were you drunk?
Todd: We were not drunk at the time, but it must have been the effects of it. We were scrambling about like cats and dogs.
Magistrate: But what happened?
Todd: There's nothing the matter with me. They've just put a lot of sheets round my head. It's not worth mentioning, I can assure you.

One morning, Detective Jerome Caminada was on duty in Charter Street, a place he described as a 'very rough quarter for any officer of the law', when a woman ran screaming past him followed by her husband, a big, powerful man. Caminada watched as the man hit her with two 'frightful blows', knocking her down and kicking her like a football. Caminada was so outraged that he rushed at the man and punched him so hard in the face that the blow lifted him off his feet. The man landed heavily on the pavement, smashing his head, and was knocked unconscious. A crowd gathered and began shouting that Caminada had 'killed the rough'.

Caminada called another policeman to the scene and they began dragging the man up Angel Street. But the aggressor recovered his senses and grabbed the officer by the groin with such force that he ripped a patch of cloth clean out of the front of his trousers. In retaliation, Caminada rained blows on the man's head, hitting him with such force that he thought he had broken his own arm. At the station, the man tried to escape. He failed to notice the station's iron gates were locked and rushed madly at them, head-first like a goat, knocking himself out.

In court the next morning, the man's wife refused to give evidence and he was sentenced to just two months in prison. When he complained about Caminada's punches, the judge said he had 'fallen into the right hands' and 'deserved all he got'. Caminada remarked: 'Fortunately my hand was only strained. I suffered from it for 15 months, not being able even to turn a door handle, but I had the satisfaction of knowing that I had administered to the big bully a thrashing he wasn't likely soon to forget.' A few months later, when Caminada saw the couple in the street, the man's wife told him: "He's very good now."

Social observers began to realise that 'home life' did not exist for many couples in Angel Meadow. A ragged school teacher wrote in the *Manchester City News*: 'Marriage is an impressive word, but when you see a lad of 17 trying to get food for a few puny children, the word loses its impressiveness.' He gave the example of Jane, a 17-year-old street waif or 'step girl' who grew up in a two-roomed house near St Michael's Church. Her case, the teacher said, was typical of half the young women in Angel Meadow. She married Bill, a 19-year-old scuttler, after 12 months of courting in 'the peculiar manner of their tribe', which meant wandering the streets as part of a gang.

Bill made his advances through wild yells and horseplay. After demonstrations of mutual affection as partners in street fights, he proposed. They took a room for two shillings a week, with a bed, table, chairs and a little crockery picked up at the market. The only clothes they owned were those on their backs. For the first few months they had enough bread and beer. They fought each other on Saturdays and were both seen with black eyes, but still appeared on the surface to be happy.

However, Jane indulged in the luxury of a hat and their finances were further stretched after buying a few gaudy pictures for the walls. A baby soon arrived and inherited the weakness of its mother, who rarely ate meat, fruit or vegetables. Bill now began to feel the responsibility of marriage. To satisfy his craving for drink, he gave less money to his wife, which meant she also had less money to spend on alcohol, and they began having daily rows. Within a few weeks, disaster struck. The baby suffocated when Bill overlaid it in bed during a drunken sleep. The teacher wrote of the couple:

> Occasionally I see Jane with companions of the same age and sex. She hangs around the public house corner gossiping, carrying another piece of wizened humanity under her shawl and with little daughters clinging to her skirts. Her only desire is for drink. She has no other aims in life. Her family will grow up with the gutter as a nursery, and so on, as it has been from generation to generation. These people are used to their life because they know no other and, ending themselves in the workhouse, leave a heritage of diseased bodies and minds to their children.

Three in ten children in Angel Meadow died before they were five-years-old. For them, according to the teacher, death was a 'merciful release' from a life of 'sickness and starvation and exposure to all weathers':

> What can be expected of the offspring of such unwholesome beings as the ordinary beer-sodden Angel Meadow parents but caricatures of humanity? The parents are a disgrace to the city so far as their bodies are concerned. Years of heredity have gifted these animals – for they are as unclean as monkeys, and their gestures and their learning unconscious of shame remind me irresistibly of apes – with peculiar characteristics which it will take a century of proper treatment to remove.

Women in the slum who fell pregnant usually worked until the very last moment and returned to their jobs when their babies were only ten-days-old. Many of these children were looked after by older women, who acted as nursemaids and washerwomen. To keep the babies quiet, these women often gave them drugs. The investigative journalist Angus Reach wrote: 'First, the child is drugged until it sleeps, and then too often it is drugged until it dies.'

The drug most often given to babies was a sweetened preparation of laudanum – a reddish-brown and bitter liquid containing opium. The drug was made by Angel Meadow's druggists and had a variety of names: Baby's Mixture, Mother's Quietness, Child's Cordial, Soothing Syrup, Sleeping Stuff and Godfrey's Cordial. It could be bought in pubs and shops, which became known as 'Godfrey shops'. It cost a penny an ounce – about the same as a pint of beer. Some shopkeepers offered it alongside other essentials – eggs, candy, bread, soap, butter, starch, herrings and cheese.

Working parents also used laudanum as a stimulant. They bought it by the teaspoon and in bad times begged shop owners for bigger doses. The drug was unregulated and each druggist devised his own concoction. The stronger he made it, the faster it sold. Some mixed it with syrup and essential oils or spices, adding double the dose of laudanum sold by rival shops.

Nursemaids sometimes give babies laudanum without the mother's knowledge. The working mother took the baby from a warm bed at 5am and carried it to the nurse, who drugged the child to keep it quiet until noon when the mother returned from the mill. The babies' bodies became so used to the drug that, within five or six weeks, they needed a stronger dose. Midwives also taught mothers how to make their own brews with aniseed and treacle.

Babies given the drug seemed to be always asleep or lay completely still, like dolls, with their eyes half open. Their heads began to swell and their fingernails turned blue. The drug also suppressed their appetite, as they were unable to cry for food, and many died from malnutrition as a result. An expert named John Greg Harrison said the system of drugging children was 'exceedingly common'. He explained: 'The child sinks into a low torpid state, wastes away to a skeleton, except the stomach, which swells, producing what is known as pot-belly. If the children survive the treatment, they are often weakly and stunted for life.'

One druggist off St George's Road claimed to Angus Reach that he 'sold nothing of the kind, at least next to nothing, nothing worth mentioning'. Reach was unsurprised to then see the druggist handing three pennyworths of the laudanum to two young girls. Reach said: 'I would have given something for that gentleman's power of face. I think it could be made useful.'

In 1845, an inquest jury was told of a suspicious case involving the death of a 10-day-old baby in Style Street. It emerged the baby, whose mother was called Catherine Hawk, had died from an overdose of 'infant's mixture'. Mrs Bannester, the wife of the druggist in St George's Road who had supplied the dose, admitted that it contained 'sufficient laudanum to poison the child'. The coroner warned that drugging children was now 'sadly too common' and that druggists were selling the mixture without labelling the bottles because they assumed people knew what they contained.

Neglect continued after the children were too old to be left drugged in their cradles. As working mothers lacked any kind of social support outside the workhouse, they were prone to leaving their children to wander the streets.

Police in Manchester searched for 3,000 lost children a year. It was estimated that 14,000 more children died than expected in Manchester. Out of 100 deaths, 48 were of children aged under five.

A single mother named Mary Sheenan went to a police station one afternoon in February 1866, carrying her dead baby in her arms. She was drunk, but she managed to tell the police the baby was 11-months-old and she had been wandering the streets with the child in her arms selling matches. She had stopped to rest on the steps of O'Neill's lodging house in Dyche Street at 1am and was still sitting there at 5.30pm when she noticed the baby was dead. He had died from exposure to the cold.

Chapter 9

Hard Times

Life was tough in the mills around Angel Meadow. Some of these great black buildings employed up to 2,000 hands in vast industrial colonies, where the working day was governed by the rise and fall of steam engines. Children risked death and serious injury to scavenge pieces of cotton beneath the fast-moving machines. The working day began at 5am, with a piece of bread and a cup of weak tea for breakfast, usually without milk. Porridge was rarely eaten in the slum.

Before dawn, the streets thronged with men, women and children heading to work. Some queued for coffee or cocoa sold by street vendors. The factory bells began to ring for five minutes before 6am. Then the engines roared into life, perfectly on time. The mill hands worked in silence amid the chattering machinery. Anyone who was late would find the doors locked and lose half a day's wages.

At 1pm, the engines fell silent and the workers stopped for dinner. Crowds of hungry people swarmed into the streets, and lanes that had been silent minutes earlier now echoed with hundreds of clogs. The workers went home and ate a few boiled potatoes or scraps of bacon fried with lard. Some visited cook shops for a meat and potato pie. After dinner, they had just enough time to smoke a pipe before the factory bells ordered them back to work.

After the Factory Acts restricted working hours in 1848, they toiled for no more than 10 hours a day. At night, exhausted, they returned home for a supper of tea mixed with spirits and some bread or perhaps cheap herrings from the Isle of Man. Families dipped their spoons into a common bowl. They bought tea and sugar on credit from small shops and as a result paid a third more than their masters, who could afford to buy in larger quantities.

Wages were paid on a Saturday, when the engines stopped at 2pm. Women spent the free afternoon cleaning and washing, and could be seen scouring or gossiping in groups on the steps outside their houses. Children staggered under pails of water fetched from the tap. Many workers went late on Saturday evenings to Smithfield Market, when the best quality food had gone and they could get a discount.

Engels said of the market: 'The potatoes which the workers buy are usually poor, the vegetables wilted, the cheese old and of poor quality, the bacon rancid, the meat lean, tough, taken from old, often diseased, cattle. The sellers are usually small hucksters who buy up inferior goods and can sell them cheaply by reason of their badness.' Their food was often adulterated too. Flour was mixed with gypsum, tea with dust, and rancid butter was sold as fresh – the lumps covered with a fresh layer or washed to make it appear new.

But as one shopkeeper in Angel Meadow found, the slum dwellers, especially those who worked on the market, were not easily tricked:

> They will not have the cheapest food, not anything that is of inferior quality. In their purchases they are prodigal and fastidious. Tongue, on account of its price, is regarded as a delicacy in most middle class homes. In any shop, it is in great demand. With boiled hams potted meats and cheese, it is the same. Only the best will satisfy. Though foodstuffs are purchased in small quantities, the best is demanded every time.

The mills were hot and stuffy and the workers breathed air clogged with dust and cotton fibres. They were exhausted by non-stop toil and a poor diet could turn their skin pale and leaden. Angus Reach described their faces as 'cadaverous and overspread by a sort of unpleasant greasy pallor'. Men working in the mills wore blue-striped shirts and trousers and the women coarse pinafores and loose jackets. Some went barefoot, flinging their clogs aside. Reach said:

> They have an essentially greasy look, which makes me sometimes think that water would run off their skins as it does off a duck's back. I fear it is very seldom that their feet see the interior of a tub, with plenty of hot water and soap. The floor which they walk upon is as dark as the darkest mahogany from the continued oily drippings with which it is anointed and it is really painful to see a pretty girl with toes and ankles the exact colour of the dingy boards.

While newspaper journalists such as Angus Reach highlighted the plight of the poor, others took practical steps to help them. The Reverend William Gadsby, a ruddy-faced and well-respected pastor of the St George's Road Baptist Chapel, erected in 1789, wrote to a friend in 1839 about the distress faced by his congregation. Gadsby, who had taken up his post in 1805, claimed Angel Street should be renamed 'Black Angel Street'. He noted: 'Trade here is worse and worse. Thousands are in deepest distress.'

Ninety people were on the chapel's poor list. Collections were made and flannels and blankets handed to more than half of them. Gadsby also hoped to 'give them a little beef at Christmas'. 'There are many of them that cannot get a morsel for months together. I have spoken to a butcher as to what price he would let me have some,' he recounted. 'They do hope trade will mend after Christmas. We have a great many poor in the church and congregation.' After the situation failed to improve, Gadsby wrote in another letter: 'Things are still very trying, and I fear that in these parts we shall have a dreadful winter.'

Charity was not enough and workers who were prepared to fight for better conditions began to find solace in a national movement for political reform. The Chartist movement was formed in the late 1830s by skilled artisans – shoemakers, printers, tailors and handloom weavers. There were 3,291 Manchester handloom weavers in 1834, compared with 18,353 cotton mill workers. The Chartists drew up a six-point 'People's Charter' aimed at making the British political system more democratic, including a demand that every man over 21 who was not a criminal or insane should have the right to vote.

They believed the Charter could give ordinary people more control over their working conditions, but the movement soon attracted others who advocated the use of strikes and violence. These men were known as 'physical force Chartists'. Irish confederates also allied themselves with the movement to pursue their separate goal of liberating Ireland from British rule. Chartists were seen as a threat to national security at a time when violent revolutions were beginning to sweep across Europe.

In 1839, the Chartists set up a meeting room in Ashley Lane led by men including Patrick Flynn, 28, an Irish immigrant handloom weaver. They began winning support among English and Irish alike in Angel Meadow and Irish Town, where some families were now living on just a penny a day.

On 11 May 1839, police received reports that Chartists were carrying out military drills on the outskirts of Manchester. Police spies made their way to a country lane three miles to the north and discovered 100 men marching. One spy was pelted with stones and he was lucky to escape alive. Another named Higginson watched as the Chartists formed two squadrons. The police later arrested eight men including the leader Edward Riley, 22, as they walked home to Manchester. Riley lived at Bank Meadow on the northern outskirts of Irish Town and worked as a dyer. Higginson told a magistrates' court he had overheard Riley telling the men: "We only want muskets now and then we shall be ready." The magistrate jailed Riley for 18 months, saying it was 'absolutely necessary' that an example be made. He warned that anyone else caught drilling 'would find the law too strong'.

Within two years, the Chartists of Angel Meadow found themselves up against a rival political movement known as the Anti-Corn Law League. The league, whose members included middle-class factory owners and warehousemen, was established in Manchester in 1838 to seek the abolition of the unpopular Corn Laws. The laws protected landowners by levying taxes on imported wheat, which raised the price of bread at a time when factory owners were cutting wages. The Leaguers had the support of sections of the Irish community in Angel Meadow who opposed the aims of the Chartists.

In late May 1841, supporters of the league began posting handbills promoting a huge rally on 5 June in Stevenson Square, a ten-minute walk from Angel Meadow. Chartists urged workers to form a rival rally in the square and to make a stand against 'tyranny and oppression'. The *Manchester Courier* told how the Leaguers responded:

> They hired 200 to 300 of the biggest and most savage Irish ragamuffins from the purlieus of St George's Road and Little Ireland and, having placed large bludgeons in their hands, stationed them in groups of a dozen or 20 on different parts of the ground. These wretches, being primed with bad gin and Irish whiskey, were soon fit for any service on which they might be commanded and they proved themselves worthy of their employers.

The weather was fine on the day of the rally and a large number of Chartists entered the square carrying flags. Within minutes, the Irish 'bludgeon men' began their first attack. They drove back the Chartists and destroyed their banners. It was said the Irish made 'the most unsparing use of their cudgels'. Large numbers of Chartists were knocked down by heavy blows. Some tried to fight back, but were beaten until the pavement was red with blood. The *Manchester Courier* said the police 'coolly witnessed the outrage' and took a few 'broken-headed Chartists' into custody instead of arresting their assailants. Eleven Chartists were taken to the infirmary with head wounds. After the battle, the Leaguers held a victory march through the city.

The following year, a huge wave of national Chartist strikes involving 500,000 workers hit factories, mills and coal mines from Dundee to Cornwall. The economy had been in dire straits for five years. Unemployment was rife and wages and working hours were being savagely cut. By July the unrest had spread to Manchester and surrounding towns. In August, mobs of strikers began storming factories and turning out workers. When they closed down a factory they removed the plugs from the boilers to stop them from being re-ignited and as a result the protest became known as the 'plug plot'.

A railway guard named William Aubrey, from St George's Road, was on a train heading north from Victoria Station on 12 August when up to 400 workers ran on to the line armed with sticks. They shouted at the passengers and threw sand in their faces. Their leader, Patrick Agnew, warned Aubrey: "If you come back, we will destroy you." Troops began patrolling Manchester's streets with fixed bayonets. Police formed a protection force for blacklegs who wanted to work during the strike.

On 22 August, news reached the town hall that a mob of 6,000 men and women were gathering at Tinker's Gardens near the Meadow. Spies believed the mob was planning to march on the city's mills. A force of 150 police officers and 250 special constables marched to the gardens.

The police formed a line at the top of St George's Road and the special constables marched through Angel Meadow and stood in a second line alongside the Irk. Chief Superintendent Richard Beswick went into the gardens and ordered the workers, who were almost all weavers, to return home. Many of them were drinking and dancing, while a large number of men stood silently in the centre of the bowling green. When they refused to leave, Beswick threatened to disperse them by force. The mob gave three cheers and left the gardens, before marching up the hill to St George's Road.

The mob made several more attempts to gather at the gardens in the following days. Two days later, a superintendent named Stevenson marched to the gardens with 60 men. Around 500 workers were already there, but Stevenson arrived just in time to prevent hundreds more from gathering. Officers were posted at the gates. One worker told Stevenson they were only meeting to 'think of how they were to get their dinners'. Another said: "We'll not work a day until we get better wages."

Eventually the crowd gave three cheers and left through a gate on St George's Road. They marched past St Patrick's Church and dispersed. The protests marked the beginning of the end of the pleasure gardens, which stayed open for just a few more years before they finally closed, when the sand once so famous for growing cucumbers was carted away by iron moulders. Manchester's workers held out until September, when they became the last in the country to return to work after negotiating a few concessions. It was an uneasy truce.

By 1848, revolution was spreading across Europe. In Manchester, Chartist weavers began making secret plans for their own insurrection. As darkness fell on 4 May, around 200 men headed north from Angel Meadow on the low road alongside the Irk. They walked silently in small groups to avoid detection until they reached Tinker's Hollow, the old sandstone quarry to the north of Tinker's Gardens. There they stood as quietly as a large crowd could stand in the natural amphitheatre, listening for the boots of marching soldiers.

They had become so enraged about conditions in the cotton mills that they felt it necessary to teach the mill owners a final lesson. The speaker was the Angel Meadow agitator Patrick Flynn, who told them of his plan to stage a huge riot in the heart of Manchester. Flynn had sent messengers across the city and to neighbouring towns, and he claimed thousands of men were now preparing to join the uprising. He urged his listeners to go home and arm themselves with cutlasses, pikes and guns, and to fight any policemen who stood in their way. With the arrangements made, the men drifted back to the Meadow. But one man kept walking. He hurried along Charter Street and kept going until he reached Manchester Town Hall in King Street. He was Constable 87C John Cookson – a police spy sent to discover the plans for insurrection. His action meant the police would be well prepared.

In the following days, a shoe shop at the corner of St George's Road and Gould Street began seeing a surprising amount of business. James Downey, the cobbler who owned the shop, was also Angel Meadow's arms dealer. Downey, an Irish confederate, offered customers a choice of weapons. He sold pike heads with 1ft long blades and makeshift cutlasses with a 2ft blade fastened to a wooden handle without a safety guard. A *Manchester Times* journalist, who ventured into the shop, wrote:

> The articles are of a very inferior quality, and whether of English or Irish manufacture, do not reflect much credit on the maker. The pike is of the ordinary size and shape. The cutlass, while of the usual length, is much narrower in the blade than the standard instrument of war. The pikes are labelled with a ticket, intimating the price of two shillings and three pence. No price is attached to the cutlasses.

He added: 'The shop has nothing of an enticing character about it, and the shopkeeper does not seem inclined to advertise his wares, the only thing in the shape of announcement in the window being a printed paper, with "Prime Pop and Nettle Beer" in large letters.'

On 30 May, another police spy went into the shop and bought a 3ft-long cutlass, which he took to the town hall. He told officers he had seen around 40 people buying pikes and cutlasses. The following morning, a crowd of up to 1,000 Chartists and Irish confederates led by Flynn and Downey gathered in the streets armed with 'dangerous and offensive weapons' and carrying flags. They intended to hold a protest in Stevenson Square at noon before marching through the streets. Police banned the march, fearing that thousands more people were planning to arrive from surrounding towns.

At 11am, the mob heard that a large crowd of 6,000 armed Chartists approaching Manchester from Oldham had been intercepted by 80 police officers at a toll-gate on the north-eastern edge of the city. The mob marched out of town to meet them, ready for a confrontation with the police. Chief Superintendent Richard Beswick stood ready for battle at the gate.

Beswick ordered a mounted officer named John Henry, the son of an MP, to ride to the town hall to muster reinforcements. He was intercepted by the mob led by Flynn and Downey, who hooted and threw stones as he galloped past. A dozen people rushed into the road and tried to grab the horse's reins, forcing Henry to lash out with his riding whip. By the time he arrived at the nearest police station, he had been hit nine times with stones and his head needed stitching. His horse had been stabbed with a pike and blood was flowing from its side.

Beswick locked the toll-gate and told his officers to draw their cutlasses and form a line across the road. At noon, two Chartist scouts from Oldham named Daniel Donovan and Edward Cropper arrived at the gate ahead of the main body of marchers. Donovan warned: "The procession must pass to Manchester." Beswick, whose words were later recorded in newspaper ink, replied: "We are stationed here by direction of the mayor to prevent any procession coming into town and, whatever the consequence, it shall not pass through the toll-bar."

Within moments the Manchester mob arrived, marching in ranks through the deserted street, as shopkeepers quickly closed their shutters. The mob was led by Flynn, who was carrying a flag. Downey was his second in command. When the mob got within about 100 yards of the police line, Flynn halted the men. He made violent threats to Beswick and ordered him to open the gate. Beswick stood firm. He told Flynn that if he tried to open the gate he would be arrested. Beswick later reported: 'I observed a gun with a bayonet at the end of it and 20 or 30 pikes held up in the centre of the procession. From the violent conduct of the people, my impression was that we should be attacked.'

At 1.30pm, a huge rain storm began lashing the streets. The Manchester mob, soaked to the skin, suddenly turned violent and launched a desperate attack on the police, who used a narrow gap in the gate to break them into smaller groups. Flynn and others were arrested, while James Downey managed to escape. Police inspector William Gifford, who was among the gate's defenders, said later that he heard Downey shouting 'come on' and 'fall in'. Beswick said: 'The neighbourhood was in a state of great alarm and many of the inhabitants had closed their doors and the shutters of their windows.'

Police armed with cutlasses occupied Stevenson Square that afternoon. They were joined by 160 soldiers, who stationed themselves in an empty building nearby. The rain continued until 5pm, when peace seemed to have been restored. The troops returned to their barracks and the police stayed at their posts. However, as the mills closed for the night, more than 20,000 people poured on to the streets. They saw the troops leaving Stevenson Square and began tearing up paving stones and throwing them at the police, forcing the soldiers to return and retake the square. One newspaper summarised what followed: 'Cavalry and infantry continued clearing the streets until near about 10pm, when a heavy rain came on and cleared the streets effectually and thus ended the Manchester revolution of 1848.'

At 11pm that night, around 50 officers led by Beswick stormed Downey's shop and arrested him. They found a huge arsenal of weapons: 30 swords, six pike heads, one bayonet, a pistol, a blunderbuss and two muskets. Some of the weapons were on display in the windows. Magistrates were told that meetings of Irish confederates were held in the shop. On the door of the upper room the following message was written in chalk: 'This club will meet at 10 o'clock tomorrow morning.' According to the *Morning Post*, at the time of Downey's arrest, 14 men were in the upper room reading the newspapers.

Houses of other suspected Chartists were also raided. Police found a 'formidable' battle axe at one address. Patrick Flynn, James Downey and others were charged with rioting. Downey was also charged with dealing in weapons. When the case eventually went before Mr Justice Creswell at the assize court, there were 47 defendants aged from 25 to 50 and they made a great noise in the dock. Downey was described as Manchester's 'principal pike vendor'.

A low-set and stout man with a 'disagreeable' face named James Abraham Ball claimed the men had been planning to fill cellars near the gasworks with gunpowder and cause a huge explosion. But he was discredited when it emerged he had made a secret deal to lie for the police, after having been arrested for neglecting his family. Flynn and Downey were jailed for 15 months with hard labour. The judge told them: "It is quite impossible that society can be safe if men are allowed to go about the country in the manner you have done, disseminating poison in the minds of the people." The Chartist revolt was over.

Chapter 10

Lodgings

The boots of the detectives scraped on the steps as they trooped into a lodging house, its crumbling brick walls covered in soot. The house had three storeys lit by windows that had gone unrepaired for decades Tattered garments, old hats, rags and scraps of brown paper were stuffed into the holes in the glass.

The detectives stomped through the lobby until they came to the common room. It was full of men and women, who responded to their arrival with a babble of tongues. Some of the inmates sat on broken chairs around a filthy table and were eating their dinner. Others were on their knees in front of a fire frying a herring. A group of women were mending their socks and appeared to have just left their beds. Some of the men were smoking and drinking on a dirty bench. Lurid prints peppered the walls and on the mantelpiece sat a blue earthenware dog with a brown tail, observing the proceedings.

The detectives could not see the man they wanted and went upstairs through a narrow passage, with plaster falling from the walls. The rotten wooden stairs were soft and shrank beneath their boots. The inmates in the upper room could hear their footsteps and were already whispering: "The Ds are coming." The room contained four wobbly bedsteads and stank of dirty clothing, foul breath and faeces.

"Now then! Sit up!" Detective Jerome Caminada shouted as he stepped confidently into the room. "Let's look at your phizzogs!" The men, women and children obeyed, pulling the rugs and coats that doubled as blankets from their heads and lifting their faces to the candlelight. "Oh, is it you, Mr Jerome?" one of the women asked.

Caminada had a reputation for finding his man, but on this night in 1861 he and his fellow officers had failed. The detectives retreated downstairs and slipped out into the gloomy street. Caminada later wrote of these lodgers: 'They sink once more into a morbid slumber until the sorrowful daylight enters and the unhallowed repose gives place to trouble, sin and debauchery. There lie old and young, grey-headed convict, wizened hag, infant and child of tender years, presenting a sickening picture of moral depravity.'

Angel Meadow was the main lodging house district for the men and women pouring into Manchester from the countryside each day in search of work. At the height of the influx in 1866, there were 88 common lodging houses in the Meadow, offering 2,653 beds at prices ranging from three pence to a shilling a night. There were 19 lodging houses in Angel Street alone. Other lodgers slept in 123 licensed houses, which offered another 1,071 beds. As a result, Angel Meadow had an ever-changing population of 3,724 lodgers on top of its permanent inhabitants.

Two of the slum's houses, Kane's and The Rest, were so cavernous that together they accommodated nearly 1,000 men. 'Here, one can get a night's sleep for 4d – and no questions asked,' the churchman William Browne remarked of the slum. A journalist from the *Manchester Guardian* wrote: 'Tramps, thieves and prostitutes of the lowest kind abound in this neighbourhood and find ample accommodation for their respective wants in these houses.' Dr James Phillips Kay dismissed them as 'disgusting abodes' haunted by vice, crime and disease. They were, however, a necessary feature of the slum and the only place where countless numbers of new arrivals could spend the night.

Some lodging houses in the Meadow were painted in bright colours, perhaps so they might be easily identified by people who could not read or write. It was said almost every house in Angel Street and Charter Street had signs in their windows or scratched on wooden boards offering 'good lodgings'. One churchman noted the 'grotesque' spelling of some of these signs, which he felt would have 'baffled even Chaucer'. One house in Charter Street even offered: 'Lodgins for travlers, three pence a nite.'

Lodging house inmates were a mixture of vagabonds, wayfarers, workmen and harvestmen who arrived and departed like swallows, following the seasons. Tradesmen, labourers and hawkers also occupied rooms. Some had regular jobs but earned too little to rent a house, others were educated men who had fallen on hard times. Philip Wentworth, a journalist from the *East Lancashire Review*, described one lodging house in the Meadow: 'In this very house are to be found broken down clergymen, demoralised doctors, shoeless solicitors, and penniless as well as briefless barristers.' One journalist from the *Manchester City News* said it took an 'iron will' for these middle-class down-and-outs to resist falling from grace. He said: 'Many of their companions are willing to teach them all the tricks of low life.'

The men, women and children who stepped inside these houses landed in a hot, damp common room, where they were eyed suspiciously by lodgers lounging on wooden benches around a large fireplace used for cooking food, boiling tea and drying clothes. Their first task was to pay the landlady or 'deputy', usually an older woman or widow, who would demand payment upfront or 'on the nail'.

The new arrivals would eat supper in the common room, borrowing a knife for a penny deposit. They would have to protect the knife from other inmates, who might try to steal it to claim the money. After a late supper, the new lodgers climbed the narrow stairs to dormitories spread over one or two floors. Some houses contained more beds higher up in attic garrets. Single lodgers were made to sleep with a stranger and latecomers faced the worst choice of beds.

One unnamed tramp who stayed in lodging houses across Britain said those in Angel Meadow were the worst 'by a long way'. He complained to the *Manchester City News* about the 'awful stench', the 'nightly brawls' and the unventilated heat that bathed him in sweat. In the ten years he had been visiting the Meadow, he had never seen a lodging house inspector. He said the bed sheets went unwashed for weeks and the black rugs that passed for blankets were never cleaned:

> Fancy turning into one of these beds in hot weather, which had been used by 30 or more people in various stages of filth before you come to it, and naked too. The beds are full of vermin, and if you slept in a shirt or anything you would find it full next morning. You roll up your clothes and put them under the mattress, and your boots and socks under the pillow.

The tramp believed that three quarters of lodging house inmates were professional loafers or thieves: "You cannot lose sight of anything – socks, boots, collar, handkerchief or hat – scarcely for a second but it vanishes." The bed sheets in one house in Charter Street were stamped with the words 'stolen from' to prevent thieves from taking them to the pawn shop.

The cunning of lodging house thieves was illustrated when a tall, saintly-looking man named James Garside was arrested following a theft at a house in Angel Street. He had slipped out of bed at 4am, tiptoed across the dormitory and slid his hand under the pillows of two fellow lodgers. He stole 11 shillings from their trouser pockets before slipping back to bed. When they got up for work, the victims discovered their pockets had been picked and told Garside he would be 'kicked into a thousand pieces' if he failed to hand back the money. He handed over his plunder and the men frogmarched him to a police station.

Two lodging house thieves picked the wrong man when they tried to rob a traveller named William Lambert in his room in Charter Street. Lambert was a tough American who had served for 15 years in the New York police. Before resting his head on the pillow, he wedged his knife in the door latch to keep it locked. He placed his cheque book in his coat pocket.

After about 15 minutes, Lambert awoke startled. Someone was trying to get into his room. "What do you want?" he shouted through the door. A voice screamed from outside: "We want you to go to sleep, you old _____." Lambert got dressed and waited. Thirty minutes later there was a loud knock at the door. Lambert tried to open it, but found it was being held shut from the outside. Two men, notorious robbers named James Greenwood and James Hurley, then pushed open the door and burst into the room. They attacked Lambert and stole his cheque book.

Lambert managed to get into the next room, but four other lodgers sprang from their beds and joined in the attack. Lambert shouted 'police' and his six attackers scurried back into their beds. He managed to get downstairs, but the landlady refused to let him leave and he only escaped after promising he would say nothing to the police. But in Charter Street, he met a constable and they returned to the house. Everybody was asleep in their beds including Greenwood, who was sleeping soundest of all. Greenwood and Hurley were shaken awake and arrested, but no trace of Lambert's cheque book was found. His 'strange story' brought laughter to Manchester's police court.

Police hunting criminals soon learned that a raid on Angel Meadow's lodging houses could produce rapid results. In 1859, when a couple named John McDermott and Ann Gintings robbed a traveller named James Morris of £60, detectives set about searching the haunts of Angel Meadow. They found McDermott, 26, and Gintings, 25, in a house off Charter Street enjoying an 'excellent breakfast' of beefsteaks, eggs and coffee.

Newspaper journalists began making undercover visits to Angel Meadow's lodging houses with the help of police bodyguards. Angus Reach visited a house in Charter Street, described by its deputy as 'the best conducted in Manchester'. As he walked in the door, he was confronted by a 'great clack of tongues'. The common room was stiflingly hot. A small candle flickered in a greased tin on a shelf, illuminating the men and women sitting on stools around a huge fireplace.

Reach wrote: 'On our entrance they became as mute as fishes, staring into the fire, and only casting furtive glances at my companion and nodding to each other when his back was turned.' Most of the women had shawls on their heads, despite the overpowering heat. Reach thought they were 'coarse-looking and repulsive' and more than one had a bruised and discoloured face. The men were 'squalid, hulking fellows'.

Reach found that the beds upstairs were packed so closely together that it was hard to walk between them. The bedclothes were bundles of rags. The landlady boasted that only two lodgers were allowed to sleep in each bed, but she was 'no ways particular' about the sexes. "Lodgers is lodgers, whether they is men or women," she said. Reach wrote: 'In the room in which we stood, more than a score of filthy vagrants often pigged together, dressed and undressed, sick and well, sober and drunk.'

Police supervised the lodging houses and restricted the numbers of beds, but the law was constantly violated. Deputies crammed beds into rooms until there was no remaining floor space. When the beds were full they threw down sacks of straw or 'shake downs' to accommodate more people. Reach's police officer companion pointed to a bundle of straw wrapped in a piece of sacking and said to the landlady: "Why here's a bed more than you are licensed for." She said: "It's my ain bed, man. Ye wad na have me sleep on the stanes?" She picked up the bed and trundled it downstairs in a huff. Asked where she usually slept, she said: "It depends on whether the hoose is full."

Reach found the dormitories were 'filthy, unscoured chambers, with stained and discoloured walls, scribbled over with names and foul expressions'. Plaster had fallen from the walls and lay in heaps in the corners. Landlords also put beds into their cellars and attics. One lodging house cellar had 15 beds which slept 60 people. A visitor from the Scotch Church Young Men's Society found attic garrets were the worst, as the air in them was so foul it made his throat sore.

Despite these conditions, the lodging house inmates still had their freedom, which they valued above all else. Philip Wentworth, writing in the *East Lancashire Review*, concluded: 'For individual freedom, men will endure the bitterest cold and the keenest hunger. In a workhouse, they would be miserable, for most of them have tried both ways of living and prefer freedom, with all its hardships, to restraint.'

Angel Meadow's lodging houses became known by the names of their masters. Fat Billy's had small rooms divided into wooden pens. The ceilings and walls were whitewashed, but the doors were coated with coal tar, which smelled so strongly of antiseptic that it saturated the whole house. Ghostly shadows lurked in dark corners in the twilight.

Another house, Murty's, was built like a fortress and guarded by thick double doors which could be barred and bolted to resist attack. The outer door was protected by a heavy crossbar which clanged noisily to the floor when it was reluctantly opened. The ground floor common room was lit by a 'sickly gas flame' and filled with thick smoke from a low fireplace, where flames smouldered as if they had been dampened down. Gusts of wind swept down the chimney in winter and leaped to the sooty ceiling. The smoke made the inmates' eyes stream. The deputy, an old woman, led the way upstairs carrying a candle in an old ginger beer bottle – the flame struggling for life.

A journalist from the *Manchester Evening News* who followed the deputy up the narrow stairs was warned to 'mind the step' as they dropped a couple of feet into a small room. Six women looking 'worn out and disreputable' were smoking pipes and talking in subdued voices. As the journalist climbed another flight of winding stairs, he stumbled and fell with a crash against a door. A terrifying voice from within shouted: "Who's there?"

More than 30 lodgers were sleeping in a long, wide attic with boxed-off sleeping compartments running down either side. Rough doors were fitted to the compartments for privacy, but they had no hinges and had to be lifted out and dragged away before the occupants could get inside. The room was whitewashed and every bit of woodwork including the rafters was 'as white as snow'. The owner had smashed through a partition wall into the attic of the next house to create another dormitory, where a man sat bolt upright in bed as others lay with hands locked behind their heads.

The journalist wrote: 'As the glare of the candle fell upon the sleepers' eyes, some stared stupidly about, while others blinked and yawned as if too overcome with sleep to care much about what was going on. As long as the light remained, a babble of oaths and invectives could be heard. This subsided as we picked our way carefully downstairs.'

Kane's lodging house stood in a commanding position at 9 Angel Street, close to the junction with Rochdale Road (formerly St George's Road). It was one of the biggest houses in Manchester, with 346 beds. The Reverend Adam Scott, a vicar who visited the house, found a large washroom in the basement where half-dressed men were having a swill. The kitchen contained large brick-built stoves where men were cooking 'bacon and bloaters' or playing dominoes at large tables in another room. 'There might be about 200 men in the house,' the Reverend Scott wrote, 'several of whom were tipsy.' He added: 'It was hard to believe that some of these were human beings. There, huddled up in a corner, is something you might take to be a bundle of rags, but it is a man, drunk and asleep.' He also came across two barefoot boys wearing oversized men's coats, whose faces were so dirty they looked as if 'they had maps outlined on them in sepia'.

Kane's was so large that its true size could not be estimated from the street. Unlike most other houses, it was kept scrupulously clean. Lodgers had access to hot water and could cook whatever they pleased. Nearby stood a provision shop where they could buy small quantities of tea, sugar, herrings, bread, butter and coffee. At a butcher's shop opposite, among the cheap cuts, some of the best meat in town could be bought.

A visitor to Kane's told the *East Lancashire Review*: 'It is not always safe for a man to turn his back upon a half-cooked or a half-eaten meal for even a minute, for hunger has no conscience. But for all that, the lodgers are fairly honest in this place.' He said the order in the dominoes rooms was 'quite as good as in most respectable social and political clubs'. The inmates slept in vast whitewashed rooms, in which iron beds were ranged along the walls.

The biggest lodging house in the whole of Manchester was known as The Rest. It stood in an old mill in Factory Yard off Charter Street and contained beds for up to 600 lodgers. It was a place where 'vice, honesty and poverty rubbed shoulders', as a journalist from the *Manchester Courier* found out. He entered the house with a bodyguard of two detectives who fortified themselves with a 'worthy disinfectant' – a plentiful supply of tobacco. One of the officers told the journalist he had a cunning plan: "You pose as a man who has been robbed. We are searching for the men."

Inside, they found a great quadrangle with a concrete floor surrounded by wooden benches. Suddenly, a man sleeping off a drinking session on a bench rolled over and fell face first on the floor. A merchant and a lawyer, who was wearing a grubby collar, laid the man back on the bench. His face, which had been resting in a pool of blood, was 'frightfully gashed'. The journalist wrote: 'The lawyer and the merchant, having flung him back on his wooden bench, walked away, not heeding the wound and he still slept on in blissful ignorance of his injury. Nobody cared. Most of the inmates went on playing dominoes, and all were completely indifferent. It was sickening.'

The names of other lodging houses have been lost in time, but their failings were recorded by journalists who bravely stepped through their doors. One house in Factory Court accommodated 40 people, who shared a privy with a collapsed wall. The attic in another had been enlarged by removing the ceiling to provide extra space for nine beds, leaving no insulation between the sleepers and the stars except for the thin slate roof.

Lodgers put their lives on the line in these houses. A 'dirty, ferocious-looking Irishman' named Darby Wiggins was charged with stabbing his countryman Patrick McDermott in one of the Meadow's lodging house dormitories. A court heard that he had been drunk and 'kicking up a great row' when McDermott got out of bed and told him to be quiet. Wiggins jumped up and stabbed him in the back before fleeing into the night – leaving McDermott fighting for his life.

Lodging house deputies faced their own dangers. Just before midnight one Saturday night, three scuttlers, Joseph Wood, Thomas Cunningham and Thomas Riley, ran into a lodging house at 61 Angel Street. Cunningham demanded to know who would fight him. Thomas Kelly, the acting lodging house deputy, asked them to leave. Cunningham knocked him down, kicked him and stabbed him in the head. Riley stabbed him in the back and Wood began kicking his body.

Cunningham then launched a lit paraffin lamp at Kelly, but one of the lodgers threw a spectacular cross-shot and extinguished the flame. When a constable named Turner arrived armed with a baton, he found Cunningham standing over Kelly holding the knife. Turner knocked Cunningham down and the knife fell to the floor and was lost. Riley and Wood escaped through the back door but were later arrested. A court later heard that Kelly was left looking 'like a Red Indian' because his face was covered in so much blood. Cunningham was jailed for 18 months, Riley for 15 and Wood for nine. Lord Chief Justice Russell spoke out against the shocking severity of the crime, but nothing was done to make the lodging houses safer.

Some housekeepers took steps to defend themselves. William Graham was charged with attacking two of his lodgers. George and Robert Newman, two brothers, appeared in court with their heads swathed in bandages. George Newman's jaw was broken and his eye badly bruised. Robert Newman had a broken nose and a gash on his head. They told the court they had been in bed when Graham and two other men burst in without warning, armed with sticks and attacked them. A constable found them sprawled on the bed with Graham standing over them. Graham was discharged at a later court hearing, after the brothers failed to appear as witnesses – amid claims they had been threatened with another beating.

Chapter 11

Underworld

A man turned off a muddy street into a rubbish-strewn alley and climbed down some steps into the pitch-blackness of a cellar. As his eyes adjusted to the darkness, the room appeared empty apart from a few bundles of rags and a bedstead. Then he realised the rags were the shapeless figures of the men, women and children who called this place home. He gagged at the sight of them and the smell.

The cellar was home to four families of 20 people, who were suffering from fever. It was so damp that drops of water were rolling down the brickwork. There were no chairs and the bed was only empty because a dead woman had just been carried off to the graveyard. Her four orphaned children were now sitting in stunned silence on the earth floor. In a corner, on a pile of straw, lay a pensioner and two other children dying from the same fever.

The pensioner lifted up a ragged blanket and showed the visitor the child lying beside him – a mere skeleton. In the opposite corner, two women from a third family lay on another pile of straw next to their mother, who sat weeping with her back to the wall. "I've been sick for two months," she said. She was only sitting upright because there was no room left for her to lie down on the straw bed. Her daughters begged the stranger to take them away. "We'll be dead before morning," they said. But the man could hold out no longer. He needed to get back to the surface.

The man, who clearly had a social conscience, for some reason felt unable to reveal his name when he later wrote an anonymous letter to the *Manchester Times* describing the 'heart sickening' scene he had witnessed beneath the alley in Angel Meadow:

Twenty human beings are struggling for existence in the pestilential air of that wretched cellar, the stench of the place being so great that I could not endure to remain in it. Most of the neighbours are afraid of the fever, and will not go in to render them assistance. The officers of the parish have known the state of this cellar for some time. Surely something should be done to save those starving, dying creatures.

A secret world lay beneath the streets of Angel Meadow – an underground labyrinth of cellars, trapdoors and passages. The cellars had originally been created to circulate air and store wares under the large merchants' houses built at the end of the eighteenth century. As the area became a slum, they were used instead for storing people. Thousands soon lived in these underground dwellings, where there was no daylight and little air. Sanitary inspectors found one 18ft-long cellar beneath Ludgate Street where the ceiling was just 3ft 3in high, which was home to 18 men, women and children.

Many cellars contained two rooms of just 10ft square inhabited by ten or more people. Each room beneath a house had a fireplace and smoke from the flames, combined with damp air, shrouded the underground rooms in a toxic fog. Most cellars only had one entrance. Others were accessed via trapdoors or underground chambers and passageways. Rear cellars were almost always dark, but a lucky few had a cellar light – a narrow slit that opened into a yard above.

Cellars were at least better than the railway arches, holes and ruined buildings where the most desperate creatures sought shelter. Despite their horrors, they were in great demand. As overcrowding increased, connected cellars were subdivided to house separate families.

In the Angel Meadow cellars lived men like John Brookes, 46, an unemployed dyer. His home was beneath Nicholas Street, one of the filthiest in the district. Brookes, a robustly built man, was a drunkard, but his wife did her best to keep their cellar clean. Four adults and four children, the Gainer family, lived next door in a one-room cellar which was damp, crowded and without a scrap of furniture. Their neighbour Ellen Roberts, 25, survived on cups of tea and hard peas. James Jenkins, a 38-year-old hatter, lived in a bare cellar beneath Nelson Street. He was a small, delicate man, who liked a drink and the cellar he shared with his family of five had no furniture, not even a chair. The bubbling Irk beneath the cellar's floor gave them no peace and they faced a constant threat of flooding.

Few outsiders were brave enough to climb down the steps of Angel Meadow's cellars to see what horrors lay hidden in the shadows. The Reverend William Gadsby, the pastor of the Rochdale Road Baptist Chapel, was one of the few who made frequent visits to Angel Meadow's underworld. Gadsby's son described in a memoir how the pastor made a shocking discovery when he ventured into the underground home of an elderly member of his congregation.

She was lying on a straw bed in a cellar 'covered in filth' from ceiling to floor. A 'dirty, lazy' daughter aged about 50 was with her, sitting with folded arms. The Reverend Gadsby said:

I found a dreadful stench on entering the cellar. Old bones, old rags, and all sorts of rubbish and dirt were piled up in different parts. "Good Lord", I said, "what a miserable place! I'll get out of this as soon as I can. I could not live here a week." I then addressed myself to the poor old woman. "Well, Mary," I said, "How are you?" "Oh", she replied, "I'm as happy as a queen. I don't think the Lord deals as mercifully with anybody as he does with me." Oh, how I blushed! This was indeed a humbling time to me, and I never can forget the preciousness of that visit.

James Phillips Kay found damp cellars overflowing with typhoid-breeding sewage from nearby privies. The inmates kept warm in winter by sleeping together on shavings or straw. 'A change of linen or clothes is an exception to the common practice,' wrote Kay. 'Many of the back rooms where they sleep have no other means of ventilation than the front rooms.' Kay said it was impossible for people to stay healthy in the 'pestilential atmosphere' of those 'obscure and damp cellars'. Some, like those in Nelson Street, were below the level of the Irk and could flood in seconds.

Cellars could also be dangerous for reasons other than the obvious health risks. Ellen McCarthy, 37, had only been out of prison a few hours when she stumbled out of a beer house and began weaving her way back to her rented room in Angel Street. She was just yards from safety in Style Street when she lost her balance and staggered sideways over a low railing and down into a cellar, where she lay unconscious and bleeding heavily from a head wound. She died later in hospital. The fall had fractured her spine.

Combatants in street fights also used cellar steps as deadly weapons, as a strongly-built labourer named Peter Craven discovered. Craven, who lived in a lodging house in Angel Street, was punched in the face and knocked to the ground by a rival named William Leather in a fight one Saturday night. Craven's badly smashed head was left hanging over the mouth of a cellar and he later died in hospital. Leather was charged with manslaughter and told a jury: "A big man met me in Angel Street and threatened to throw me and 20 more like me down a cellar and I replied that I could do the same game."

But cellars had advantages too. If not dry, they were warm. A cellar beneath a house was better than an attic with a hole in the roof. Cellars also offered a degree of privacy compared with the lodging houses above ground. Dr Peter Gaskell discovered uninhabited cellars accessed by secret trap doors which provided perfect hiding places for illicit distilleries that produced illegal liquor or 'poteen' at the highest strength. He wrote: 'These generally are dark cellars, having no outlet except a trap door, opening into some obscure court, half filled with filth, or excavations dug in the sandstone rock, beneath tenements occupied by persons either knowing nothing of their subterranean neighbours, or being in league with them'.

Criminals also used the cellars as hiding places for stolen goods. Newspapers were littered with stories of men like John Owen and Joseph Riley, two 'rough looking fellows' who were caught concealing shoes and boots in an empty cellar in Angel Street after raiding a shoe shop in Long Millgate. At 6am on 8 October 1856, Mr Dobbie, the landlord of the Greyhound Inn in Ludgate Hill, was woken in bed by a noise in the parlour below. He tiptoed downstairs and found that burglars had broken in during the night and fled with his takings. A cupboard drawer sat empty on the bar alongside a box of cigars ready to be carried away. Another drawer containing £3 in coppers was gone.

A witness, James Gill, told police he had seen three men running away down Ludgate Hill in the grey dawn accompanied by the sound of jingling coins. A police sergeant named Duckworth later entered a cellar in Charter Street and surprised a thief named Thomas Smith. In Smith's cupboard, Duckworth found a crowbar that matched an imprint on the damaged drawers in the Greyhound. Another crowbar was found under Smith's bed, alongside a stash of stolen money.

Some of the worst cellars were hidden away in the back streets of Angel Meadow. Beneath Factory Street were two cellars filled with 'little else than dirt, misery and people'. The cellars were connected by a doorway, which was later bricked up to create separate dwellings as the landlord sought to double his profits. A journalist from the *Manchester Guardian* descended into another passageway in Back Old Mount Street, with a cigarette in his mouth to mask the 'reeking stench', and discovered a set of filthy underground privies which served 200 people living in 11 houses. The privies had no doors and even the stones that held up the seats had been stolen.

Sanitary inspectors discovered other horrors. When they climbed down into a cellar in No.1 Yard, off Simpson Street, they found it was home to a donkey. They noted in their report: 'The effluvia proceeding from this place occasioned the most noxious smell even in the next house.' In Gibraltar, at least six cellars stood 2ft beneath the level of the river and just 6ft away from the water. One cellar there was in a 'most fearful state of darkness and dirt' and another 'totally unfit for human habitation'. A temperance worker also said of another cellar in Rochdale Road: 'The cockroaches eat the bugs.'

The deepest cellars in the whole of Manchester were beneath Old Mount Street and Style Street, below the Old Burying Ground. At the Old Mount Street end, they were just a few steps below the surface, but at the Style Street end they were at least 15ft below ground, down a flight of ten steps. These deep chasms were surrounded by the same earth holding the corpses in the neighbouring cemetery and their inhabitants were prone to scarlet fever. Inspectors descended into a 12ft-square cellar that was home to 11 people. They said the stench was 'almost intolerable' and the air was 'highly poisoned'. Prisoners had more space and better air in Strangeways, they observed. In addition, the alleyways between the neighbouring streets contained 'malaria-producing filth' and the houses above in No.1 Court off New Mount Street were full of casual lodgers who had 'no regard for cleanliness'.

In November 1849, Inspector William Gifford climbed down ten steps into the cellar beneath 8 Style Street. In the darkness, on the brick floor he found a boy of six named Patrick Stewart dying from scarlet fever. Patrick lived there with his father, Michael Doonan, and his mother, Bridget Stewart, who was also very sick. Their bed was a heap of wood shavings covered by a sheet. Gifford spied two underground doors. One led to a rear cellar occupied by Martin Kelly and four women, the other to a neighbouring cellar occupied by a man named Carney and his wife, who were also suffering from fever.

Gifford decided to get the inhabitants out and contacted the workhouse. But it was two days before the workhouse van rattled into Style Street and took only the Carneys, who were frightened and did not want to leave their home. The driver said he had no orders from Manchester's Board of Guardians to take Patrick Stewart and his mother, so he left them to die in the damp cellar.

Patrick died that day, his lungs inflamed by the fever that had gripped him for over a month. His inquest began at the infirmary the next morning and lasted five hours. The jury blamed the Board of Guardians for his death and recommended that fever victims be removed from cellars with 'utmost haste'. They asked the coroner, Edward Herford, to write to Whitehall. Mr Nobel, the board's medical officer, said he had known the cellar for several years and it was the most notorious 'fever nest' in town. Nobel kept a list of slum dwellings that supplied the hospital with the most fever cases – and the Style Street cellar was right at the top.

In retaliation, the board tried to blame Inspector Gifford. They claimed Gifford had told their clerk about the Carneys but had failed to notify him about Patrick Stewart. They also claimed they had repeatedly told Gifford to turn cellar occupants out on to the streets because they had no power to take people from cellars. Before they could enter the workhouse, the poor had to declare themselves homeless. In a final effort to blacken Gifford's name, the board claimed he had been heard boasting that he had nearly sent one of the board's relieving officers to prison.

Politicians began closing the cellars in a bid to rid Angel Meadow of its hellish underworld. Manchester was slow to catch up with national legislation and only after the city introduced the New Streets Act in 1853 were property owners finally banned from turning their cellars into dwellings. In Manchester, the ceilings of cellars now had to be 6ft 6in high, which was still lower than the national regulations. Drains only had to be a minimum of 6in beneath the floor.

By 1854, 16,400 people were living in Manchester's 4,643 cellars. Six years later, 17,478 people were living in 4,467 cellars – a sign that overcrowding was increasing. In 1861, Manchester's Building and Sanitary Committee closed 341 cellars and altered 1,121 more to make them more hospitable. When a newspaper called *The Builder* carried out its own investigation the following year it found that 'the evil of cellar dwellings' was even worse than previously thought. The newspaper located the worst cellars in Angel Meadow. It argued that these damp 'caves' were responsible for the city's high death rate: 'When the door is closed, these ill-planned homes must be little better, from a sanitary point of view, than a burial vault, and yet in such situations it is permitted that children shall be born, and that, struggling for life, they, as well as persons of more mature years, shall be left to die before their time.'

By 1865, the cellar closure rate had dropped to just 37 per year. There were still 3,700 cellars in the city and it was estimated by inspectors that it would take until 1965 to close them all. In 1866, it emerged the corporation was now reopening a handful of cellars each year. Some councillors had sympathy for the landlords and were deeply opposed to the closures. Councillor Ashmore assured his colleagues that there were people living in Angel Meadow's cellars who had reached the grand age of 90 and were 'much more comfortable than they would be in crowded garrets'.

The Manchester Property Owners' Association claimed that closing 'good and useful cellars' had left large numbers of people 'huddled together' in small tenements 'breathing adulterated air over and over again until it became rank poison'. The Ladies' Sanitary Association seemed to agree. In 1870 they toured Angel Meadow handing out carbolic acid for 'purifying the dirty courts and filthy and overcrowded houses'. In their annual report they noted the 'improvements' made by Manchester Corporation in closing cellars, but added: 'Unless cheap dwellings and lodging houses elsewhere are provided, the mere closing of cellars only increases the overcrowding.'

Others, including Councillor Joseph Lamb, were outraged at news that the cellars in Style Street, where Patrick Stewart had died, were now being declared fit for occupation by the corporation. He complained: 'Why, they are eight or ten steps down and though they are double cellars, they are in such a state that it made me ill to go into them.' It emerged that Alderman Boardman, the chairman of the Sanitary Committee, was a member of an organisation

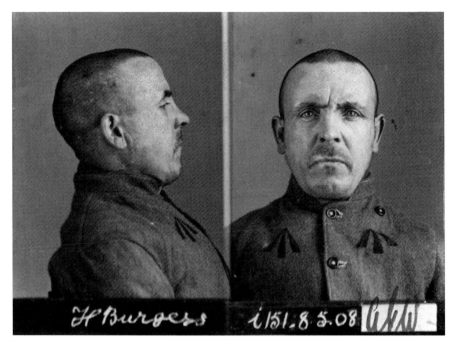

The scuttler Henry Burgess was the most feared man in Angel Meadow. (Staffordshire Record Office.)

A sketch of Angel Street looking downhill towards St Michael's Church. (Manchester Libraries, Information and Archives, Manchester City Council.)

Lodging houses in Angel Street. Note the gentrified door columns and gallery windows in the attics, relics of former prosperity. (Manchester Libraries, Information and Archives, Manchester City Council.)

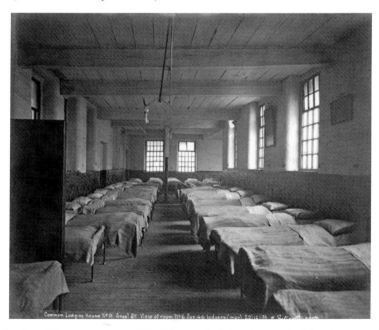

Kane's in Angel Street was one of the biggest lodging houses in Manchester, with 346 beds. Note the keys hanging from the ceiling. (Manchester Libraries, Information and Archives, Manchester City Council.)

An uncommon Villain.

John Williams' lodging house in Charter Street, formerly The Grapes. The front window of Cabbage Ann's den can be seen on the right. (Manchester Libraries, Information and Archives, Manchester City Council.)

Benjamin Redfern's sketch of a lodging house thief trainer, who had a 'lame leg' and a 'grizzled, military moustache'. (Manchester Libraries, Information and Archives, Manchester City Council.)

An attic garret above John Williams' lodging house in Charter Street. He knocked through into a room above the neighbouring house to extend his 'vile trade'. (Manchester Libraries, Information and Archives, Manchester City Council.)

Sketches by the churchman William Browne of some of the 'angels' who could be found in the slum. (Together Trust/ Manchester Libraries, Information and Archives, Manchester City Council.)

Women wearing shawls sit on steps half way down the hill of Angel Street. Note the blocked up cellar entrance. (Manchester Libraries, Information and Archives, Manchester City Council.)

Lodgers sleep on the floor and sit around a roaring fire smoking clay pipes in a dingy lodging house. (Salford Diocesan Archives.)

A family of 10 try to sleep on the floor in a damp cellar. They have barely a bedsheet between them. (Salford Diocesan Archives.)

The gaunt bell tower of St Michael's Church looms out of the mist, viewed from the foot of Angel Street. The demolished building on the left was the Victory Tavern. (Manchester Libraries, Information and Archives, Manchester City Council.)

Charter Street Ragged School in all its splendour. (Charter Street Ragged School.)

A woman pulls at a rival's hair in a fight to the death outside a pub. (*Illustrated Police News*, 10 March 1883. Image © The British Library Board, courtesy of the British Newspaper Archive: www.britishnewspaperarchive.co.uk.)

(The Dealer in Bitters)

A sketch by Benjamin Redfern of Molly Trainor, a quack who sold useless tonics on the streets of the slum. (Manchester Libraries, Information and Archives, Manchester City Council.)

An idealised sketch of Friedrich Engels' visit to Angel Meadow, from an old Soviet postcard. (Author's own collection.)

Friedrich Engels, from an old Soviet postcard. (Author's own collection.)

Riots were common in Angel Meadow. (*Illustrated Police News*, 21 July 1888. Image © The British Library Board, courtesy of the British Newspaper Archive: www. britishnewspaperarchive.co.uk.)

A WELL-KNOWN HOUSE IN CHARTER STREET.

A SCENE IN ANGEL MEADOW.

Sketches of street scenes in Angel Meadow. (Together Trust/ Manchester Libraries, Information and Archives, Manchester City Council.)

Jemmie the Crawler went around Angel Meadow on a wheeled cart, wearing a sailor's uniform. He was a notorious conman or 'dry land sailor'. (Manchester Libraries, Information and Archives, Manchester City Council.)

A woman shouts abuse at a landlord after she is thrown out of a pub in Angel Meadow. (Salford Diocesan Archives.)

Bob Horridge, Angel Meadow's most dangerous criminal, was jailed for life after shooting two police officers in an armed robbery. (Courtesy of Angela Buckley.)

Police search the River Irk after Bob Horridge leaps into the filthy water in a desperate bid to escape arrest. (Courtesy of Angela Buckley.)

Men work the furnaces and haul carts of hot coke through the Rochdale Road Gasworks. (Author's own collection.)

Two Angel Meadow characters, 'Joe' and 'Joe's pal'. (Salford Diocesan Archives.)

Scuttlers from Angel Meadow stab Joseph Brady to death in his lodging house. (*Illustrated Police News*, 19 February 1887: Image © The British Library Board, courtesy of the British Newspaper Archive: www.britishnewspaperarchive.co.uk.)

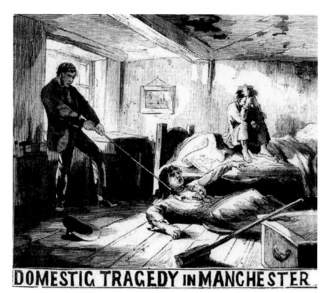

Patrick Durr murders his wife Catherine by hanging her in their bedroom. He is watched by their son Paddy, 14, who is too terrified to attempt to save her. (*Illustrated Police News*, 27 August 1870. Image © The British Library Board, courtesy of the British Newspaper Archive: www.britishnewspaperarchive.co.uk.)

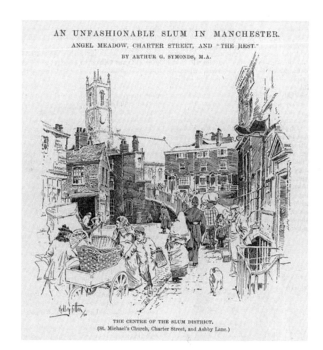

A sketch of St Michael's Square and Charter Street, looking towards St Michael's Church. The Victory Tavern stands in front of the church in the middle distance. (Mary Evans Picture Library.)

Thomas Johnson, the Superintendent of the Charter Street Ragged School. (*Manchester Evening News*, 21 December 1914. Image © Trinity Mirror. Image created courtesy of The British Library Board, courtesy of the British Newspaper Archive: www.britishnewspaperarchive.co.uk.)

Father Daniel Hearne, the fierce Irish priest, broke up fights in the slum armed with a mahogany stick. (Salford Diocesan Archives.)

The Rev John Mercer, the Rector of St Michael's Church, called for guerrilla warfare against the slum's insanitary conditions. (W. L. Crowther Library, Tasmanian Archive and Heritage Office.)

William Wiggins, a Charter Street pickpocket. His long police record said he had one leg shorter than the other. (Greater Manchester Police Museum and Archives.)

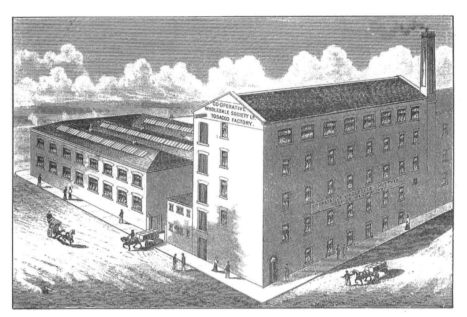

The CWS tobacco factory in Sharp Street. (National Co-operative Archive.)

Workers at the tobacco factory pose for a rare photograph. The factory employed no workers from the slum, preferring those from 'better class districts'. (National Co-operative Archive.)

A train steams towards Angel Meadow on the grey-bricked railway viaduct. The skyline is dominated by the Rochdale Road Gasworks. (Author's own collection.)

A sketch by Benjamin Redfern of the one-armed street fighters Bacup Billy and Stumpy before their deadly battle on the Old Burying Ground. (Manchester Libraries, Information and Archives, Manchester City Council.)

Slum dwellers buy coke for their fires from the Rochdale Road Gasworks. (Author's own collection.)

Scott (alias John) Harrison, a notorious Charter Street thief. (Greater Manchester Police Museum and Archives.)

Samuel Bebbington, another Charter Street thief. Note the handcuffs on his right wrist. (Greater Manchester Police Museum and Archives.)

Three finely-dressed 'megs men' or swindlers lie in wait for potential victims outside the Highland Laddie in Charter Street. (Manchester Libraries, Information and Archives, Manchester City Council.)

Smithfield Market was one of the main places of work for people who lived in Angel Meadow. (Author's own collection.)

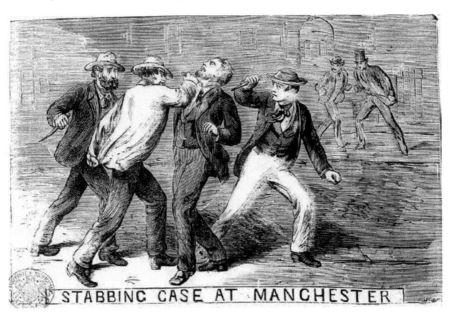

John Bernadotti, Joseph Restron and Bartholomew Galgani stab John Oldham to death near Smithfield Market. (*Illustrated Police News*, 6 March 1869. Image © The British Library Board, courtesy of the British Newspaper Archive: www. britishnewspaperarchive.co.uk.)

campaigning against the closure of cellars. Boardman owned 20 cellars in Back Style Street, two in Style Street and eight in Old Mount Street.

Anyone in doubt about the horrors of the cellar underworld had only to read journalist Angus Reach's account of his visit to Angel Meadow, in which he recounted having followed a woman lighting their way with a candle into the 'worst cellar in Manchester'. He described the interior to readers as follows:

> The vaults were mere subterranean holes, utterly without light. The flicker of the candle showed their grimy walls, reeking with foetid damp, which trickled in greasy drops down to the floor. Beds were huddled in every corner, some of them on frames – I cannot call them bedsteads – others on the floor. In one of these a man was lying dressed, and beside him slept a well-grown calf.

Reach found a drunken old man sitting on another bed with saliva running down his chin, who was trying unsuccessfully to remove his trousers and roaring for help. In the next cellar, two boys were snoring together in one bed and beside them was a man sleeping in an old battered hat. Reach asked: "Is he undressed?" The police officer accompanying him turned down the bedsheet and revealed a naked man, black with filth. Undeterred by the 'dreadful' smell in the 'hot and wet' atmosphere of the cellar, he continued to explore:

> "What's this you have being doing?" said my conductor to the landlady, stooping down and examining the lower part of one of the walls. I joined him, and saw that a sort of hole or shallow cave, about six feet long, two deep, and a little more than one high, had been scooped out through the wall into the earth on the outside of the foundation, there being probably some yard on the other side, and in this hole or earthen cupboard there was stretched, upon a scanty litter of foul-smelling straw, a human being – an old man. As he lay on his back, his face was not two inches beneath the roof – so to speak – of the hole. "He's a poor old body," said the landlady, in a tone of deprecation, "and if we didn't let him crawl in there he would have to sleep in the streets." I turned away, and was glad when I found myself breathing such comparatively fresh air as can be found in Angel Meadow.

Chapter 12

Street Life

T he two beggars squared up to each other on the rough slope of the Old Burying Ground and prepared for their pre-arranged battle. It was a Sunday afternoon, the usual time and place for settling grudges with a fight, and hundreds of spectators had gathered in a big circle around them. In this hotly-anticipated bout it was impossible to predict the winner. The opponents were perfectly matched – they both only had one arm.

One of the fighters was known as Bacup Billy (possibly because he came from the Lancashire village of Bacup). He had lost his left arm in a colliery explosion and was generally a quiet, peaceful man until his anger was roused, when he became dangerous. His opponent, Stumpy, was a bully and more treacherous for it. He was as strong as a horse and had been a navvy until his right arm was severed in a railway accident. Stumpy had been bullying Billy and had finally provoked him into a fight.

In the first few rounds, the fight was going in Stumpy's favour. Most of the crowd, who hated Stumpy and were cheering for Billy, the underdog, were disgusted. Then, in the sixth or seventh round, came a decisive blow. Stumpy grabbed Billy with his one good arm and threw him to the ground, before giving him a crashing kick in the ribs. The spectators' disgust turned to outrage. They threw themselves on Stumpy and might have killed him but for Billy, who screamed with tears of rage that he should be allowed to continue the fight, as his honour was at stake. The spectators backed off and the two men returned to business.

Stumpy, after being set upon by the crowd, was cowed. It finally looked as though Stumpy might be beaten, but then he made an unusual and decisive move that would change the course of both their lives. Benjamin Redfern described what happened next: 'The men were rolling on the ground, when the bigger villain bit through Billy's hand – completely through – and the consequence was that the crowd smashed him into a crushed, shapeless and bleeding mass in their indignation at such foul play.'

Billy did not recover from his horrific injury. His arm became infected and he later died. Stumpy recovered but was sent into exile from Angel Meadow, having committed the worst of all crimes by not engaging in a fair fight. He ended up in a far corner of the city where his badly-damaged and villainous face told its own story.

Their battle was immortalised by Redfern, who drew a remarkable sketch of Billy and Stumpy in *Odds and Ends* magazine, which has been preserved in Manchester Archives. Billy is wearing a cap, waistcoat and jacket – his armless left sleeve buttoned to his chest. He has thin eyes, a large nose and a neat beard covers the line of his jaw. Stumpy is depicted jacket-less, ready for a fight, with his right sleeve held up by a piece of string tied over his shoulder and his left sleeve rolled up to reveal a tattoo of a sailing ship. He wears trouser braces and a neckerchief, above which his eyes appear wild and his hair is in shaggy curls. A scraggy goatee covers his chin.

The Old Burying Ground became the scene of weekly fights – a favourite spectator sport for slum dwellers. Men who threw punches in the beer houses on Saturday nights would settle their differences on the cemetery's uneven ground on Sunday afternoons, watched by huge crowds who gambled their wages on the winners. The district's medical officer, Dr Edward Meacham, said in 1866 there had only been three Sundays in 12 months when no fighting took place: 'If any disturbance occurs in the neighbouring public houses, the advice generally is given to fight it out on the burying ground.' If the combatants were too hungover from the previous night, the fight would be postponed until they were both sufficiently sober.

Women also fought in the burying ground half-stripped like the men, punching and biting one another in 'true Lancashire fashion' with crowds of up to 400 people cheering them. A fight was known as a 'mill', which one Victorian writer described as follows in a dictionary of Manchester slang: 'We presume it refers to the pounding which one gets when in a fight, such as a mutilation we might expect if we got fast in a huge coffee mill or other grinding machine.'

A working man named Holland said he had seen four or five fights take place in the cemetery in as many hours and it was sometimes 40 minutes before a constable arrived. He had seen combatants doing battle with pokers, iron bars and other weapons, and police officers attempting to intervene were 'shamefully knocked about'. Even in the days when constables were armed with cutlasses, it often took them a whole day with their weapons drawn to break up the fighting. Most were too afraid to enter the cemetery alone and after a while they only went there in groups of three.

The cemetery was also a no-go-zone for the Reverend Thomas Wolstencroft, the rector of St Michael's Church. He marched across it one Sunday to break up a game of pitch and toss and limped back to the church with two broken ribs. Parishioners found it hard to concentrate on his sermons because of the 'yelling and shouting and blasphemous oaths' outside. It was not uncommon for stones to crash through the church's windows on Sundays, leaving the congregation in 'bodily fear'.

An anonymous letter from a parishioner in the *Manchester Guardian* expressed outrage at the 'pugilistic encounters' that had taken place there for 25 years. It was, the correspondent said, enough to 'sear the eye and grieve the heart'. He added: 'The assistance of the police has been repeatedly solicited but, though they have endeavoured to do their duty, they are powerless against the numbers that frequently congregate here.' Another letter writer said the graveyard was a 'disgrace to Manchester':

> The ground is very often the arena for various gladiatorial exhibitions, such as a fight generally got up in some of the low drinking places of the neighbourhood. I have often seen some hundreds of the poor inhabitants of the district congregated together to witness two of their species stand up to be knocked down and frequently kicked while in that position and this takes place over a spot where 40,000 bodies are said to be buried.

William Browne was visiting St Michael's in the gloom of a Sunday evening with a slum guide, who whistled a melancholy tune as they walked. Browne suddenly heard a series of unearthly screams and saw people running towards the cemetery. He and his guide followed and found two prostitutes named Bridget and Kate battling it out at the centre of a large crowd. Kate, who had big muscles and was 'a regular bruiser', had objected to Bridget poaching on her domain. Browne wrote:

> They are like wild beasts. They kick, they scratch, they pull each other's hair, bite – now down, now up. Amid the cheers of the crowd, and breathing terrible curses, Kate goes down with a heavy thud, the bigger woman on top of her, and a faint "Oh!" proceeds from her bleeding lips. The crowd presses closer. Surely she is dead. No. Again, the ring is made wider – again the populace urge them on with "Well done Kate!" and "Mill her, Bridget – stop her little game!" Murder will be done tonight.

The fight was eventually stopped by a brave police officer, his collar number 999B glinting in the near darkness. "What's up?" he asked, and someone replied: "Only a mill". The crowd vanished in an instant and, as the officer went on his way, Browne heard a woman say: "Ain't it a blooming pity, Billy, a prime mill like that 'ere wos spoiled."

The streets surrounding the church were just as dangerous as the cemetery. Police were called to Charter Street one Thursday in August, 1851. Three 'disreputable looking fellows', Henry Carter, Thomas Smith and John Eden, had stripped down to the waist and were fighting at the centre of a large crowd. A police officer seized hold of Eden, but his hands slipped off his sweat-soaked body and the officer suffered a severe beating before a brick was finally thrown at his head, destroying his hat and leaving him with a large cut.

W R Jordan, a writer who visited Angel Meadow, warned his readers: 'A sight which may frequently be witnessed is the neighbourly row which ends in a fight. Take care not to interfere, for your chances are that one or both of the combatants will turn upon you.'

Mass brawls were one thing, casual violence was quite another. William Browne was walking along Dyche Street on another night when he witnessed a shocking attack on an old woman by her husband. The thug, apparently annoyed by her pestering him to return home, gave his wife a brutal blow that caused her to reel like a drunkard into the middle of the street. Browne said: 'As her head goes with a heavy thud against the hard, cruel stones, and the cry of pain finds utterance, we feel a cold shudder take possession of us.' He warned: 'Such scenes are of frequent occurrence here. The only variation is that sometimes it may not be a wife, but a child or sweetheart. And who can wonder when real Irish whiskey or London gin gets into the brain. Then the human beings under its influence are converted into fiends.'

Casual violence led to a number of deaths. One Sunday night in April 1867, a widow named Fanny Halliday, 65, was heading out of a lodging house in Charter Street to buy some tobacco when a boy punched her in the face and ran away. By Monday, her face and eyes were badly swollen and the next day tears of blood were streaming down her face. She died at the workhouse five days later from a bacterial infection known as St Anthony's Fire. An inquest jury found her death was caused by the blow.

The Reverend Adam Scott came across other badly beaten women when he visited a large beer house known as the Beggars' Resort:

Several women in a most wretched condition – in rags, dirty and dazed with drink – hover about the doors. One of them has a pair of black eyes – one out of about a score of women I saw in the same condition. Looking inside the house we see about 40 people around the bar having drink, and, as nearly as I can estimate, about the half are women.

Police officers dealing with street fights were ordered to keep their tempers under control and never to handle prisoners 'more roughly than absolutely necessary'. They had no powers to arrest anyone arguing in the street until they threatened violence or drew a weapon. They could only use their staffs in self-defence and were ordered to keep them hidden until needed.

However, officers knew the realities of street life in Angel Meadow and they were prepared to do anything necessary to keep the peace. Their orders even demanded that they step into the fray once a fight had started and 'immediately interfere to separate the combatants'. A handbook issued to officers stated: 'Do everything in your power to restore peace and quiet.'

A report by Manchester's Chief Constable in August, 1856, recognised that Angel Meadow needed extra policing. He said: 'The district is inhabited generally by a large number of thieves as well as a low class of Irish persons, and sometimes fights suddenly occur which the policeman on the beat is not able to suppress without first obtaining additional assistance.' He proposed to add four extra constables a day, but the move seemed to have little effect. Assaults on police in Manchester increased from 381 in 1858 to 504 in 1864. Manslaughter convictions rose from 9 to 15, shootings and stabbings leapt from 15 to 29. Only murders and attempted murders fell – from eight in 1859 to three in 1865.

The police were now dealing with violent assaults and robberies every single day in the streets of Angel Meadow and anyone entering the slum risked becoming a target. In 1853, William Fone was leaving the Weaver's Arms in Angel Street when a robber named Thomas Darey grabbed him by the throat with such force that blood spurted from his mouth. Darey put his knees on Fone's chest and rifled through his pockets, taking six half-crowns.

Joseph Bradley, a stoker, was walking home along Charter Street at 11pm on a Saturday in October 1852, when a thug named James Bates rushed up behind him and seized him tightly around the neck with a garrotte while another man emptied his pockets. They left him for dead. When the case went to court, Bradley withdrew his complaint and it was clear that he had been threatened by Bates' friends. The prisoner walked free.

An even more shocking garrotte robbery took place outside the Highland Laddie beer house in Charter Street in February, 1851. A young woman named Mary Anne Mutch was walking past when two 14-year-old girls, Mary Anne Welch and Mary O'Brien, emerged from the vault and followed her to a secluded alley. One of the girls tried to strangle her using a piece of wire rope, while the other put a hand in Mutch's pockets and stole a shilling and seven pence. A judge prosecuting the two girls said it was one of the strangest robberies he had come across.

Another common tactic used by robbers was the 'honey trap'. Women would hang around coaching inns in better parts of Manchester looking for wealthy travellers who had just arrived in the city and would try to entice them back to the idyllic-sounding Angel Meadow. Instead, once inside the slum's maze of alleyways, the victim would be set upon by a gang of thugs. One well-known 'honey trap' artiste was Ellen Hatton, who lured a traveller named John Seddon to the Meadow on a hot summer's night. Seddon was followed by two men who knocked him down and took his watch. Police later found Hatton lounging in bed in a 'house of ill fame' deep in the Meadow.

Another traveller named Thomas Goulden, 23, was so badly beaten that he was almost killed when a woman led him to the lair of thugs who stole his watch and purse. Goulden, a stranger to Manchester, was looking for a bed before getting the early morning mail coach. He was intercepted by an unknown woman who invited him to accompany her to Angel Meadow, where she claimed 'she would take care that he should be accommodated with as comfortable a bed as a gentleman need to lie on'. When they reached the slum, she took him down an alley where four robbers savagely beat him before emptying his pockets.

When he eventually recovered his senses, Goulden shouted out for a policeman, who arrived quickly and struck up a plan. The officer waited with Goulden in the alley, guessing that the thugs would return. The pair then grabbed the first two men who appeared in the gloom. One escaped, but the other, Edward Griffiths, was caught and Goulden's watch was found in his coat pocket.

Women in Angel Meadow also carried out their own robberies. A venetian blind maker named Henry Neill was walking along Ledger Street when two women named Mary Ann Johnson and Susannah Brierley grabbed hold of him and dragged him into a house. They threw him to the floor and stuffed his handkerchief into his mouth, then cut open his trouser pockets with a large bread knife and stole his money. They ran off, leaving him on the floor, but were later caught.

Despite all they were up against, police officers had to keep a clear head. 'Remember,' they were told in their handbook, 'neglect of duty in any way not only brings disgrace upon the force, but also gives thieves the opportunity of committing their depredations.' Officers were banned from drinking on duty and told that their 'sobriety and decision of character' would be respected. The handbook added: 'Experience has proved that coffee is better adapted for keeping the body warm and comfortable in cold and wet weather than spirits or beer.' Entering beer houses in uniform was strictly forbidden unless they were arresting a criminal or helping a landlord eject a drunken customer. Officers were told that any offers of a drink should be politely declined.

But at 2am one Saturday in July, 1863, a police officer named Peter Egan snapped. Egan, 25, had been drinking on the beat when he claimed lodging house keeper John Wild's wife had pelted him with stones and bricks in Charter Street. Egan chased Mrs Wild into the house and kicked her savagely as she tumbled to the floor. Egan then began attacking everyone in the house, thumping John Wild in the face and beating him with his staff. He later claimed Wild had attacked him with a poker. A police officer named Kendal ran into the house after hearing a scream and found John Wild on the floor holding Egan's legs, while Egan held Wild by the hair. Egan had torn the shirt from Wild's back. Egan shouted: "Wild has knocked me down and I will pay him for old times."

Bridget Devitt, whose face was badly disfigured during Egan's rampage, said he had nearly killed her. Her shoulder was black with bruises and Egan had blinded her in one eye. A widow named Harriet Greenhaulgh was carrying a baby in her arms when Egan beat her with a thick stick and tore a fistful of hair from her head. William Downs, a boy who was sleeping at the lodging house, said Egan burst into his room and hit him on the head. Ann Powell, a notorious thief trainer nicknamed Cabbage Ann, who was then living in Crown Street, had been visiting her dying daughter at the house when Egan punched and kicked her.

Other officers rallied round Egan in court and one even said he had seen bricks flying in the street. Egan, who was 5ft 9in with brown hair and grey eyes, was a married with a son. Magistrates said he had been a 'most excellent' officer, but they had no choice but to jail him for 12 months. Egan told the prison warder he was a labourer, perhaps seeking to mask his true identity from fellow convicts who might have known him from the streets of Angel Meadow.

Chapter 13

Drinking Dens

The silence of a winter's night was shattered by a piercing scream and the sound of unsteady footsteps. Michael Kirby, 55, staggered out of an alley near Victoria Station. His grey eyes were flushed red by the alcohol in his bloodstream and his sallow skin appeared sickly yellow in the jaundiced glow of the street lamps. It was too late. A woman named Ann Queary had seen him and was already calling out for a constable. He turned awkwardly on unsteady legs and was swallowed by the darkness.

A constable named Smith was first to arrive. Queary told him she had seen a drunken man and woman stagger into the alley, before hearing a chilling scream. Smith took a candle and picked his way into the shadows. The alley led into the jaws of an unfinished warehouse and was lined with deep, uncovered cellars. It was only when Smith lowered the flame into one of the cavernous holes that he finally saw her. Charlotte Stott was lying on her back 13ft below ground, moaning and insensible. Smith found Kirby hiding nearby in the shadows. "I ain't seen no woman," Kirby protested as he struggled like a cat to break free from Smith's grasp. Kirby was a scavenger from Angel Meadow – and a steaming drunk.

Charlotte Stott died in hospital four days later. She had fractured her spine in the fall. Kirby had been released on bail but was re-arrested at his home in Irk Street and taken to the New Bailey Prison. The house he shared with his wife Mary and four children stood in the shadow of the railway and within sniffing distance of the river.

Kirby was 5ft 5in and had dark brown hair and a tattoo of two pears on his left arm. He had moved to Manchester from Castlebar on the west coast of Ireland following the Great Famine. Now he was charged with 'feloniously killing and slaying' Charlotte Stott in the alley. In court, the prosecutor claimed Kirby had deliberately pushed Stott down the hole. The strongest evidence was a statement taken from the victim before she died. Stott claimed she had entered the alley with Kirby and he had pushed her into the cellar – and had killed her. The judge brought the trial to an immediate halt. It was impossible, he said, for Stott to give evidence about her own death. Kirby was cleared.

The quickest way out of Victorian Manchester was through the doors of the city's beer houses. Ale, whisky and gin had been part of life in Angel Meadow since the slum's earliest days. The district containing the slum had 44 taverns and 33 gin shops by the 1830s. Dr James Phillips Kay observed: 'Where there are the most paupers, the gin shops, taverns and beer houses are the most numerous.' Benjamin Braidley, the borough reeve, reported seeing 112 men and 163 women entering one gin shop in just 40 minutes during one Saturday night.

Angel Meadow's pubs had colourful names: the Dog and Duck, the Flying Ass, the Gas Tavern, the Sun Vaults, the Flower Pot and the Barley Mow, among others. One pub, the Angel's Whisper, which overlooked the Old Burying Ground, was named after a call sign used by army deserters. Others were named by the Irish: The Duke of Connaught, the Harp and Shamrock, the Exile of Erin and Tara's Hall.

The Crown and Cushion in Long Millgate was a world away from the small, cramped houses it overshadowed. It had three storeys, with five rooms to a floor, cellars beneath, and a brew house, water pump and stable in the yard. The Church Inn on Charter Street, also known as St Michael's Tavern, contained a brew house and two vaulted cellars. One landlord of the tavern, a notorious swindler named Walter Griffiths Lloyd, kept a huge dog behind the bar for protection against police raids.

Friedrich Engels was appalled by the excessive drinking he saw in Manchester. He found mothers with babies in their arms hanging around beer houses and mixing with thieves and swindlers. 'When one reflects that many a mother gives the baby on her arm gin to drink, the demoralising effects of frequenting such places cannot be denied,' he remarked. Engels frequently saw people staggering about drunk or lying in the gutter. Even young women could be seen slipping into Angel Meadow's liquor vaults. Angus Reach said he found drunken men and women 'shouting, hallooing and romping' in streets a short walk from the slum: 'Rows, fights and scuffles were every moment taking place within doors and in the streets. The whole street rung with shouting, screaming and swearing, mingled with the jarring music of half a dozen bands.'

Recorded cases of drunkenness in Manchester rose rapidly during the mid-nineteenth century. There were 1,806 cases in 1858 and 3,679 in 1865. Heavy drinking was part of every family event in Angel Meadow – baptisms, marriages and funerals. Death was seen as an occasion for 'drowning grief by getting drunk', noted one journalist who toured the slum with a census taker. He wrote:

One house was shut up, and on applying at the neighbour for particulars, the answer given by one of its occupants was, "Oh, they're drunk". The other objected, and said, "No, they're burying a relation", which elicited the reply, "Well, it's all the same". In two other instances, the state of the room and of the 'head' was excused on the grounds of a death in the family.

Funeral wakes were huge affairs and occasionally led to drunken outrages on the dead. One Irish priest banned wakes and began reading out the names of participants during Mass to discourage the practice. Another banned a widower from having a wake for his wife and marched to his house with a thick stick when he discovered the ban was being flouted. The priest stormed through the front door and took down the names of six mourners, but the man defiantly wrapped his wife's corpse in a bed sheet and carried her to a house in another parish, where the wake continued.

A journalist described an even more shocking incident:

A friend of mine, a priest, once came suddenly upon one of these gatherings and found the corpse lying in a bed with a lighted pipe stuck in its mouth and the drunken wakers enjoying the sight. Of course this was an extreme case for, as a rule, the Irish have a great veneration for the dead. It is generally the living who suffer from the amount of drink consumed.

Manchester's coroners and magistrates witnessed the devastating effects of rampant alcoholism at first-hand. Jerry Scott, who lived in lodgings in Charter Street, staggered into the Crown and Cushion one night and became 'mad drunk' after downing several glasses of whisky in an hour. He then jumped up and began fighting everyone who came through the door. His 'capering about' lasted until he suddenly collapsed. He was carried back to his lodgings, but died in his bed. An inquest heard he had been drinking almost non-stop for a week.

Violence flared easily in the slum's beer houses. The backroom bare-knuckle boxing matches that made some Manchester pubs legendary took place in other parts of the city. In Angel Meadow, drinkers preferred brawling and stabbing each other in the front room. One reporter who visited Long Millgate on a Saturday night with a bodyguard of two detectives wrote:

The first hotel we passed had a large plate-glass window broken, and the landlord stood at the door complacently smoking a cigar. "Hallo – how's business? Anything doing?" one of the genial officers asked. "Oh, very quiet," replied the publican from behind a cloud of smoke. "We've only had five fights and a stabbing since eight o'clock. It's very quiet indeed." And yet the street resounded with midsummer night's screams of revelry and riot.

A magistrate named Fowler said the courts should fine pub landlords who allowed customers to drink too heavily. "If this course were adopted there would not be seen at court on Monday mornings 120 drunken men brought forward," he argued. One court regular, Ellen Williams, had 89 convictions for drunkenness.

It was unsurprising that the poor found solace in Angel Meadow's taverns. With their brightly-lit vaults, warm fires and cheap ale, they were palaces compared with their own cold, dark homes. The Reverend Adam Scott wrote:

In all of this district, with its hungry thousands, I did not see a single handsome provision shop, but the temptations to drink are manifold. Its dwellings are mean and poor in the extreme, but at its head there stands a gin palace upon which no expense has been spared. It is lighted with electricity, and made in every way tempting for men and women with the love of drink to enter.

Another writer, W R Jordan, sympathised: 'It is no wonder then that he who can scrape a copper or two together will find the nearest beer house a more comfortable place than his own house – for he will at least have light and warmth and congenial companions.'

When drinkers blew their money on drink, they would go to the nearest pawn shop and hand over everything they could carry – furniture, clothes and even knives and forks – to buy more beer. They would return to the shop midweek to repay the loan, until one day they would finally run out of funds and find themselves left with no furniture.

The biggest pawn shop in Angel Meadow stood near St Michael's Church. It was owned by a man named Platt, but was known as My Uncle's, a common nickname for pawnbrokers. William Browne, who went inside, said: 'It is well stocked – a sign that the times are bad. Just going in, we see a somewhat seedy individual. He is a regular habitué, and therefore goes in with an easy, nonchalant air.'

Men could smoke their short clay pipes in the pubs, buy snacks of bread and cheese, and gamble at cards, skittles or dominoes. W R Jordan found that pub-goers in the Meadow would bet on anything: 'If by laying down a shilling he thinks it probable it will be returned to him twenty fold, you may be quite sure that by some means or other the shilling will be obtained.'

One of the most popular pub sports was the ratting match, in which terriers were pitted against rats. The Dog and Duck in Charter Street had both a skittle alley and a rat pit. The rules were strict and the stakes were high, with the dogs weighed like boxers to determine how many rats they would fight in the waist-high, circular pit. Bets were taken on how long they would take to kill the rats and their owners could win prizes including teapots, silver cups and dog collars.

A man named Rafferty who lived in an Angel Meadow lodging house told investigators:

Some low fellows bring the dog – ugly little bull terrier – and a lot of rats are let loose in a pit, and it nips their spines one by one as if it enjoyed it. Then a man will nip their spines too with his teeth, just like a dog. Then the doors will be locked and two dogs will fight, or a badger will be drawn, or two men will slog each other in an amusing and indiscriminate manner and I, and any other fellows who are there, will tip them half-sovereigns.

A journalist from the *Free Lance* described a match in a room above another pub across town. Squeaks from behind the counter alerted him that he was 'in rat land' and he saw the pub's pipe-smoking dog owners nursing their pets 'as if they had been babies'. The rats were thrown into the pit over the spectators' heads and scurried around with 'the innocence of kittens'. They did all they could to escape – even climbing up the dog owner's trouser legs. The rules stated that he had to stand in a chalk circle and was not allowed to move.

The journalist recounted: 'Down goes the dog and he has seized a rat before your eye has had time to twinkle. Everybody seems to shout something that nobody distinctly hears. His master becomes fearfully energetic. We certainly never did see a man beat his hand so hard upon a wooden floor before, and probably there never was a dog so shouted at since dogs were invented.'

Secret dog fights were also held in Angel Meadow. Twenty-five men appeared in court one morning charged with dog fighting at the Grapes in Charter Street. Two police officers crept into the house at noon one Monday and locked the doors. As they crept upstairs, they heard shouts of "Now Joe!" and saw two men in a ring of wooden benches releasing the dogs. The men rushed from the room, but were caught. The landlord and two men were jailed for two months and the others were fined.

Drinking in Angel Meadow's pubs meant mixing with the slum's thieves, who used them as their dens. Angus Reach stepped into an unnamed pub in Charter Street with a police inspector and found a large number of men and women whose 'faded finery' suggested they had seen better times. Barefooted boys were drinking beer and Reach could hear the rattle of dominoes on every side. Candles flickered amid the swirling tobacco smoke. Reach said: 'Ensconced in the seat of honour by the fire was a villainous-looking black man without shoes, who said that he had just come to town, having cadged it from Stafford, and in a corner sat two pedlars, each upon his box.'

As Reach and the inspector were leaving, a teenage boy passed them at the threshold. He was smartly dressed, with a tassel dangling from his cap. "Well, young un," the inspector said. "Whose pockets have your hands been in this evening?" According to Reach: 'The boy stared coolly at the inspector. The light from the lamp fell on his face, and I never saw a worse one – little deep-sunk eyes, and square bony jaw, with a vile expression.' The boy told the officer: "What do you mean talking about pockets to me? I don't know nothing about pockets." Then he turned on his heels and entered the house. The inspector told Reach the boy had been twice convicted.

For many years, the Dog and Duck in Charter Street boasted the title of the worst pub in Manchester. So bad was its reputation that the police said it was 'the greatest resort of professional thieves in the town'. Pictures of boxers decorated the walls. When Reach ventured into the Dog with his police guide that same night, he noted: 'This is the house of call for the swell mob of Manchester and the superior class of prigs.'

The Victory, a triangular-shaped building squashed into a small plot of land near the foot of Angel Street, was another notorious beer house. It stood in a raised position overlooking the lower half of the slum and had a large drop to the rear. The interior was split into two levels with a lower rear door opening down on Ashley Lane. The Victory went up for sale in 1840, when a newspaper advert described the pub as a 'desirable opportunity'.

The Victory was famed for its wild nights. Eventually the landlord lost his licence and the premises was turned into a hostel for lost boys. One visitor said: 'Angel Meadow abounds in thieving dens and infamous plague spots, common lodging houses and gin palaces. Among the latter, none was viler than the Victory, which stood on an eminence overlooking squalor and misery of which it was one of the prime causes.' He added:

The lower part of this notorious public house had earned the distinction of the 'hole-in-the-wall' on account of a general practice being made of passing intoxicating liquor through a hole in the wall, during illegal hours. This house was the resort of thieves and one who was there tells us of bank notes to the extent of fifties being changed within its walls, which had been the booty of burglars. A drunken frowsy mob hourly besieged its counters, and its deadly poison was administered alike to men, women and children, till at last it was deprived of its licence.

Pubs were not the only places where a man could find a drink in Angel Meadow. There were dozens of secret, unlicensed dens in houses and underground vaults. A gang of 11 thieves were caught hiding in an upper room when their drunken antics awoke the neighbourhood. Police found the gang of boys and girls singing, swearing and shouting. Four were jailed for two months, the rest for a month with hard labour.

A journalist from the *Manchester Courier* accidentally discovered a drinking den in a lodging house in Crown Lane when he entered with two detectives. A crowd of filthy and drunken men and women were crowded into the common room. A young man with a prison haircut, a week-old beard and a 'villainous expanse of jaw' was entertaining them. 'He held a teacup full of beer in one hand, and a quart jug in the other,' the journalist wrote. With his eyes fixed on the grimy wall opposite, the man began to sing with serious feeling: "Oh 'e talks just like a picture book, does Inky. At argiment 'e's quite a furrough-bred. Tho' e' deals in coule an' coke, e's a hedicated bloke an' a cove wot's got some big fings in 'is 'ed." The men and women in the packed room joined in the chorus. The journalist wrote: 'The only audible notice of our entrance was a unanimous request that we should pay for a gallon, but still the men contracted their brows in hatred of the detectives.'

Another infamous drinking den stood in Nelson Street. It had a good-sized room, which was used for the 'most immoral and degrading purposes' as a 'free and easy', a venue where visitors would compete at singing and dancing. It was badly lit, poorly ventilated and had a steep, dark staircase leading to an upper room. Teachers at the Charter Street Ragged School, who later took over the building, said it was the 'Devil's house' and the 'meeting house of thieves and the rendezvous of prostitutes': 'The very Sunday night before we entered into possession, it was used as a dancing saloon and for some weeks our services were carried on with flimsy and gaudy decorations still decking its walls.'

One writer saw how a 'free and easy' in Angel Meadow could swiftly turn violent. After being invited to see 'a hop', he was taken down a dark passageway into a long room, which was crowded with Irishmen and as hot as an oven. A tall, lanky youth nicknamed Lamp Post was standing on a box furiously playing a jig on a tin whistle. The writer said: 'The dancers are almost mad. They jump, they shout, they rattle their feet as if they were strung on wires.

The fun grows fast and furious. The dance is far from decent. The whistle player only stopped through exhaustion. The dancers stood still, downed jugs of ale and lit their pipes.'

During the lull, a red-faced giant entered the room with a swagger. Someone shouted: "Ah, 'tis Conny. Shure he'll chuck a move." Lamp Post began playing a jig called the Leg of the Duck. The dancers formed a ring and Conny jumped into the middle. The writer continued: 'It is simply wonderful. Heel and toe, toe and heel – piano-forte – shake, trill, on, on, on, ever dancing. To use the words of the assembled crowd, "Shure there's music in the bhoy's heels."'

A man with a jealous eye stood in the corner. He was 'dwarfish', the writer noted, and had a large head. "He dance? So can a cat on hot iron," he shouted. The writer said:

> The grin on Conny's face relaxes. Clouds are gathering in its place. The look-out is ominous. He stops, casts a withering look at the fellow and says: "Get out wid yer, ye omadhaun" (Gaelic for a fool). "Faith, I'll split open yer silly skull, I will, in de twinkle of an oye." What a change – an explosion of curses. They close. Amid a scene of the wildest confusion, chairs are broken as well as heads. Over goes the paraffin lamp – darkness – and under its cover we slip out, thanking our stars we are none the worse for the visit.

Irish bootleggers supplied the alcohol for these dens, producing gallons of whiskey in stills hidden in cellars. Joshua Pritchard, a customs officer, said these stills could hold up to 50 gallons of whiskey made from treacle or dregs of beer. Pritchard explained: 'It is made in so hurried a way that in general it is of an inferior quality. They make all kinds of spirits of this whiskey – or poteen as they call it – gin, brandy or rum, by colouring it. I have been told that this illicit spirit is sold to a considerable extent at the beer shops, and I believe this to be the case.' He added: 'Some of my informers have told me that the illicit distillers cannot execute their orders fast enough.' Pritchard believed that over 100 stills were in operation in Manchester and Salford, while Dr Peter Gaskell estimated they were producing 156,000 gallons of 'genuine poteen of the highest strength' every year.

Police efforts to find these stills became a game of cat and mouse. In a single year, they jailed 30 people for distilling and hawking illicit spirits. One December night, officers raided a couple's house in Angel Meadow and seized an active still. The man was jailed for three months, but his wife received double his sentence amid claims she was 'an old offender'. The Irish began hiding stills in the deepest, darkest and most obscure places they could find.

The kit was so cheap and simple that it could be quickly replaced if police carried out a raid.

The Manchester and Salford Temperance Society was formed in 1851 in a bid to end the scourge of alcohol. Members pledged to abstain and the society's missionary, John Ripley, visited homes handing out tracts on the evils of drink. In one house he found a man confined to bed for eight weeks with an abscess caused by drinking. Ripley wrote: 'For the last 17 years he was in the habit of fiddling at public houses, drinking very hard and eating very little. "No one can tell," confessed the poor creature, "how hard it is when a man's sober to have to sit in a public house and to crack jokes and sing songs to amuse a lot of drunken men for a living."'

In another house he found a 'decent woman' nursing a baby made lame by its drunken father, who had knocked it down and stood on its foot. She had buried another child a fortnight earlier and was so poor she had to go begging to pay for the funeral. She planned to leave her unemployed husband, who had been drinking non-stop for four days. In a third house, Ripley found a man and wife who had been married 23 years, during which she had never known him to be sober for a full week. Despite this, she told Ripley that he had now been teetotal for seven weeks and they had seen more 'domestic bliss' in that time than in all their years of marriage.

Members of the temperance society called on Parliament to abolish Sunday drinking. One temperance worker claimed a 'successful resistance' was being made against the demon drink, even in the slums. 'I attended a temperance meeting in Angel Meadow – the most profligate part of the town,' he noted, 'and was much pleased to hear the sensible and hearty declarations of the temperance disciples.'

In truth, the movement had only limited success in the Meadow, where it was said that anyone standing in one particular street could throw a stone into eight beer houses. The Reverend Mercer was still bemoaning the slum's 'besotted drinking' and 'gross intemperance' decades later.

Chapter 14

The Cotton Famine

Thomas Burke was unafraid of hard graft. He faced a daily battle to find labouring work to feed his wife Catherine, 33, and their five-year-old daughter, Alice. But one night, unemployed with a badly injured leg, 48-year-old Burke had no money left for the bed in a Charter Street lodging house that had become their refuge. As the door of the house clanged shut, he was left with no choice: he had to cross the Irk and throw his family on the mercy of the workhouse.

From Charter Street, the journey to the workhouse was less than half a mile, but it was one that struck fear into the hearts of slum dwellers in Angel Meadow. Conditions within its thick walls were deliberately harsh, the food was appalling and the shame alone of being unable to make a living was enough to scar a man's soul.

The workhouse had been built in 1792 just across the Irk from Angel Meadow. The house rules stated that paupers had to 'demean themselves orderly and peaceable' and be 'diligent in their work'. Once inside, they were only allowed out with a ticket of leave. Entering the workhouse was a last resort and some preferred to sleep in the slum's alleyways and yards or under the railway arches.

The workhouse was enlarged in 1843, with operations overseen by the Board of Guardians. Friedrich Engels, writing in 1845, described it as a 'citadel' that looked 'threateningly down from behind its high walls and parapets' on the slum below. The paupers' cemetery of Walker's Croft, which stood just beneath the workhouse walls, only added to the building's sinister aspect. Engels observed that most people would rather starve to death in their miserable homes than enter the 'hell' of the workhouse.

The authorities felt the slum's Irish inmates were often trying to trick them into getting help for free. One overseer, Mr Rose, claimed the Irish had a 'cringing' way of asking for relief and became violent when it was refused: 'They seem never to be satisfied – very few of them are thankful.' He claimed some would borrow children and fake illness to obtain aid: 'There is a great deal of pilfering and making smuggled whiskey, and living by sleight of hand, and begging among the Irish – all which things accustom them to deceit.'

By 1866, on the bitterly cold night when Thomas Burke crossed the Irk, the workhouse had more than 1,600 inmates. Burke sent his wife and daughter ahead, perhaps believing that they had a better chance of getting inside without him. Eventually, he dragged his lame leg across the old bridge and thumped on the huge wooden door of the workhouse's night asylum. The gatehouse keeper came to the hatch and asked Thomas what he wanted. "A night's shelter," he said.

The huge door creaked open and Thomas stepped inside. He was led down a flight of stone steps past a bench where three other men sat frozen, waiting to see the workhouse doctor. Francis Dalton, the tramp master, was waiting. He told Burke he had to work if he wanted to stay. "Grind some corn," Dalton ordered. "I can't," Burke said. "I have a bad leg." Burke asked to sit on the bench and await the doctor, but Dalton grabbed him by the scruff of the neck, tearing his coat. He dragged Burke up the steps, pulled open the door and threw him face down on the road. Then he slammed the door firmly shut behind him.

As Thomas Burke was thrown out in the cold, thousands of mills workers across Manchester were trying to get back on their feet after the worst famine in the city's history, which had been caused by a shortage of cotton. By the early 1860s, Lancashire's vast cotton industry employed 440,000 workers in 2,400 mills. The slave fields of the southern United States were the main source of Manchester's cotton. When the American Civil War began, Union ships blockaded Confederate ports and the cotton supply was cut off. Manchester's giant weaving machines fell silent and, by the winter of 1861, tens of thousands of mill workers were unable to feed their families. The Cotton Famine had begun.

The workers of Angel Meadow were hit hardest that winter. The factories surrounding the slum were their main source of income and whole families, including children, worked together in the same mills. Shopkeepers in the slum also began to suffer, as many of their customers relied on credit and even shoemakers were paid in instalments.

In January 1862, the Reverend Thomas Wolstencroft, the Rector of St Michael's Church, made an urgent plea for help in a letter to the *Manchester Courier*. He had only been in post since October and his ministry had begun with a lavish tea party attended by 500 people at the parish school in a large room adorned with flags, banners and garlands of evergreens for the occasion. Wolstencroft explained to readers of the *Courier*:

During the past week I have visited at least 200 families and I have not seen in any case an ounce of butcher's meat. In many houses there was not a morsel of food and frequently parents declared that they had not had anything to eat for 24 hours. In one house the mother was placing the kettle on the fire and I asked her what she was preparing for dinner. She replied that the boy had gone to get three pence on the saucepan and the father wept before me like a child and said they had sold and pawned everything that they could until they had nothing left.

Wolstencroft said many people had sold their bed sheets and in some cases were now lying sick on the floor of their homes.

In just one week, up to 250 parishioners called at the house Wolstencroft shared with his wife and daughter, 'earnestly craving' some help for their families. Wolstencroft was given permission by the city's main famine relief organisation, the District Provident Society, to send 120 families two miles across town to their depot, where they would receive parcels of food. He later discovered that starving workers from the Meadow were queuing in the rain outside the depot from 5am until noon, only to be told to return the next day for a few pieces of bread. Some of the workers were queuing for two or three days before they were able to get a foot in the door.

Wolstencroft launched his own appeal, the Angel Meadow Relief Fund, and began providing bread for 100 families he feared would otherwise starve to death. Donations began to arrive straight away. One gentleman braved a journey through Angel Meadow to leave £1 in an envelope at Wolstencroft's house and the wives of two working men posted some food stamps from Warwickshire. Others sent bundles of old clothes. A middle–class schoolgirl named Lizzie sent four shillings she had raised through selling her pet rabbits. Wolstencroft was able to distribute £20 worth of bread and oatmeal. However, his success only encouraged others to apply for relief and he was soon receiving hundreds of fresh applicants every day. One of his assistants had to sit from dawn until dusk taking down their names.

Local businessmen including Murray Gladstone, a cousin of future Prime Minister William Gladstone, joined the relief fund's management committee. Donors sent bed sheets and scraps of cloth to make into clothing. The editor of the *Manchester Courier* backed Wolstencroft's campaign as the Cotton Famine worsened. Out of more than 47,000 cotton workers in Manchester, over 12,500 were now working short time and 6,200 were unemployed, the newspaper revealed. Those on short hours were unable to claim poor relief because they still had jobs.

On 23 January, the Board of Guardians gathered in the workhouse's wood panelled boardroom. They were joined around the table by a group of business leaders and churchmen, including the Reverend Wolstencroft and a deputation from the District Provident Society. Wolstencroft stood up and presented the guardians with a list of 600 starving people. Murray Gladstone asked if the guardians could change their rules so that workers left starving by short hours could claim poor relief. He said many 'sober, industrious, but destitute workmen' who had been earning 15 shillings a week were now receiving just sixpence a week, which was insufficient to 'keep body and soul together'.

But Charles Rickards, a magistrate who was chairman of the board, said the guardians could only help the 'destitute' unemployed and not those going without food because their hours had been cut. The law could not be changed, he said, because it was based on 'well-established principles'. Rickards also claimed that widespread fraud and deception was practised by poor relief claimants. He reserved special criticism for the people of Angel Meadow. In one case, he said, a coffin was ordered for a family who claimed they were too poor to afford a proper funeral. Later he discovered the family had hired two mourning coaches and had gone to the expense of having the coffin 'nicely lined and trimmed'. The guardians' task, Rickards claimed, was to instil discipline. 'We are the best judges of what is necessary,' he said.

Wolstencroft was forced to step up his work following Rickards' refusal to help. The *Manchester Times* said he was 'indefatigable' in his support for the poor. The *Manchester Guardian* acknowledged there was a 'great amount of distress' in Angel Meadow, adding: 'We understand that in other parts of the city, there is also a large amount of privation and suffering, though not perhaps so intense, and certainly not so general, as in St Michael's district.'

More than 500 starving people gathered in the parish school on Miller Street. Wolstencroft gave them bread, butter and tea – and a talk on patience and temperance. As they headed back out into the cold night, he handed them another thick slice of bread. By February he had spent £140 on soup alone (around £6,500 today) and he had helped more than 10,000 people. Up to 200 at a time ate soup at the school, which served 70 gallons a day. By March, Wolstencroft was dealing with 980 cases a week and distributing groceries, clothing and coal. He was still appealing for donations.

Despite Wolstencroft's sterling work, the famine only grew worse. On 10 May, the *Courier* warned: 'We are requested by the committee of the St Michael's and the Angel Meadow Relief Fund to state that the distress in these districts is on the increase. The funds are exhausted and, but for the intervention of a few friends, the relief would have had to be discontinued on this day.' In response, Wolstencroft and his parishioners held an urgent meeting with members of the Rochdale Road Baptist Chapel on 7 August. As a result, they formed a joint committee and pledged to 'use every effort' to raise funds and distribute relief. The new committee was so well organised that 3,138 people were receiving aid by November.

That Christmas, another group of businessmen stepped into the fray. Joseph Morgan from the Ducie Works, a warehouse and workshop beside the Irk, formed another relief organisation: the Ducie Relief Committee. Its members opened a dining room in Nelson Street for distressed cotton workers. The room had a lofty ceiling and a section of it was partitioned off to create a separate area for women. The kitchen contained two huge boilers, each capable of holding 100 gallons, for making soup and potato hash, and a potato steamer. The dining room opened daily from 8am to 6pm and the food was half the price of soup kitchens in other parts of town.

A journalist who visited the dining room described what was on offer to the unemployed cotton mill worker:

> He can procure a cup of good coffee or a cup of tea, or a plate of bread and butter, while for three-halfpence he may have a bowl of broth or soup, a plate of potato hash, and a plate of potatoes. One penny will cover the cost of bread and cheese, while for two-pence the poor fellow may enjoy the unwonted luxury of a plate of beef or bacon. By such means as these, the self-respect of the poor cotton spinner may be preserved unimpaired.

It was important to them, he explained, that they 'paid a trifle' instead of receiving charity, as they would rather suffer in silence than 'degrade' themselves by falling on the workhouse.

That winter a travelling minister, the Reverend Arthur Mursell, gave a series of lectures at Manchester's Free Trade Hall. In one talk entitled 'the Wolf at the Door', he described how snow stood 6in deep at cottage doors in Angel Meadow: 'Talk about empty cupboards, cold hearthstones, thin wives, hungry husbands, and crying children. I feel they are to be sadly abundant for some months to come, unless our cut-throat cousins across the water come to their right senses a little faster.'

Manchester's cotton workers could have been forgiven for calling for an end to the Union's blockade and siding with the slave-owning South. But on New Year's Eve, 1862, thousands of them left their soup kitchens and packed into the Free Trade Hall, built on the site of the Peterloo Massacre. They gathered to show their support for the Union, whose ships were causing them to starve – a selfless act, putting the freedom of slaves over their own hunger. They passed a motion urging Abraham Lincoln to continue the war and abolish slavery and affirmed their support for the blockade. One worker, Thomas Evans, drew cheers when he said the workers of Manchester 'shook hands with the North' and the philosopher John Stuart Mill sent a letter praising the workers' 'moral greatness'.

The American Civil War drew parallels with the workers' own fight for electoral reform, which had led to the Peterloo Massacre. Lincoln sent a letter to Manchester's cotton workers in January, 1863, in which he expressed his gratitude for their support: 'I know and deeply deplore the sufferings which the working men of Manchester, and in all Europe, are called to endure in this crisis… Under the circumstances, I cannot but regard your decisive utterances upon the question as an instance of sublime Christian heroism which has not been surpassed in any age or in any country.'

Wolstencroft's time in Angel Meadow was coming to an end. Two months later, his ministry finished as it had begun – with a tea party. A large crowd gathered at the parish school in Miller Street in March and presented him with a copy of a Bible and a silver inkstand. They cheered as Murray Gladstone made the presentation. So many people signed his written address that the paper stretched several yards in length. The Cotton Famine rolled on for two more years until the American Civil War ended in 1865.

The following year, a major investigation was launched into the conditions in Manchester Workhouse that had so terrified starving cotton workers and men like Thomas Burke. Inmates claimed the food was inedible and that they were being subjected to appalling abuse. One woman said she had been left vomiting for two days and received no help. Another inmate, Sarah Corfield, complained that the potatoes contained black lumps and were unfit for pigs, and the bread was soft, clammy and dark. Of the pea soup, she said: "They called it pea soup, but I did not. I never saw a pea in it." She added:

On Wednesday, the dinner was what they called suet pudding. I tasted it, but could not dine upon it. It was heavy, like lead. On Saturday we had what they called potato hash, but I did not call it potato hash. When I make such, I peel the potatoes, and cut them and the meat into small pieces and then, with pepper and salt, it is very good. The workhouse hash was potatoes boiled in their skins and cold soup, warmed and mixed with water, poured over them.

One night seven women queued for a bath. The first had consumption, the next four had bad legs, one had a broken arm and the seventh a cut head. They were given 15 minutes each in the same dirty water, which had scum floating on its surface. Ann Lyons, who lived in Charter Street and was heavily pregnant, was told to follow them into the greasy and dirty bath. She said:

I went to the bathroom soon after I got in, with the night nurse. I put my hand into the water, which was dirty and cold. I told her I would not go in a cold, dirty bath like that, and that it was not fit for a woman in my condition. She said I should have to go in and brought the day and night officers. They both said if I did not go in I should not go to bed. As I had my clothes off, I went into the bath, the water of which was unchanged.

The workhouse also contained a fever hospital, venereal wards, foul wards, and paralysis wards. The inmates slept on straw mattresses and the bedding went unwashed for weeks. Patients on the hospital wing reported that the matron walked through the rooms jangling her keys at night and gave inmates medicine from an egg cup, while the night nurse fell asleep in a chair. Another nurse failed to get a doctor for a dying woman and then took four pence from her belongings after she had died to cover the cost of her food.

An inspector noted in his report: 'The rice is distasteful to many, while the pea soup disagrees with some of the aged poor. The old women especially complain that their tea is not good and that it is too weak.' He found the ventilation 'especially defective' in the workhouse's Magdalen wards. But Christopher Severs, the master of the workhouse, blamed the poor for the workhouse's bad conditions. He claimed the bread was never more than three days out of date and the paupers in the kitchen failed to pick out the bad potatoes.

Chapter 15

Cross Cribs

When John 'Patsey' Reardon and his wife Emma took over the Dog and Duck in Charter Street in 1866, the pub was already known as greatest thieving den in Manchester. It cast a shadow over the entire city – and across the north of England. Dublin-born Reardon should have been intimidated when he passed beneath the green lantern fixed above the entrance and stepped into the vault, but he was the perfect man for the job – and he knew it.

Although Reardon's skills behind the bar were no better than those of any other publican in the city, he had another secret talent. Reardon, 33, was an expert 'fence' – a criminal who would receive stolen goods and sell them on the black market. He and many others in Angel Meadow, including Joe Hyde, Bob Butterworth, Bob MacFarlane and the fantastically nicknamed Cabbage Ann and One-Armed Kitty, were keepers of snide liquor vaults and lodging houses known throughout the land by travelling thieves as 'safe harbours'.

The thieves who visited Reardon at the Dog travelled many miles in pursuit of victims. The pub's close proximity to Victoria Station meant they could head to distant towns for a day's thieving and return to the pub in time for last orders. They carried out raids in Halifax, Leeds, Lancaster, Kendal and even Glasgow. When a woman named Lucy Wilson was robbed of her watch at Rochdale train station in 1857, news quickly filtered back to Manchester's detectives and they knew where to look.

A detective named Henry Bateman headed straight to the Dog in search of the culprits. The landlady at the time, Elizabeth Pearson, was keeping watch at the door and she ran inside when she spotted Bateman. He burst through the front door and saw the landlord, William Pearson, in the vault examining a fine gold watch in the glare of the gaslight. Bateman tried to snatch it, but Pearson tossed it to a barmaid, who ran into the kitchen and escaped out of a door. Pearson also fled and went on the run, but was later caught. He told Bateman the barmaid was blameless: "Well Henry. It's a bad job, but she's innocent and I'm guilty." At his trial, the jury heard that the Dog was Manchester's most notorious 'resort for travelling thieves'.

John Reardon's appointment as gatekeeper to Manchester's criminal underworld was short-lived. In 1866, he was jailed for seven years along with John Williams, the landlord of another notorious Charter Street pub, the Grapes, after a cotton broker was robbed of £170 on a train at Victoria Station. Reardon and Williams took no part in the robbery, but they were caught trying to launder a £100 note taken from the victim. Prison warders described Reardon as a 'reputed thief'. He was 5ft 4in, with brown hair and sallow skin. A scar on his nose and a large boil on the back of his neck completed the picture.

By 1868, Bob MacFarlane was running the still notorious Dog and Duck. Detectives searched the pub one day while looking for James Gibb, a dangerous and expert thief nicknamed 'Flying Gibb'. His career began with the theft of a rabbit, but he was soon behind a series of high-profile burglaries and he was now wanted for stealing 12 gold watches from a jeweller's shop.

Detectives found Gibb and his partner, Mary Ann Parr, hiding in the Dog. As Mary Ann tried to hide two of the watches in a towel, Gibb ran upstairs and leaped from a window. Detective Jerome Caminada later arrested him after a 'very tough struggle' in torrential rain. Caminada was hit by several blows and was almost thrown down a cellar, but he eventually managed to drag Gibb to the police station, where Gibb collapsed and pretended to be dead. He was jailed for three months.

Another notorious pub, the Highland Laddie in Charter Street, was the headquarters of an infamous gang of 'reputed and clever swindlers', who lay in wait for passengers at Victoria Station as they stepped off the trains. These swindlers or 'megs men' dressed in fine clothes. One pretended he knew his victim and another posed as an 'unemployed gentleman', who would graciously offer to show the new arrival around town. A third acted the part of a 'straightforward John Bull', who pretended to take pity on a victim because he 'liked his face'. Once hooked, the unsuspecting soul was whisked off to the Laddie with the promise of a pint of ale and a plate of bread and cheese, where other members of the gang were waiting to empty his pockets. They were more sophisticated than thieves such as Thomas Williams and John Stafford, who bit the hand of a man named Thomas Moorhouse while trying to steal his watch on one of the station platforms.

It was said that the Laddie's crooks were 'deeply steeped in vice' and selected victims who were carrying their life-savings in carpet bags. Benjamin Redfern drew a sketch of three of the gang members who often stood in a knot outside the beer house. In the sketch, which still survives, one of the thieves has sideburns and whiskers. He is depicted smoking a large pipe and wearing a top hat and chequered waistcoat. Another carries an umbrella and wears a smart jacket with a pocket watch. The third sports a cravat and spats, has a handkerchief in his pocket and carries a cane. A large but docile-looking dog stands at his side.

Matthew Falkner, 21, an 'innocent-looking rustic' from Lincolnshire, had just arrived in Manchester when he was befriended by John Williams and invited to the Laddie for a friendly glass of ale. A welcoming party of swindlers named Thomas Jackson, Charles Booth and Margaret Brown were waiting. They bought Falkner beer and cheese before tricking him into handing over £25 – a small fortune. The gang then slipped out of the pub, but Falkner later recognised them in the street and they were caught by the police.

A journalist from the *Manchester Evening News* disguised himself as a rogue and entered the beer houses in Charter Street with a burglar acting as his guide. He was able to get within earshot of a group of thieves inside a pub where the well-lit bar was long enough to seat 50 people. His guide led him down a passage into the smoke-room, where four thieves were dividing some money on the table. They stopped talking and stared in silence when the pair stepped into the room, but then carried on counting. The journalist wrote:

> Each man eventually got a couple of sovereigns and some loose silver that was spent in glasses of whisky. All of them had been convicted of felony and one, a little stumpy man with a face bespeaking low cunning, was just out 'on ticket'. With a convict's carelessness, he was again associating with his old companions in spite of the risk of being sent back to finish his time.

Two of the men were back in Manchester after recently being released from a penal colony in Australia. They had only been in town a few days and were staying to the north of Angel Meadow. They steered clear of the lodging houses of Charter Street, however, where they would be recognised by the police.

Pub landlords were often in league with their criminal customers. Samuel Lowe, who kept the Victory, was arrested for handling some stolen textile prints, which were found in his scullery. Five women wearing lilac dresses fashioned from the same printed material were also arrested.

The most famously corrupt landlord was Walter Griffiths Lloyd, who ran the Church Inn. He was charged with possessing identity certificates belonging to army reservists. Detective Jerome Caminada raided the pub and clambered over the bar just in time to see Lloyd fleeing into the cellar carrying a black bag. Caminada managed to evade the huge dog that Lloyd kept behind the bar and followed him up through a trap door. He finally caught him in Miller Street, where he also found the bag hidden behind some barrels. It contained more than 240 papers belonging to old soldiers. Lloyd had made hundreds of pounds by lending money to reservists and keeping their papers as insurance. They fell into his debt and spent what remained of their cash in his pub.

Landlords would allow almost anything on their premises, but they would not stand being cheated by customers. Richard Singleton was caught trying to buy ale at the Victory with two forged sixpences. He fled when his trick was discovered, but was roused from a drunken slumber by the police the next morning and sent to prison. It was a common ruse. Two women and two men were also spotted trying to spend some forged sixpences on rum and cheese in four different pubs during a high-risk pub crawl. Each time they were rumbled, they downed the rum and ran off. Landlords also had to keep an eye on their fixtures and fittings as thieves were liable to steal anything not nailed down. Thomas Flavell stole the weather glass from the Gas Tavern and was caught trying to sell it in a nearby street.

Thieves also used lodging houses in Angel Meadow as dens where they met to hatch plans and stash stolen goods. A *Manchester Evening News* journalist went into one of these 'cross cribs' in the early hours and found a dozen men and women smoking cheap tobacco with a relish that was 'absolutely startling'. They sucked at their stumpy pipes with such determination that a cloud of dense smoke 'curled lovingly round their necks'. The journalist struck up conversation with one woman, Irish Kate, who had 'the dirtiest pipe, the rankest weed, and the most garrulous tongue'.

He wrote: 'She was a withered, dried-up specimen of the hoisting sisterhood, with a little puckered up face, expressionless in repose and yet mobile when the eyes peered out sharply at a strange question. Sucking the stem of her pipe with great gusto, she told me how cleverly she had been pinched for lifting cheese.' Irish Kate described how a clever policeman had matched the buttons on her dress with the holes they had imprinted in the cheese. "I got off wid two months," she chuckled.

Thieves who specialised in training young pickpockets used these lodging houses as their recruiting grounds and training schools. Benjamin Redfern said one thief trainer was a 'military-looking man' who was lame in one leg. A journalist acquainted with the man described him as prematurely old with a 'grizzled, military moustache'. He found him sitting in a private room in a lodging house in front of a roaring fire, which threw 'strange shadows' over his 'villainous face'.

Another thieves' den had a notice in the window proclaiming it to be a 'home from home', but the kitchen was crowded with men and women – each distinguished by the same 'criminal features'. The owner was a stout old lady who presided over affairs from a bed in the window. Hushed whispers greeted any police officers who entered, but the woman was a cute diplomat who wished them: "Good morning, gentlemen." One police officer said: "The old woman always lets on to be ill, but the chief use of the bed is to hide swag. It's not long since we took a fellow and a side of bacon from under it."

Other dens appeared more respectable and these often contained the 'fly' men – clever thieves who were hardly ever caught. Joe Hyde ran an establishment frequented by the most intelligent criminals, who were well dressed and always had money to spend. One man said: "I've seen a dozen of them playing cards all night, and the table covered with sovereigns – £5 a corner – and all paid up at the finish."

A journalist, who went inside one of these dens with a slum guide named Mack, wrote:

> One of the front doors stood wide open and at the end of the low narrow passage leading to the back kitchen a brilliant light was shining. We walked in and there, comfortably enjoying their midnight drink and smoke, were two respectably-dressed men who might have passed for clerks or warehousemen. There was nothing in their appearance to create suspicion and after resting for a few minutes and joining them in a pipe, I left with the impression that they must have retired long ago from public life.

Mack laughed sarcastically and told him they were in fact the craftiest 'hooks' or pickpockets in the city and were rarely jailed.

Men could steal because they had places to sell their goods. These marine stores or 'putty shops' were run by men who did not have the standing of pawnbrokers and were often unscrupulous. Stolen goods could be deposited there until it was safe to retrieve them. It was a lucrative business. One Angel Street marine store dealer, Frederick Wilde, left £4,000 in his will when he died in 1878.

John Williams, who ran the Grapes in Charter Street, turned the pub into a lodging house after losing his licence to serve alcohol, following his conviction for money laundering with his partner in crime John 'Patsey' Reardon. The house was a nest of thieves. Williams, 55, who had a scar on his forehead, turned a blind eye to his customers' comings and goings.

In 1871, a census taker was left so frustrated by Williams' failure to hand over his customers' names that he vented his fury in a remarkable note on the census page. 'Gross carelessness on the part of the lodging house keeper,' he wrote. 'When I informed him to read the schedule and told him the penalty, it was all to no purpose. He said he asked them their names and they would not tell him.' The census taker then listed the names of a dozen lodgers as 'not known'. The anonymous lodgers soon had a chance to return the favour, as two police officers were attacked when they entered the house to arrest Williams for drunkenness. The lodgers pelted them with mud and tin cans and attacked them with brooms.

Cabbage Ann was another character who ran one of the Charter Street cross cribs. It was said she was known to thieves across England. Her real name was Ann Powell. A widow by 42, she ran a grocery shop and lodging house next door to the Grapes, perhaps taking her nickname from the cabbages she sold. She was a notorious thief trainer too, but appears to have escaped justice despite having a few brushes with the law.

In February 1867, Ann was hauled before a judge charged with receiving stolen goods. A constable named James Plumb had raided Ann's house one Friday night. The cellar beneath the kitchen had been condemned as unfit for habitation, but Plumb clambered down the stairs on a hunch and found an overcoat hidden in a sack. It had been stolen the previous evening from a milkman doing his rounds in Charter Street.

Cabbage Ann claimed two boys had brought the coat into the house. She pointed out one of them, Michael Crane, aged 13, in the courtroom, where he was facing a separate charge of stealing some eggs. The judge asked Crane what he knew about the coat and he claimed two other boys had hidden it in Cabbage Ann's cellar without her knowledge. He was jailed for a month and sent to a reformatory for five years.

Constable Plumb informed the court: "This woman keeps a lodging house where half a dozen young thieves constantly live. Indeed, it is a regular place for harbouring thieves." Mr Fowler, the judge, told Cabbage Ann: "You are a regular trainer of young thieves – one of the worst women in Manchester – and I will take care to help the police in every possible way to get you transported as soon as possible." Cabbage Ann shouted from the dock: "I want justice." Mr Fowler said: "You will get justice, but we will go out of our way to give it to you, and I promise to say a word or two to the recorder when you come here again." But Cabbage Ann walked free after being discharged due to the lack of evidence.

A journalist keen to get a glimpse of Cabbage Ann slipped into her kitchen with his criminal guide. There were a number of men and women in the room, but Cabbage Ann was nowhere to be seen. He described the scene:

> From the upper regions came noises which showed that something unusual was taking place, and great was our surprise when, in answer to a question as to what was up there, one of the women jerked out, "A dead man, if ye want to know." Such, indeed, was the case, for a member of the

fraternity, eminent as a pickpocket – he might indeed have been called a great 'gun' – had died a day or two before, and the wake was now being held with all due honours.

The journalist was warned by Mack not to go upstairs, as Cabbage Ann was aloft superintending the wake. The woman who had shouted at the journalist puffed savagely at her pipe and eyed him suspiciously through the rank tobacco smoke. 'The place looked squalid and miserable,' he wrote, 'and the people in it were of poor, miserable appearance as if they found it hard to live at all. The walls were bare and dirty, and the furniture of the rudest and scantiest kind – a rough wooden form doing duty for half a dozen chairs.'

He added: 'It did not seem as if much money would be forthcoming in such a barn of a place, and as the youths were mere "snow-droppers" or "linen-lifters" from clothes lines and hedges, it was not to be expected that they could play the part of generous donors.' Mack told him the 'crooked community' had paid for the lavish wake after a collection was made at local pubs, raising three or four pounds. It was left to the parish to organise the funeral though, and the corpse was buried at the expense of the city's ratepayers. Those at the wake supped five times the undertaker's fee.

One of Cabbage Ann's lodgers was a hardened 22-year-old thief named 'Leeds Jemmy'. He used a number of aliases but his real name was David Gamble and he claimed at various times that he was born not in Leeds but in Manchester, Salford and Ireland. Jemmy had six previous convictions and on one occasion had been jailed for stealing 20 cigars. He was 5ft 4in and highly conspicuous: his throat was badly pockmarked by smallpox, his hands were covered with warts and a large boil stood out on his back. He refused to give his address to prison warders and claimed he had no friends.

Jemmy's accomplice was John Currie, nicknamed the Badger, possibly because his neck was bloated and badly scarred by scrofula, an infection of the lymph nodes caused by tuberculosis. But, it may also have been because his favoured method of breaking into houses was by climbing down coal grids to get into the cellars.

Leeds Jemmy threatened to hunt down Jerome Caminada after the detective saw him jailed for eight months for burglary. One Sunday morning, Jemmy was at Cabbage Ann's when he spotted Caminada strolling confidently down Charter Street. He flew out of the house and punched the detective on the side of the head. A large crowd gathered as they fought in the street.

Another well-known Angel Meadow character named One Armed Kitty lived nearby. Her son, Joseph, rushed out behind Jemmy and threw a bottle at Caminada's face. Caminada ducked, but the bottle struck the helmet of a policeman running to his aid. He fell down bleeding – his helmet badge driven into his head by the blow. Caminada chased Jemmy, who darted up an alley and barricaded himself into a yard. The crowd blocked Caminada's escape and he had to fight his way out as blows rained down on him from all sides. He finally rescued the constable and took him to a druggist's shop as One Armed Kitty's son escaped through the back streets. Leeds Jemmy and the Badger were both later jailed following another burglary and transported to Millbank Prison in London.

The warren of alleyways behind the slum's pubs and lodging houses provided perfect escape routes for those on the run from the police. During a chase, thieves would run straight through a house and out the back door and then vanish into the labyrinth. One journalist who went into an alley behind a lodging house noted: 'Here was another warren of dilapidated property, more complicated than any we had yet seen.' A man running through the yard could flee in nearly a dozen directions. A police officer told the journalist: "If it comes to a chase, and a man gets in here, it's almost impossible to take him." Another officer added, as he took a journalist into a narrow courtyard with half a dozen doorways and small passages running in all directions: "These are the runs in which old hands slip us – a rare place for hide and seek. They dodge through these places like rabbits in warrens."

Another journalist found out the truth of this for himself when he went on the run with Mack, the criminal guide, in the back alleys of Angel Meadow and found himself in a 'lost city of the dead'. He was following two men out of a beer house, when two detectives approached. Mack dragged him into a narrow alleyway to escape:

> With a sense of utter helplessness I stumbled along as best I could, the ground being rough and uneven, and not a ray of light visible to show whither I was going. I nearly came to grief several times in treacherous puddles that had collected in stray holes, and it was only by touching either wall with my outstretched hands that I could progress at all.

They suddenly entered an enclosed court so dark that the journalist could see no way out. "We mustn't be seen," said Mack, tapping quietly at a door that suddenly appeared in the darkness. A dog inside began barking and rushed from behind the door with such ferocity that the journalist feared it would smash right through and maul them. When the occupants began stirring, he beat a rapid retreat as Mack shouted: "Follow me, sharp!" The journalist wrote:

We were again off in the darkness through such a devious maze of courts and passages that I wondered what particular part of the city we should arrive at. We got out safely, albeit I was bruised and dirty, from falling against such trifling obstacles as the corners of walls and a few broken-down steps, and to my surprise we were in Charter Street.

Back at the Dog and Duck, the Manchester-born wife of landlord John Reardon was caught by the police handling some stolen watches. Emma Reardon, 26, was 5ft 6in with mousey hair, a light complexion and grey eyes. She had a mole on each cheek, her ears were pierced and she had lost several teeth. Mrs Reardon was caught fencing stolen goods after police raided the home of a silver dealer named Joseph Bloor in February 1866, following a series of burglaries. They discovered 140 watches and a stash of cutlery hidden beneath a trap door in the floor. Bloor claimed he had bought the watches from Emma Reardon for £18 (worth around £1,400 today).

Police raided the Dog and found she had exactly £18 in her pocket. In a bid to prove their case, the constables pushed Bloor into Reardon's cell at the police station and sparked an argument. Reardon told the police: "It's all spite because I wouldn't do business for him. When I took the Dog and Duck, he came and said he would advance me money to buy stolen property and, because I wouldn't do it, he has put this job on me."

Bloor, 45, was jailed for seven years. Reardon, who had no previous convictions, was jailed for five years. A newspaper report described the moment she was sent down: 'The prisoner seemed weak and ill, and was very much distressed.'

Chapter 16

The Martyrs

John Francis Nugent awoke with a shudder and lay staring wide-eyed into the blackness of his room in Buckley Street in the Irish enclave of New Town. He was fully dressed and sweating, and his waking mind was a sea of confusion. Autumn darkness pressed heavily against the window, but when the gasworks clock struck 3am, its familiarity was comforting and he began to drift back to sleep. It was only then that he heard it – a soft rumbling like distant thunder getting closer and closer. Adrenaline surged through his veins. They were coming.

Nine police officers were marching quick-time towards Nugent's rented house. The noise he could hear was the scraping of their boots on the cobbles just a few streets away. It was 5 October 1867 and Nugent was a wanted man. The constables were the vanguard of the largest manhunt in Manchester's history. Irish Republicans, or Fenians as they were known, had shot and killed a police officer named Sergeant Charles Brett a few days earlier, as they freed two comrades from a prison van during a riot in Hyde Road on the other side of Manchester. Hundreds of police officers were now carrying out lightning raids in Irish areas, including New Town and Angel Meadow, which were said to be 'infected with the Fenian taint'.

Police believed Nugent, 22, from Drogheda in County Lough, was one of the rioters. At 6ft 2in with a hollow scar in the centre of his forehead, he was a distinctive man. Nugent had a fresh complexion, brown hair and grey eyes. He was a joiner with a powerful physique – so strong that police superintendent John Gee was now bringing a whole squad of officers to arrest him.

But Nugent had no intention of being caught. As the officers turned into Buckley Street, he jumped out of bed and ran into the back yard, picking up a wood saw before he disappeared into the foul-smelling outhouse. Seconds later, the officers smashed through the front door. Gee burst into the lower room as his officers stormed upstairs. They arrested two Irish brothers, James and John Sherry, who shared the house with Nugent and were also wanted. Their main suspect, however, seemed to have disappeared.

Gee believed that Nugent and the Sherry brothers were members of the Irish Republican Brotherhood, a group of Fenians formed in Dublin in 1858 with the objective of freeing Ireland from British rule. The brotherhood's leader in 1867 was Thomas Kelly, the goatee-wearing son of a Galway farmer, who had been shot through the jaw while serving as a colonel in the US Army during the American Civil War. Kelly had joined the Brotherhood in New York and then travelled to Ireland where he attempted to launch an insurrection. After this failed he made plans to take the Irish rebellion to the British mainland, hoping to win support from Irish immigrants in Manchester and other cities. Fenian circles in Manchester and Liverpool planned an attack on Chester Castle, but the plot was foiled by informants.

On St Patrick's Day that year, rumours spread through Manchester that Fenians were planning to attack the city. Gangs of men were seen gathering on street corners in Angel Meadow. The threat came to nothing and by 11pm, telegrams were dispatched from the town hall to police stations saying: 'All Quiet. No disturbance.' The *Manchester Courier* reported: 'Two or three scattered rascals of banditti-like appearance were lurking in sundry holes and corners, but it is very evident that the Fenian sentiment is at a discount in this commercial and eminently sensible city.'

When Kelly travelled to Manchester in September with Timothy Deasey, another Fenian who had served in the Civil War, spies alerted the police. On 11 September, a constable spotted Kelly and Deasey outside a house owned by a Dublin-born clothes dealer named Henry Wilson near Smithfield Market. The constable watched from the shadows as Deasey tapped twice at Wilson's window and Kelly went to the corner of the market and stood listening to the night. Kelly then turned and entered the house, returning to the door several times. The constable was joined in the shadows by a sergeant and, when Kelly and Deasey finally emerged, the officers jumped out of hiding. Deasey drew a revolver, which was wrestled from his grasp.

The officers took the men to a police station, where another revolver was found in Kelly's pocket. Deasey, who had an American accent, claimed he was a travelling hatter. Kelly claimed he was an unemployed American bookbinder and that they were visiting Wilson because his child was sick.

The Fenians quickly began plotting to rescue Kelly and Deasey. Their chance came on 19 September, when Kelly and Deasey were being escorted from court to Belle Vue Prison, which stood on Hyde Road in the south-east of the city. Fenians attacked their prison van as it travelled under a railway bridge and shot Sergeant Brett, an 'old and dependable' officer. Newspapers described the attack as the 'most daring and unprecedented outrage' ever committed in the city.

Ellen Cooper, a factory girl with a pock-marked face who lived on Red Bank, a slum district across the Irk from Angel Meadow, was among the prisoners in the van. She was being jailed for robbery with nine convictions already to her name. Cooper later said in court: "I heard several pistol shots and many stones struck the van. There was one shot fired through the ventilator beneath the driver's seat and went past my bonnet. Two shots were fired through the door. After that a pistol was fired through the ventilator and Brett turned his face to the door and fell."

Cooper claimed an Irishman named William O'Mara Allen pointed a pistol at her head and threatened to blow out her brains unless she passed Brett's keys through the trap door. When the doors were finally wrenched open, she fled. Another prisoner, Emma Halliday, an 18-year-old thief, said that Brett had looked out and shouted: "I will stick to my post till the last." He fell in a stooping position with his head against the door.

A police officer claimed a second man, William Gould, fired a revolver at one of the van's horses, while a third, Michael Larkin, fired at the driver on top of the van. Other witnesses said they saw Allen smashing open the roof with an adze – a carpenter's tool with an axe and a hammer head – while Larkin banged on the door with a stone.

An omnibus driver claimed to have spotted John Francis Nugent among the crowd and a local tobacconist claimed Nugent was throwing stones to keep the crowd away. A police officer named John Thompson also said Nugent tried to smash open the van with a large stone. It was alleged that the fugitives then split up: Larkin made off with Deasey, Gould and Allen with Kelly.

Prison guards raced to the scene and chased the attackers up the railway embankment and across the tracks. Prison warder Mark Baxter chased Gould and Allen. He said Allen threatened to 'scatter his brains' with his revolver and pulled the trigger twice, but it failed to fire. Another prison officer, Joseph Howard, arrested Allen after a struggle and seized the gun, which still had a bullet in the chamber. Baxter picked up a brick and struck Gould, knocking him down. A railway worker grabbed Larkin.

Sergeant Brett died at the infirmary. A bullet had passed through his head. Police launched a huge manhunt for Kelly, Deasey and their rescuers. One newspaper declared: 'Many houses in the city have been searched, and though these proceedings have not yet led to the capture of the two principal persons who are wanted, they have revealed the existence of more Fenians in the district than was ever before suspected.' Police began raiding homes in Angel Meadow and New Town, arresting more than 40 suspects. Almost all of them were poorly educated, out of work and from the 'lowest class of Irish'.

John Francis Nugent was still in the outhouse when the officers crept into the yard. They knew there was only one place he could be hiding and ordered him to surrender. Nugent kept them at bay for 15 minutes, swinging the large saw each time they tried to open the door. Newspapers reported later how he fought with 'great determination', cutting an officer's hand.

A constable named Goode finally dragged Nugent to the police station, where officers produced an artist's impression which they claimed matched Nugent's face. A letter found in Nugent's pocket from a fellow Fenian congratulated him on 'many heroic escapes' from the police. The following day, Nugent was picked out at an identity parade by five witnesses who claimed he was the 'most conspicuous' rioter, clad in a dark shooting coat and a cap with a large peak.

John Brannon, a widowed clothes dealer with four children who lived in Cable Street just outside Angel Meadow, was among those arrested following the rescue. Four witnesses put him at the scene. One claimed he was armed with a pistol and had commanded onlookers to stay away, while another said he threw a big stone at the prison van. Brannon, 40, was originally from Roscommon. At 5ft 8in with sallow skin and black hair, he was dishevelled, with two missing front teeth and a pockmarked face marked by his fondness for drink.

Thousands of people gathered at the police station where the prisoners were being held – some standing on rooftops to get a better view. Soldiers stood guard in front of the cells and others armed with bayonets formed an outer perimeter. A stream of witnesses trooped past the accused men. According to one newspaper reporter at the scene: 'Many of the prisoners are hangdog looking fellows and it required a good deal of resolution to pass down an alley with 25 such men on one side and only about a yard of retreating room on the other. On several occasions, witnesses hesitated and had to be urged forward by the police.'

One prisoner, James Woods, stood on the cold floor of the corridor in bare feet. Police found his boots were daubed with clay, as if he had been running cross-country, and took them as evidence. When it was time for the prisoners to go to court, soldiers with bayonets followed their van. The crowd outside hooted as they passed.

The alleged ringleader, William O'Mara Allen, was born in Tipperary. He was just 19, 5ft 9in with pale skin, his face marked by several cuts. He was dressed in shabby black trousers, a dirty light coat, a waistcoat, and a brown hat. Like Nugent, he worked as a joiner and lived near him in Suddell Street, across Rochdale Road from Angel Meadow. He had travelled to Manchester in search of work in 1864 and it was said he had secured the affections of a young woman from a respectable family. Newspapers claimed he was 'one of the most active agents' of Fenianism.

Michael Larkin, 32, was a tailor from King's County. He was married and had four children. He was 5ft 5in, with a large scar under his jaw. William

Gould, 30, was well-educated and had trained as a clerk, but was out of work. He was 5ft 8in and strongly built, with a fresh complexion. An Irish American, Gould was from New York.

A reporter from the *Free Lance* wrote during the trial that Allen looked calm and dogged, and nothing could be read in the 'pale, round, unbearded face of the murderer or desperado'. Gould had the 'flabby face of a drunkard' and a black eye, and in court he spent time passing folded notes to his legal adviser. Larkin was 'a little man, with a thin, sharp face and sunken eyes'. He had 'longish hair combed straight' and his beard was 'growing on his chin in Yankee fashion'. His neighbours claimed he had as much to do with the Fenians as the Bishop of Manchester.

Allen, Larkin and Gould were found guilty of murdering Brett. The *Manchester Guardian* claimed there appeared 'no doubt whatever' that Allen was guilty. The judge placed a black cap on his head and sentenced them to death. Allen claimed he was a victim of mistaken identity. Gould denied the murder but told the court his real name was Captain Michael O'Brien, formerly of the US Army and that he had been in the same regiment as Colonel Thomas Kelly. Before he was taken down, he read out a long speech on the wrongs committed by the British in Ireland.

Four other prisoners were sentenced to hang alongside them. Thomas Maguire was pardoned after it emerged that he was a Royal Marine on home leave. He had an anchor tattooed on his right arm. Edward O'Meagher Condon, a 27-year-old Irish American and captain in the US Army, also known as Edward Shore, had his death sentence commuted to life. Two others, William Pherson Thompson, 28, and Patrick Melody, 24, also had their sentences commuted. Thompson died later in prison, but Melody travelled to New York and tried to kill himself in Madison Square. He was later pardoned.

Witnesses from Angel Meadow saved John Brannon from the gallows. Elizabeth Healy, a seamstress who lived off Rochdale Road, said she was with him on the afternoon of the attack. She first saw him on Angel Street when she went to buy some cream and later saw him drinking at the George Inn on Rochdale Road at 4pm. They had shared a glass of porter until just after 5pm, the hour during which the attack took place. She denied that they were lovers.

A tailor named Patrick McTighe said he saw Brannon at 1.30pm and they went for a drink at Charles Crompton's beer house in Simpson Street, Angel Meadow. He said they played cards for nearly an hour and went to Smithfield Market, where they stayed for half an hour before later heading to the George Inn. William Brickall, a barman at the George Inn, confirmed that Brannon had been with McTighe and Healy between 4.15pm and 4.30pm.

Several of Brannon's neighbours also came forward to testify to his good character. Mary Bird, 18, from Style Street, said she had lived in the neighbourhood all her life and had known Brannon for as long as she could remember. She said he was a 'respectable, decent man'. John Francis Doyle, who worked in a clothes shop near the market, told the courtroom: "He's a working man, occasionally fond of a drop of drink, as I am myself." Despite his alibi, Brannon was jailed for five years – two of them with hard labour.

A scaffold was erected on the east wall of New Bailey Prison on the banks of the Irwell so that Allen, Larkin and O'Brien could be hanged on 23 November. The top section of the prison wall was pulled down to make room for the platform. Black drapes were hung so that only the men's heads would be seen when they fell through the platform.

More than 800 police officers and 2,000 special constables with white badges on their sleeves stood guard outside the prison, along with 500 soldiers, including 100 kilted men from the 72nd Highlanders. Some kept watch from the railway viaduct overlooking the prison and trains were banned from stopping. Other police officers guarded gas stations and public buildings, while Manchester's fire brigade stayed on duty. Warehouses were guarded by men with revolvers. That night a letter was sent to the bearded hangman, William Calcraft. It said: 'If you hang any of the gentlemen condemned to death at the New Bailey Prison, it will be worse for you. You will not survive afterwards.'

Spectators began arriving the day before to get the best positions. By 3am more than 2,000 people were already in their places – pitmen, mill hands and factory girls. One journalist wrote of the crowd: 'The keen pallid faces and ragged clothing of some exhibited deep traces of hard working or hard drinking. There were sharp, precocious lads of the criminal class, whose language and behaviour showed an acquaintance with some of the sternest realities of early life and there were girls and women whose habits form the darkest chapters of our social history.'

Angel Meadow folk loved a hanging. When James Burrows, 18, was hanged the previous year for beating to death a labourer who had refused to lend him a few shillings, it seemed as though the whole of Angel Meadow had turned out. Hulking men and ill-looking women gazed with morbid interest at the scaffold. But few Catholics from Angel Meadow would be in the crowd as dawn broke that morning. Their priests had urged them to stay away.

At 5am a mist began to climb out of the River Irwell, steadily thickening into a yellow, murky fog. Around 12,000 people stood waiting. There was a cry of 'hat's off' as the moment neared, followed by a slight cheer. Allen, Larkin and O'Brien were supported by three priests: Allen by his parish priest, Canon Cantwell from St Patrick's, and Fathers Quick and Gadd. As dawn broke, they prayed together, kneeling on the stone floor of their cells behind heavy, nail-studded doors. Father Gadd wrote later:

> A dank mist had arisen from the river that crawled its slimy length beneath the prison walls, and a wintry fog enshrouded the city – the battlements of the New Bailey Prison through the November gloom assuming the proportions of a huge fortress. A crowd of inhuman ghouls from the purlieus of Deansgate and the slums of the city had been gathered for hours in the streets abutting the gaol.

But, he added, the Irish of Angel Meadow and other areas of Manchester stayed away:

> No Irish mingled with the throng to gaze on the scene on the scaffold. They had obeyed the instructions of the clergy. Throughout Manchester and Salford silent congregations, with tear-stained faces and hearts throbbing with a thousand emotions, assembled in the various churches for the celebration of early Mass for the eternal welfare of the young Irishmen doomed to die a dreadful death that morning.

At 7.45am, the condemned men marched up the rough steps to the scaffold with the three priests and the prison officials. The priests could be heard praying on the battlements behind the blanket of fog. Allen was deadly pale and clasped a crucifix. Larkin needed help to mount the stairs. Gould calmly took his place above the drop. As a white cap was placed over Allen's face, Gould leaned slightly aside, shook his hand and kissed his right cheek. When Gould was capped and placed in the noose, he prayed in a loud voice that could be heard across the street. Larkin fainted and had to be supported by Calcraft, the hangman. Then the bolt was swiftly drawn and the three bodies dropped.

Allen was dead in a minute, but Larkin and O'Brien struggled. The drop was too short. Calcraft went down and killed Larkin but Father Gadd stopped him from touching O'Brien. The priest held the dying man for three quarters of an hour and recited the prayers of the dying as his life slipped away.

The bodies were placed in a pit of quick lime and buried in the prison yard. Their clothes were burned. They were later exhumed and moved to Strangeways, where they were buried behind the forbidding brick walls in a spot known as Murderers' Cemetery. Cabalistic marks on the walls were said to indicate their resting place, which no-one but the warders understood.

On 1 December, hundreds of Irish people from Angel Meadow and other parts of the city marched in memory of the three men, who were now considered martyrs to the Irish cause. Handbills were posted on walls on green paper with a black border stating: 'A procession in honour of the Irish martyrs will take place on Sunday at 2pm. The utmost order is requested. Remember that every improper act gives strength to the enemy.' Catholic priests urged their congregations to stay away once again, but their plea was ignored. A small brass band led the way.

One newspaper said the procession was composed of 'very motley elements' and contained several thousand people, who 'seemed to belong exclusively to the lower grades of the Irish labouring classes'. Many of the young men wore green scarves. The brass band played the 'Dead March'. Heavy rain began to fall as they marched slowly past Irish areas of the city, including Angel Meadow.

There was one final twist to the story. When John Francis Nugent was hauled before the court, he had alibis from more than a dozen witnesses. All of them lived in and around Buckley Street in New Town. William Saunders said he had seen Nugent in Burton Street, off Buckley Street, where Nugent and his father, Robert, were repairing a window. Elizabeth Massey, who lived next door but one to Nugent, saw him at his own door, holding a hammer and asked him the time. Nugent's father Robert Nugent, who had lived with his son in Manchester for seven months, said they were working in Burton Street all afternoon and had walked along Charter Street to give a customer an estimate for a job. The customer, a surgeon named John Bedale, confirmed they had been to see him. The jury was told there was 'no defence on earth as strong as an honest alibi'.

Nugent was acquitted but as he stepped confidently out of the dock at the assize court, he was immediately handcuffed by Thomas Welby from the Irish Constabulary. It emerged after the trial that Nugent was wanted in Ireland, as he had staged a 'very daring' escape from police in Drogheda back in May. He had locked himself in a room and leaped from a very high window before fleeing Ireland for Manchester.

The Irish Constabulary had originally arrested Nugent that spring after a spy claimed he had taken an oath to free Ireland from the 'tyrant yoke of England' and 'wade to the knees in Saxon and Protestant blood'. After his acquittal in Manchester, he was taken home to Drogheda by steamer on a charge of Fenianism. He was jailed for a month in Dublin. The *Cork Examiner* described him as 'a very respectable young man of fine appearance and, saving the alleged political offences with which he is charged, of high character.'

Chapter 17

Red Bank

When the Kuetski family arrived in Manchester from Poland, they headed straight for a lodging house in Angel Meadow. The journey had been long and the house in Back Joiner Street appeared to be a place where they could find refuge. The landlord, Peter Samsel, spoke their language. He was 42, born in Russian Poland and married to a Welsh woman named Eleanor Morris. They had a 12-year-old son. Samsel spoke only a smattering of English and had worked as a slipper maker across the Irk in Lydia Street, Red Bank, before taking over the lodging house in Back Joiner Street.

The house, however, was in a bad state. The Kuetskis shared an ancient four-poster bed in a room where the floor was full of holes, the walls were stained with dirt and damp and the roof was badly leaking. They had been there only a few weeks when they began to get behind with the rent, as they struggled to find work. One Saturday afternoon, Samsel and his deputy Joseph Harkowski got drunk and went upstairs to demand the rent money owed by the family. An argument broke out and Harkowski grabbed hold of Mrs Kuetski and dragged her across the floor by her hair. He then punched and kicked her husband into a corner. Then he ran into the back room and fetched an axe, smashing Mr Kuetski on the head seven times before finally kicking him downstairs.

Constable Joseph Grundy was first on the scene. He found Mr Kuetski bleeding heavily at the foot of the stairs with devastating wounds to his head and face. Samsel and Harkowski claimed they never touched him. Later, when they gave evidence in court through an interpreter, Samsel admitted he had wanted to 'get rid' of the Kuetskis, while Harkowski claimed he remembered nothing of the incident. Harkowski was jailed for a month and Samsel was fined 10 shillings. The court heard that Mr Kuetski had recovered but was expected to lose his sight in one eye.

Angel Meadow's lodging houses were a first port of call for immigrants from across Europe and beyond. There were so many nationalities in the slum that Benjamin Redfern described it as an 'olla podrida' – a Spanish stew containing lots of mixed ingredients. Redfern said the slum's residents included

Chinese, German and French nationals, Middle Eastern sailors or 'lascars' and 'representatives of every nation on the face of the earth'. German bandsmen and foreign musicians including 'Tyrolese minstrels' competed for space with Lancashire bell ringers.

Among the earliest visitors to Manchester's lodging houses were former slaves. The British government abolished the slave trade within the British Empire in 1807 and banned slavery altogether in 1834. Former slaves worked as labourers, entertainers, street sweepers and domestic servants in Manchester. Victims of the 1832 cholera outbreak included John Thomas, described by Dr Gaulter as a 'black man of fine athletic form', who walked the streets carrying a placard advertising the work of a portrait painter. In 1849, African-born John Abdella was jailed for 14 days for begging in Manchester. He was 39, just over 5ft tall and described as possessing dark grey hair and black eyes, a slightly crooked nose, a scar on his left cheek and boil marks on his back. He lived with his wife in Ashley Lane, Angel Meadow.

Racism was rife as one incident showed. A journalist from the *Manchester Evening News* who visited an Angel Meadow lodging house found a black man upstairs suffering from a terrible toothache. The room, he said, looked 'weird and desolate' in the half light and the people appeared strange in the gloom. Other lodgers were mocking the man with 'merciless severity'. The journalist decided to join in the joke and pulled a penknife from his pocket. He proposed to ease the man's pain by cutting off his gums. He said it brought 'roars of delight' from the 'rough spirits' in the room, but the man 'cried off' when he saw the blade. The man asked the journalist to put a finger into his mouth to feel the tooth. 'I had too much respect for my own flesh and blood to tempt the unfortunate contraband into cannibalism,' the journalist wrote.

Families from Eastern Europe formed the largest foreign settlement in Manchester. They included Catholics from Ukraine and Jews from Russia, Poland, Austria and Romania. The first Jewish settlers arrived in the eighteenth century and set up home along Long Millgate. A flower dealer named Hamilton Levi is thought to have been the city's first recorded Jewish resident, noted in a trade directory in 1788. The first Jewish community was formed mainly by German pedlars dealing in jewellery, optical lenses, umbrellas and old clothes. Later they became shopkeepers and were joined by merchants and professional men, including Sephardi traders from the coasts of the Mediterranean.

Another wave of Jewish settlers arrived from Russia and Poland as they sought to escape poverty and persecution during a series of pogroms. Many settled in Manchester when they found the route across the Atlantic blocked by the American Civil War. Arrivals increased rapidly over the coming decades as the persecution peaked on the continent. Manchester's Jewish population rose from less than 10,000 in 1875 to more than 35,000 within 40 years – the largest Jewish community outside London.

The new arrivals found jobs as glaziers, tailors and makers of caps, waterproofs, cabinets and cigarettes in the workshops of Red Bank, the steep embankment across the Irk from Angel Meadow which became the heart of the city's Jewish quarter. Red Bank, named after the sandstone bedrock that formed its foundations, had opened up in 1816 when a new bridge was built across the Irk. Three-quarters of shops in Red Bank had German and Russian names. Living conditions were just as bad as those in the Meadow – the ash-pits in many of the courts lay in ruins. The community's synagogues, schools, charities and social organisations offered a support network that was missing across the river.

On a frosty winter's day, a journalist found his way to the exotic-sounding Odessa Café to the north of Red Bank. From the outside it looked like any other house, but a sign hanging in the parlour window offered 'coffee served in the Russian style'. Russian elders shuffled with bent backs down a passageway leading to the door, which was lit by an oil lamp. Customers wore sheepskin overcoats trimmed with brown fur. The younger men smoked Russian cigarettes wrapped in brown paper and stood discussing the latest horse racing odds. The journalist wrote:

> Houses used as provision shops are doing a roaring trade. The tinned sardines and anchovies are going with great rapidity, and in the crowded lobbies the shopkeepers experience difficulty in finding the whereabouts of the fish boxes. Add swarms of children and a babble of talk: imagine most of the young women to be buxom brunettes and good looking and the middle aged and elders to be minus the later quality, give adults an average height of about 5ft 4in and you possess some notion of a Russian street.

He added: 'Another feature, probably due to the nearness of Angel Meadow, is the number of itinerant musicians and showmen.' Red Bank was home to two 16-strong German brass bands who were sometimes supported by a string quartet. The journalist also described other performances: 'Russian dancing bears give weekly exhibitions. Some inventor has also devised a barrel organ which sets in motion a number of marionettes on the top. But the pedlar of small wares is the most unmitigated nuisance.'

Another reporter from *The Shadow*, who stepped into the streets of Red Bank in 1868, said the 'rat-att-att' of sewing machines could be heard constantly from upper windows. Fried fish were displayed in one window, seed bread in another. The sign on a druggist's door announced that he was 'Agentur for Deutch Medicines', while another advertised a 'Deutch Beerhaus'.

Fernie Street in the heart of Red Bank was filthy and full of tailoring businesses. The journalist wrote: 'The name itself is pleasant enough. It leads the thoughts to cool and shady retreats, but there is no more fern to be seen here than there is grass in Angel Meadow.' He added: 'Ugly and slatternly women sit on the doorsteps half-naked, dirt-begrimed children wallow on the flags and yet in Fernie Street there is much industry.'

Few outsiders were said to enter Red Bank, but the Irish of Angel Meadow were frequent visitors. Every Sunday, they trooped across the Irk in their hundreds for Mass at a Catholic church dedicated to St Chad, a monk who went on a mission to Ireland. St Chad's was erected at a cost of £7,000 and opened on 4 August 1847. It replaced an earlier chapel in Rook Street in the centre of Manchester and was equipped with a 130ft tower and enough seats for 1,000 people.

The church's opening was celebrated with 'all possible pomp and circumstance' with a Mass led by 80 priests. The *Manchester Guardian* said the singing was 'disappointingly poor' and the old organ, brought over from Rook Street for a last performance, broke down. A small sister chapel, St William's, opened in Simpson Street in Angel Meadow in 1864. It was paid for with subscriptions after the parish priest of St Chad's made a last-ditch public appeal from the chapel's upper windows. On 23 December 1878, Bishop Herbert Vaughan of Salford wrote to the priest: 'Tell the people not to spend the last night of the year in public houses, in drinking and in foolish feasting, and in silly and dangerous dancing. Invite them to church, exhort them to pray at home, remind them of the uncertainty of life, of the shortness of time, and of the length of eternity.'

As the Irish flowed through Red Bank, the Jewish community also flowed through Angel Meadow. Red Bank had few lodging houses, but they were as badly kept as those in Angel Meadow. One of them was run by Harris Gaskie who, in 1877, was convicted for the fourth time of keeping houses that were 'injurious to the health of the inmates'. Henry Moses' lodging house was so filthy that chickens were paddling about in the muddy pools in the scullery.

Some newly-arrived Jewish immigrants seeking lodging houses chose to cross the Irk and set up temporary home in the Irish heartland of Angel Meadow. A journalist from the *Manchester City News* estimated that three out of four shops on Miller Street were occupied by Jewish tailors and waterproof makers. A colony of around a hundred Polish and Lithuanian immigrants set up home in several large tenements near the Old Burying Ground. 'In uncleanliness, both Poles and Russians rather surpass the average tramp,' one journalist claimed, 'but they are quiet and inoffensive, and on the whole better residents than those whom they propose to displace.' Reflecting racial stereotypes of the time, he added: 'With their pallid faces, black beards, and furtive – even dangerous – looks, the Poles and their neighbours, the Lithuanians, bear close resemblance to the Russians. They possess the same fondness for squalid surroundings and for brown bread and onions diversified with a vegetable soup.'

Newspapers editors were keen to point out any evidence of foreignness among those who committed crimes and drew attention to their broken English. When a watch thief named Isaac Jacob was arrested, he was reported to have told police: "Me hungry belly, no money, so me took tic-tac." Benjamin Redfern described one of the leading thief trainers in Angel Meadow as an 'English Jew with just a touch of negro blood in his veins'. But the truth was that German, Russian and Polish nationals largely kept out of trouble and rarely entered the beer houses of Angel Meadow.

Around 50 'wandering Germans' occupied a block of four houses in Crown Lane in Meadow, where it was said they kept the houses much cleaner than their English and Irish neighbours. One journalist who paid them a visit said:

> The walls are gay with coloured prints which have come from the Fatherland. The benches and tables, instead of being black with dirt, are white with scrubbing and there are many more appliances for comfort and decency than we have seen elsewhere. But here, too, the roof and walls are in much disrepair. There is no window or ventilator in the staircase and the smell ascends from the kitchen into all the upper rooms. As German cooking is somewhat pungent, and as German smoking is pretty constant, a good deal of smell does go up there.

The occupants of these houses shared one privy with a waste outlet that flowed through an open gutter connecting the yards. They had to fetch water from a tap in the street. The visiting journalist concluded: 'When we think that at least 50 people occupy these houses, we wonder how it is they are so clean and leave with a very high opinion of their keepers.'

Foreigners in Angel Meadow were usually described as Germans unless their nationality was known. German Peter was Italian. Two other well-known foreigners in Angel Meadow were German Dick and German Johnny. They were actually Chinese scent dealers, who went round the slum wearing their national costume. Their nicknames stuck until people learned they were Chinese and that Johnny was actually Dick's wife. Afterwards they were renamed Chinese Dick and Young Hyson. Colourful characters of all nationalities passed through the slum. One Friday night, two Frenchmen – and their dancing bear – were arrested and taken into custody at Goulden Street police station. Constable John Smith told magistrates how a large crowd had gathered around them in the street. The men, and presumably the bear, were later cautioned and discharged.

To the east of Angel Meadow stood a collection of streets known as Little Italy, where the Italians lived in their own lodging houses. Some earned a living selling ice-cream in summer and hot chestnuts in winter, while others worked plaster of Paris or played barrel organs. Journalists reported that they dined on a stew made from cheap cuts of meat, potatoes, cabbage leaves, a little macaroni and a few drops of olive oil.

The barrel organs were repaired in shops along Rochdale Road. The machines needed constant tuning and fitting with new melodies. The organ grinders sometimes delighted passers-by with performances by monkeys, raccoons and white mice. One journalist wrote: 'On the whole, the Italian colony does not give much trouble, except when the males quarrel through drink or jealousy and then they become very dangerous, owing to the use of the knife.'

His assertion was borne out in one case in March, 1869, when a plaster of Paris modeller named John Bernadotti was jailed for 20 years for stabbing to death John Oldham near Smithfield Market. Bernadotti was 24, with brown hair, hazel eyes and a dark moustache. Two other Italians, Joseph Restron and Bartholomew Galgani, were also jailed as accomplices. John Oldham had been walking home from a beer house when drunken Bernadotti pulled a knife from his trouser pocket and stabbed him in the neck. Restron and Galgani then stabbed him. Oldham was found lying in a pool of blood and died later at the infirmary. His brother James Oldham caught Bernadotti, who was still armed with the knife. Galgani was very drunk when he was arrested and was also carrying a blood-soaked knife. A judge said none but the 'most cowardly miscreants' used a knife when they knew their opponents were unarmed and he declared that this act was 'as un-Italian as it was un-English'.

A journalist from the *Manchester Courier* also claimed Victorian Manchester 'swarmed' with gypsies. They were 'swarthy men bartering dubious horseflesh at the public fairs' and 'dusky women huckstering wickerwork, brooms, carpets and wheedling money from fortune telling'. In Ashley Lane stood a tenement occupied by a group described as travelling tinkers and tin men, which could only be reached through a narrow entry from the street. Benjamin Redfern said these men led the 'most uncivilised and purely animal kind of life'. One of them, he claimed, earned a living by whistling like a canary: 'This man's face is truly beautiful for he has such a meek and patient look of humility and innocence that would charm anyone. What is better, he is as good as he looks.'

The twin worlds of Angel Meadow and Red Bank were brought together by the Manchester Medical Mission, which saw 350,000 patients from both sides of the Irk over 24 years. It was run by Dr Edward Meacham, a former soldier and a surgeon, who was appointed medical officer for the district. Meacham ran the mission until he retired aged 73 in 1896, by which time he was known in the slum as 'the old doctor'. It was said by one Victorian writer that the medical mission's customers included 'jail birds, victims of drink, young women fighting a lonely battle amid terrible dangers and representatives of all kinds of poverty, misery and degradation'.

The mission mainly treated cases of bronchitis, consumption, influenza, rheumatism and stomach disorders, but also specialised in early treatments for diabetes, heart disease, arsenic poisoning and even cancer. One woman told Meacham that her head wound had been inflicted by her husband with a poker. "That's not all," she added, "I was stabbed there by my husband with a penknife. See doctor, this place in my skull, some bone came away from there, where my husband kicked me. He got six months for that. See this collar bone which he broke with his fist."

The mission had an ulterior motive: it aimed to save people's souls as well as their bodies. Patients were subjected to Bible classes and prayer meetings as they waited for treatment. Up to 150 at a time were given a numbered card and a book containing their medical notes. They had to go to the hall and sit through a religious service before they received their medicine. The drugs were free, but patients had to pay a penny for the bottle. One 28-year-old man, who became paralysed for months after a life of drunkenness, had an electric battery applied to his arm while he received the 'good news of salvation'.

The mission attracted both Jews and Christians, Protestants and Catholics, including some who spoke no English. The doctors used interpreters to communicate with patients in French, German, Spanish, Russian, Turkish and Yiddish. A third of the regulars were Jews from Red Bank. One Jewish woman said: "I know the doctor. He is very good to our people and I have faith in him, but I cannot say I believe in Jesus." Others found their faith at the mission and one patient went on to set up a prayer meeting in her Angel Meadow cellar, which became known as the 'Hallelujah cellar'.

Of all nationalities, it was an Irishman who finally brought Red Bank to the world's attention. Patrick Durr was born in Roscommon and had settled in Manchester with his wife Catherine in the 1850s. Aged 42, he had sallow skin, brown hair and was blind in one eye. He was a bricklayer, while Catherine, also 42, worked as a hawker. They were drunkards who regularly fought, and

Patrick had served time for assault. By 1870, they were living in Brighton Court in Red Bank.

On the moonlit night of 17 August that year, the couple went drinking in a nearby beer house and returned home just after 11pm. Before going inside, they sat singing on the steps at the end of the court. Their eldest son John, 16, was away from home, while Paddy, 14, was upstairs in the family's one bed. Durr had been unemployed for weeks and their only remaining furniture, apart from the bed, was a broken rocking chair, a table and a mangle. Catherine kept pawning their clothes to buy beer and they often went without food, but tonight they had a loaf of stale bread.

The argument began almost as soon as they staggered through the door. Durr could not find his shirt and when Catherine said it was near the mangle, he snapped. He claimed the shirt was 'where everything else was – at the pawnshop' and ordered her to get up from the bed, but she refused. Then he went downstairs and shouted to his son: "Paddy, where's the knife?" Durr ordered him to fetch the table knife from the mantelpiece and began cutting a thin piece of rope from the back of the rocking chair. After shaping it carefully into a noose, he stomped upstairs.

Durr found Catherine sitting on the bed. He threw the noose over her head and pulled the knot tight under her left ear. Then he dragged her to towards the window. She fell to the floor and began shouting: "Murder! Murder!" Durr pulled on the rope for 20 minutes, standing in the window silhouetted by bright moonlight. Finally, he put his knee on Catherine's chest and strangled her to death. As she struggled, she cried: "God forgive you, Patsy." A neighbour named Ann Lea heard Catherine's shuddering screams, which grew fainter as she began to die.

Durr's son, Patrick, was still in bed, too terrified to move. Durr gave him sixpence and said: "She's dead now Paddy. You'd better be off." Police officers found Catherine's body on the floor near the window with the rope still around her neck. Her face was swollen, her eyes sunken and her teeth clamped like a vice around her tongue. Durr was arrested and later found guilty of murder following a trial. A report by the *Manchester Evening News* stated simply: 'The prisoner was found guilty and sentenced to death – the judge saying that there was no hope for him.'

Durr awoke early on Boxing Day, 1870, in the condemned cell in the western wing of Strangeways. It was more spacious than an ordinary cell, but the extra space was taken up by a huge iron cage, in which a warder sat watching the doomed man day and night in case he tried to take his own life and 'deprive the law of her victim'. Durr's death was to be a relatively private affair, overseen by prison officials and half a dozen reporters. Calcraft, the executioner, had arrived at Strangeways that night for dinner and was introduced to Durr in the morning. A black flag was hoisted above the prison walls before the execution and the death bell began to toll at 8am. Durr walked to the scaffold with a firm step wearing a blue shooting coat, dark corduroy trousers and a cloth vest – the same clothes he had worn on the night of the murder.

One journalist watching the scene reported that Durr appeared 'wonderfully calm', though his face appeared 'pale and troubled' and the twitching of his fingers betrayed his mental agony. Standing before the drop, he lifted his eyes to the lofty prison wall in front of him and said: "I believe my two boys are outside. I wish to speak to them." Calcraft grunted: "You can't." But Durr ignored him and began loudly reciting a poem:

> *Dear boys, don't fret,*
> *This is a debt,*
> *To nature due.*
> *I must go to the earth,*
> *Which gave me birth,*
> *And so must you.*

It was gone 8am when Calcraft placed the noose over Durr's head and shook his hand before pulling the bolt. Durr plunged into the drop, still alive. Calcraft had bungled his measurements. The hangman steadied the rope, took Durr by the shoulders and leaned on him as he struggled violently, before finally falling still. 'He appeared to die hard,' one journalist observed as Durr was buried within the prison walls, less than five minutes' walk from Red Bank.

Chapter 18

Cracksmen

Bob Horridge was a first class workman. Born to industrious parents on Rochdale Road in 1849, he followed his father and became a blacksmith. He toiled with fire and anvil in a workshop formed by three cellars below Style Street – growing muscular and athletic like a boxer. Men who knew Bob said he could work harder and quicker than any other blacksmith in England. But at night, he cast a long shadow in the streets of Manchester. He was an expert safe breaker and one of the most accomplished thieves in the city.

Bob showed signs of 'unusual depravity' at the age of 13, when he was jailed for six months, according to Detective Jerome Caminada. As a teenager he was always ready to fight the police – a hobby he continued even after he married and became a father. Whenever he was in prison, the amount of robberies in Manchester would fall dramatically, but when he was out, a safe in a secluded part of the city would soon be overturned and peeled open like a sardine tin.

In the 1860s, police were alerted to a series of robberies on a furrier's shop, a silk merchant's and a jeweller's in rapid succession. Bob was finally seen running back to his house in Gould Street at 6.30am carrying a lump hammer. Gould Street contained 'very dirty' courts in which an 'offensive' smell rose from the ash-pits and privies.

Up to 30 police officers surrounded the house, gave a loud knock and shouted: "Open up!" Bob jumped out of bed and gave a friendly tap at the window, as if to signal that he would open the door. Instead of going downstairs, he then smashed through the plaster ceiling and clambered onto the roofs of the neighbouring houses. He scampered high above the slum wearing only a shirt and trousers until he reached Ludgate Hill, where he smashed a hole in a roof and dropped into a lodging house attic where a group of harvesters were sleeping. They were startled but did nothing to stop Bob as he ran downstairs and threw open the door – making a flying leap over the heads of two officers who had given chase. Before they had time to react, he disappeared into the warren of streets.

Angel Meadow was known throughout Manchester and across the country for being 'deeply stained' by crime and vice. 'In Angel Meadow,' Jerome

Caminada wrote, 'the wicked never ceased from troubling, nor were the weary ever at rest.' The detective claimed that thieves had turned Angel Meadow into 'an abscess in the side of a great and wealthy city'.

One unnamed criminal described how up to a hundred professional thieves – the 'cross men' – could be seen loitering on corners in Charter Street at midday and discussing their plans for their next 'lay'. If a detective showed his face, they would disappear into houses and alleyways in seconds – leaving the street deserted. He said: "In at the front door and out at the back, over the yard as quick as fear could make them scramble, for each one knew they might have been spotted for some little job he had done, and it would not be worthwhile to wait and be lagged."

Thieves began their criminal careers at a young age in the slum. They embarked on a career path that saw them graduate from 'snow droppers' or strippers of clothes lines to experienced 'guns' or pickpockets and then burglars. Nothing was sacred to these young thieves. On a Friday night in February 1851, two brothers named John and James Leech, aged 14 and 12, clambered out of their cellar in Gibraltar and set off through the streets in the darkness. They were about to commit a burglary that would have shocked even hardened criminals.

It was after 8pm and the boys knew that Richard Jones, the warden of St Michael's Church, would already be on his way home. They carefully removed the lead and eight small panes of glass from the vestry window and then smashed through the panel of an inner door. Once inside, the boys worked quickly, ripping 35 bronze gas pendants from the walls, stealing the silver knobs from the tops of the staves and finally grabbing the fire irons from the vestry. Their theft was only discovered the following morning.

A constable named Duckworth went to the boys' cellar after a tip-off and caught John Leech trying to bury some of the silver under the floor. Witnesses also saw Leech throwing the gas pendants into the Irk to hide them, before later diving into the slimy water to rescue them. James Leech was armed with a chisel when they found him. The police believed the boys were behind a separate burglary at the school attached to the church, which had taken place four days earlier.

Thieves would steal almost anything and Victorian Manchester's court records were full of unusual thefts. One man was arrested for stealing a cart pulled by dogs, while a sailor woke up in an Angel Meadow lodging house one morning to find that his uniform had been stolen. Thomas Griffin, 31, who lived in Angel Street, was a prolific thief with varied tastes. He spent more than eight years in jail for stealing items including tobacco, butter, fruit, two coats and a cart.

The thieves' sworn enemies were the 'slops' – policemen who patrolled the streets of the slum. These officers could be seen goose-stepping at a slow but steady pace along Charter Street with military precision, dressed in blue coats studded with metal buttons and stiff leather collars. Strict rules meant they had to reach set points on their beat at exact times so that their superiors and any officers who needed assistance knew where to find them. This also meant criminals knew exactly how much time they had to carry out a burglary before another officer would swing around the corner. A reporter from the *Free Lance* described one of these officers in 1867: 'He is never in a particular hurry and he has a way, as he walks along, of looking into shop windows without turning his head sideways, and without cutting his throat with his leather collar.'

It was said that the Meadow's policemen, who were paid 24 shillings a week, had a habit of scrutinising anyone who approached them for a few seconds before speaking as they tried to remember their face. The tools of their trade included a truncheon, a whistle, a lamp and handcuffs, while their two pairs of regulation boots had to be kept in perfect condition. If they survived 20 years on the beat, the officers would get a pension. The widows of those killed on duty were paid an annual allowance.

At night their blue uniform, greatcoat, helmet and cape appeared sombre grey in the darkness. They walked cautiously close to the houses, keeping in the shadows. Their main task after dark was to check that all coal grids, cellars and shop doors were locked. They paid special attention to pawnbrokers' shops, where a gas light was left burning so officers could see if anyone was inside. They had powers to arrest anyone carrying housebreaking tools or weapons, or loitering with their face blackened. They could also detain anyone removing furniture from a house at night until receiving confirmation that they were not burglars or doing a 'midnight flit' to avoid paying the rent. *The Manchester Police Force Constables' Guide* of 1882 advised:

Attention should be directed to unusual noises in the night including barking dogs and breaking glass. Should thieves have already entered, you will best secure their apprehension by secreting yourself where you can command a view of their exit from the premises and at the same time taking the best means of getting assistance from other constables and surrounding the premises. You must also be on alert to discover and get removed ladders placed against buildings in positions which enable thieves to enter premises and commit robberies.

Officers put the advice to good use. Two burglars named George Thompson and James Kelly, who lived in an Angel Meadow lodging house, were arrested after a pair of plucky police constables caught them trying to steal some jewellery from a shop. The officers removed their boots, climbed onto the roof and caught the thieves hiding behind some chimneys.

Angel Meadow scuttlers Henry Burgess, 20, and Alexander Pearson, 19, were also experienced shop breakers with a string of convictions. In June 1891, they were jailed with hard labour for breaking into a confectionery shop run by Mary Lamb. They stole a quarter pound of coffee and some toffee, which they were caught eating in the street at 1am.

The toughest of all of Angel Meadow's criminals were the 'cracksmen' – house-breakers and burglars who were unafraid of using violence. The tools of their trade included picklocks, keys, chisels, wrenches, jacks and crowbars, and their weapons were knives, pistols, bludgeons and even cutlasses.

John Royle and John Holland, both 18, were already hardened cracksmen when they broke into the home of a shopkeeper named Charles Grenville Smart. They had assumed Smart would be asleep, but he was sitting up in bed reading a newspaper. His room on the ground floor was well lit with candles and his fire was blazing. Royle and Holland burst through the door. "Don't be afraid," Royle said. "I think I've good cause to be alarmed," Smart replied. He jumped up and tried to rush past them, but Holland pushed him back onto the bed and hit him in the face with a chisel, causing a severe wound. Smart cried out and his niece, who was sleeping upstairs, threw open a window and began shouting for the police. Royle and Holland were later arrested at a house in Angel Meadow, after leaving behind a crowbar, a chisel and a pair of boots at the scene.

Cracksmen arrested by the police would find themselves thrown into a horse-drawn prison van – the dreaded Black Maria – and whisked off to court and then to one of the city's prisons. Inmates being transported to prison after being sentenced at court were packed into the vans 'like herrings in a barrel'. Each van was divided into separate cubicles for each inmate but, on busy court days, two inmates might be placed in each cubicle and many more were crammed into the central passageway. Jerome Caminada saw 27 people spill out of one prison van in 1870, with misery etched into their pinched faces.

Manchester's Strangeways prison was built on top of a park to the west of Angel Meadow. It was designed by architect Alfred Waterhouse, who went on to create Manchester Town Hall and the Natural History Museum in London. The prison opened its doors in 1868 as a replacement for the New Bailey in Salford and was designed to house 1,000 prisoners. At more than 230ft high, its ventilation tower could be seen from the upper reaches of Angel Meadow – a constant reminder of what awaited those intent on breaking the law.

A churchman who visited Strangeways described the 'awesome' gloom within the small courtyard behind the gatehouse's thick, red-brick walls. From inside the prison's central dome, he could peer into five wings banked with cells. Iron steps led to each storey and warders patrolled each corridor. Inside the prison chapel, female prisoners sat on benches inside a cage backed by black boards so they could not be seen by the men. Condemned prisoners listened to the sermon from a box surrounded on three sides by black curtains.

On the door of each prison cell was a ticket giving the prisoner's name, age, offence, length of sentence and date of conviction. Catholics were given a red ticket and Protestants a white one. The cells contained a bedstead, a table and a small bracket for soap, a towel and a hairbrush. Prisoners' days were spent cleaning their cells, attending chapel, picking cotton or making hemp mats.

Those condemned to hard labour had to face the treadmill, which stood in a forbidding room separated from the cells by a yard. Each prisoner stood in a box stacked three tiers high – their feet rising and falling from the motion of the wheel. Men sometimes fainted in their boxes though exhaustion and would have to be carried out. The wheel was used to grind flour for the prison's bakehouse below. 'Oh I'm a bloke who gets my livin' by takin' things what isn't given,' went an old Manchester song. 'With my hand, with my fist, with my juke, with my mauler, I wish there was no Bobbies. I do. I do. For the treadmill, it does make me ill.'

Jerome Caminada claimed prison reduced men to nothing more than 'disciplined brutes' and was the city's 'best school of crime': 'Our prisons are nothing more but organised sewers. They poison, brutalise, depress and corrupt. Looking at our present system of dealing with thieves, examining it from every side, it is clear that nothing can be more clumsy and inefficient as a means of reformation, or more effectual in the production of crime.'

One of Manchester's toughest cracksmen kept returning to his wicked ways, despite repeated stretches in prison. One night, Bob Horridge robbed a fancy goods shop in Thomas Street with his accomplice Long Dick. When a police officer spotted them through the shutters and tried to arrest them, Bob smashed him in the face with a violent blow and escaped. Later he also stole a safe from a factory, weighing 450lb and containing £600 in gold and silver (worth more than £28,000 today) using a skeleton key to get into the office.

Jerome Caminada discovered that Horridge had pushed the safe into a reservoir behind his workshop, which supplied the water for an old mill. Caminada ordered the mill owner to drain the 5ft-deep water and had the safe hoisted to the surface using lifting tackle. The back of the safe had been smashed open.

Weeks later, a police officer checked the door of a warehouse and found it unlocked. It yielded a little when he pressed his body against it, and then suddenly gave way as Horridge rushed out into the street. Horridge punched the officer to the ground and then ran off towards Long Millgate. The officer struggled to his feet and set off in hot pursuit, shouting: "Stop thief!" Another policeman raced to the rescue, but toppled like a skittle under Horridge's heavy blows. A journalist also tried to make a citizen's arrest and was knocked down.

Horridge raced down some steps near Victoria Station and leaped over the parapet of a footbridge into the filthy River Irk. He disappeared into the black tunnel running under Walker's Croft and emerged in the River Irwell, where he continued swimming until he came to a croft in Strangeways from which he got clean away.

It would be months because he was finally caught – tricked into meeting an undercover police officer in a beer house – and jailed for seven years.

Chapter 19

Conmen

Jemmie the Crawler had no legs. Every morning, he dressed in a sailor's uniform and set off through Angel Meadow on a wheeled trolley, pushing himself along with his hands. Jemmie was no sailor. He was a professional beggar who told everyone who would listen that he had lost the use of his legs while doing battle on a Royal Navy warship. Everyone in the Meadow knew the truth. Jemmie had been disabled from birth and he had never been within 40 miles of the sea. He was a 'shallow cove' or 'dry land sailor', a man who posed as an injured seaman to stoke pity and national fervour and earn a few coppers.

Benjamin Redfern drew a remarkable pencil sketch of Jemmie. It shows the beggar wheeling himself along on his cart wearing a jaunty sailor's hat, a short jacket and a neckerchief. He has a broad smile, mutton-chop whiskers and wears a large earring like a pirate. Redfern said Jemmie had a 'cheery look' and an 'ever ready song'. He added:

> The only humbug about him was his cry of "pity a poor old man o' war's man as has lost the use in his low's timbers" which he repeated so often that at last he began to believe that he actually had served in the Navy. Peace to his memory! He was happy as man can be under greater disadvantages than most men, and the alms he received was money well spent by the giver. Why he couldn't at first tell the charitable that he was born a cripple – which was the patent fact to any ordinary observer – cannot now be told.

Professional beggars were as common in Angel Meadow as the rats. They learned their trade from seasoned conmen and spent years perfecting their skills. The slum's lodging houses and beer houses were their workshops and the streets and lanes of respectable Manchester were their finishing schools. Begging was the only source of survival for many in a world offering little security and, for many, the only other option was to fall on the workhouse.

Begging also had its advantages and skilled conmen who mingled with genuine beggars and prayed on people's generosity were able to make a good living. The Reverend Mercer said the majority of the Meadow's 'army of paupers' believed that 'only fools and horses work' and some became so skilled that they were able to eat and drink like 'pauper kings'. Angel Meadow was the place 'where beggars grew fat', he claimed.

Philip Wentworth from the *East Lancashire Review* came across two tramps who were 'fluent in speech, full of knowledge of the world, adventurous and ready'. He said they penned no end of begging letters asking likely benefactors for help. 'On occasions they try a spell at church or chapel going and continue to lay their case before the over-taxed and often deceived parson,' he wrote.

Each beggar had their own preferred technique or 'dodge'. The Reverend Mercer gave an insight in the range of dodges performed each day on Manchester's streets. The slum was home to a company of hawkers who dirtied people's doorsteps and an army of 'itinerant musicians, conjurers, tipsters, lurkers and mouchers'. He said: 'There are the begging letter writers, who have sounded every depth of human woe. There is the "puller up", who stops his victims, and there is the man who "stands pad", who never asks, but stands with an averted look of suffering angelically borne, and who appeals to you the more affectingly.'

Sham sailors like Jemmie the Crawler were a common sight as they limped around the streets in their navy uniforms. In 1851, around 300 genuine seadogs poured into the city as they sought to collect subscriptions for a strike at Liverpool Docks. Unlike them, the sham sailors had never seen the sea. They pulled on their begging uniforms and headed to Market Street with their legs and arms supposedly crippled in shipwrecks and naval battles. They told tall tales of heroic escapes, collected their money and returned to the pubs of Angel Meadow at night.

John Milner was one member of this 'land navy' caught out by a detective named Somerville. Milner was standing on a street corner wearing a navy jersey with his chest partially exposed. He appeared to have only one arm and was singing a mariners' hymn, 'Rocked in the Cradle of the Deep'. Milner, who also walked with a fake limp, asked the undercover officer if he could 'help a poor sailor', but when Somerville told Milner he was a police officer, the beggar's lameness suddenly disappeared and his missing arm slipped out of the jumper. Somerville only caught him after he had sprinted for nearly a mile. Milner brazenly denied the offence in court, but the magistrates described him as 'an idle fellow' and jailed him for 14 days.

Dry land sharks were a separate breed of conmen, who were even more unscrupulous than the 'sham sailors'. Their preferred technique was to hang around street corners and beer house doorways like hermit crabs, waiting to pounce on country rustics who had only recently arrived in Manchester.

These 'sharks', who also wore navy uniforms and chewed tobacco in seaman-like fashion, would lead victims into a quiet back room and whisper that they were selling smuggled goods. Their wares, small pieces of silk or cigars, were damaged goods bought cheaply on Smithfield Market. They sold them at three times their real value and cautioned customers against saying a word to others. After a parting glass and a shake of the hand, the victim would sneak off, fearing arrest for being in possession of 'smuggled' goods. Detective Jerome Caminada was of the opinion that these imposters deserved 'nothing better than a good flogging'.

Another trick used by Angel Meadow's conmen was the 'fit' dodge. A man walking along the street would suddenly fall down theatrically, as though he had been shot. His limbs would twitch and he would foam at the mouth, while a crowd of people ran to his aid and tried to calm him. They failed to notice the small piece of soap he had slipped into his mouth to make it froth. The rescuers would find that his health could only be restored by a drop of brandy and a few coins. He would keep a grimace on his face until he was safely around the corner and then attempt the same trick just a few streets away. By night, the health of these imposters would be miraculously restored and they could be seen in the beer houses of Charter Street spending their earnings.

Other rogues worked in pairs and practised a trick called 'the bread touch'. One would craftily drop a piece of mouldy bread on the cobbles while the other would pretend to spot the bread and snatch at it. The pair would then begin fighting, before one of them finally devoured the bread like it was the last morsel of food left on earth. The Reverend Mercer described how victims were suckered into helping them: 'The hair of the benevolent one stands on end. His eyes moisten, his fingers search for a substantial coin and the pals divide the booty.' He added: 'My experiences in Angel Meadow, and my glimpse into the lives and takings of many of this class, have enabled me to harden my heart on occasions when, but for those experiences, I should have fallen a helpless victim. We must learn not to give casually if we would heal this particular social sore.'

A journalist from the *Manchester Evening News* managed to get into an Angel Meadow 'begging ken' – one of the lodging houses frequented by professional beggars. He was led by a guide down a long passage into a large room where a dozen men and women were sitting around a table, while a great fire roared in the huge fireplace. 'They seemed as much at home as it was possible to imagine and were smoking filthy clay pipes and exchanging confidences with perfect freedom,' he reported. 'There was no whining cant in their voices now, for they had only fellow-cheaters to deal with and they appeared in their true colours.'

The beggars ate supper from a huge iron pot bubbling on the fire. Clean plates and a knife and fork 'of exceedingly venerable aspect' were laid out on the table for each person. Pipes were put out carefully and tenderly placed in their owners' pockets before a huge pot of beefsteak and onions was shared out with a huge loaf. The journalist wrote: 'This "ken" has an immense reputation among the cadging and tramp fraternity as they can always ensure good treatment if they have the means of paying a very small charge. Here they arrange the districts in which they shall work the city and the neighbourhood, and map out with wonderful cuteness the route each shall take.' A sketch was found by police in one of these houses, which pinpointed the best begging grounds in the city.

In 1880, a member of this begging fraternity gave away some of the tricks of his trade. The unnamed 63-year-old revealed in a letter published in a newspaper how he had earned his living for nearly 20 years, during which he had been jailed more than 100 times. He had been a begging letter writer, a member of the 'land navy' and had also tried his hand at the 'cripple dodge', despite at times also having a semi-legitimate job hawking pens, razors and shoelaces.

Once, he even posed as a preacher. 'This game pays well in remote village streets on Sunday evenings,' he wrote, 'but I was not fit for it. Once, when I was invited to hold forth in a small chapel, I was in no little danger of grinning in the pulpit at my own roguery.' The mystery man had also been an assistant to a 'quack' doctor who sold useless, sugar-coated pills that he claimed were a miracle cure for liver disease. 'I have been a rogue, imposter and vagabond of each and every denomination,' he admitted.

One hawker staying in an Angel Meadow lodging house told a writer named Austin Oates how his begging career had progressed. He had graduated from selling rings or 'fawneys' to watches or 'kettles', but he said the best game of all was quack-doctoring or 'crocusing', which could earn a successful 'quack' £500 a day: "There's no job like it. I know chaps to get two shillings and sixpence for a bottle of water, coloured with Spanish juice. Aye, sold it for sarsaparilla and quinine, and the blooming mugs came back the next day for another bottle, and told people the stuff did them good."

One of the best-known quacks in Angel Meadow was Molly Trainor, a 'fine, healthy-looking old dame' according to Benjamin Redfern. She walked the streets selling 'bitters' and tonics for indigestion. She claimed she could tell if a man had not chewed his food properly by looking into his eyes. Redfern warned: 'You may taste the bitters which she sells and is sure to prescribe for you, but don't be swindled into buying.'

Another con trick was the 'bereavement lurk', in which the trickster pretended to have been recently widowed with a young family. One beggar paid three shillings to borrow three children from a family in a Charter Street lodging house, promising their parents to give them breakfast and a few pence on their return. The man took up position at one of the entrances to Smithfield Market with the children wearing placards inscribed with the word 'motherless'. The beggar later admitted to a journalist: "In five hours I had more than 30 shillings given to me in silver and copper. I should think I drank at least a shillings-worth of rum during the time, besides buying some cakes for the children and giving them four pence each for themselves, after which I had £1 and eight shillings for myself."

On another day, he tried the same ruse with two girls, including one who was aged about 12. But she began causing trouble in the middle of his performance and the rogue gave her a slap on shoulders, which 'inflamed her Irish blood to fury'. He said he was compelled to 'pitch the crack' with only seven shillings in his pocket.

John Walsh, who lived at No.1 Court off Charter Street, was caught carrying out the bereavement lurk with two children, aged six and three. One had a card around her neck claiming her father had been a mill owner who had lost his property in a fire. The children were taken to a shelter and Walsh, who had more than £1 in his pockets in coppers, was jailed for a month with hard labour. Herbert Gilbertson from Style Street was also jailed for a month after he and his wife were caught begging with their three children. She was discharged to look after them.

Angel Meadow's most famous beggar Jemmie the Crawler was not quite the happy soul depicted by Benjamin Redfern. Jemmie, whose real name was Francis Vose, was arrested in 1851 with his accomplice James Morris and charged with causing a riot in the Highland Laddie. Vose and Morris both appeared in the dock dressed in 'regular Jack Tar fashion'. They only had one leg between them, the court reporters noted. Morris was 19-years-old, 6ft and wore a pair of earrings as well as having nautical tattoos of anchors and sea creatures on his arms. James Hilton, the landlord of the Highland Laddie, said the pair were playing cards in the vault at 3pm when an old man accused Vose of picking his pocket.

A row broke out and Vose and Morris began attacking everyone in the room with their crutches. They smashed nearly every window, jug and glass and beat the old man so badly that he was carted off home dangerously ill. Two other witnesses said their behaviour was 'the most violent, savage and reckless' they had ever seen. Morris claimed he and Vose went into the pub for a pint of ale and started playing cards with some other men for sixpence a game. He said some of the men tried to cheat him after he won two shillings and he and Vose 'got very badly treated'.

Vose was discharged and Morris was jailed for 14 days with hard labour. The magistrate said it was clear that Vose and Morris had been obtaining a living by fraud at the expense of real paupers and were profligate with their money. "I will take care that the police have orders as will stop your proceedings in future," he warned.

Chapter 20

Fallen Angels

It was just after dawn when a night-soil man approached the covered alleyway off Back Style Street to remove the cans from beneath the privies. Even in his line of work, it was a job he dreaded. This particular privy was so vile and the fumes so sickening that two of his workmates fell unconscious on an earlier visit and had to be dragged outside by their feet. The night-soil man took a deep breath and stepped inside.

He worked quickly, ignoring the filth covering the floor and walls and holding his breath as he dragged the heavy cans outside. Their foul load splashed over as he bumped them over the threshold and slopped against his leather apron. He was bending down to pull the last can from beneath the privy seats when he saw it: face down in the filth was the body of a woman.

Annie Chapman had been lying dead on the filthy floor of the privy, unseen for two or three days. The night-soil man noticed her red hair and freckles as he turned her over, as well as the gouges where rats had gnawed the flesh on her right arm. He turned and stumbled out into the open air, gagging as he tried to shout for a constable.

Chapman was well-known to the police officers who patrolled the streets of the slum. She was a 43-year-old prostitute with more than 70 convictions for being drunk and disorderly, as well as rioting, smashing windows, assault and wandering without any obvious means of subsistence. Detectives from Goulden Street police station suspected Chapman had been murdered by a punter in one of the nearby houses, before being dumped in the alley.

Prostitution was rife in Angel Meadow. The Reverend John Mercer noted that the slum's class of 'fallen girls and women' was 'very large and aggressive' and warned that syphilis was being continually injected into the veins of 'poor humanity' in Angel Meadow. Mercer estimated that, out of 42 streets in the slum, only 18 were free of prostitutes – and even some of those were doubtful. In some streets, most of the houses were used as brothels. Prostitutes operated from 46 out of 54 houses in Angel Street and 58 of 79 houses in Charter Street.

Prostitutes had been working the streets since the early days of the slum. One victim of the 1832 cholera outbreak was a 20-year-old prostitute named Sarah Clough, who rented a filthy room above some pigsties in No.1 Court, off Charter Street. It was a grim hovel surrounded by high buildings and a narrow entrance guarded by a stable. Clough's horrific death from cholera at least saved her from the advanced stages of syphilis, with had already infected her body.

In 1847, a visitor from the Scotch Church Young Men's Society discovered houses in Angel Meadow occupied by no-one but prostitutes and thieves. In one house he stumbled upon a thief and two prostitutes sharing a bed. He said girls as young as 15 were known to police as 'street walkers' and that prostitution was looked upon by slum dwellers as just one more way of making a living.

Early one morning, he visited the home of a mother who was living off her daughter's 'horrid and unnatural livelihood'. He wrote: 'The daughter had just returned home, and it appeared the mother regularly sits up for her return and has her tea ready with as much care as if she were a good mother waiting for the return of her child from an honest and hard day's work.' The following year, Manchester author Elizabeth Gaskell chose Nicholas Street in Angel Meadow for the home of Esther Fergusson, a character who turns to prostitution when she is deserted by her lover, in her novel *Mary Barton*.

Cases of prostitution and begging, which were lumped together in police statistics, rose dramatically in Manchester during the Cotton Famine. In 1862 they topped 1,240. The Watch Committee warned that prostitution was 'very much on the increase'. It reported 'It is not a rare circumstance to find police talking to females in the street and to servant girls at the doors of houses.'

One woman dedicated her life to helping prostitutes on both sides of the Irk. Elizabeth Prout, a Sister of the Cross and Passion, arrived in Manchester in 1851 and set up home in Stocks Street, Red Bank, behind St Chad's Church. When she became a nun, she changed her name to Mother Mary Joseph and founded a community of sisters who taught children and young factory girls and provided them with support. The sisters lived in extreme poverty, dyeing their own clothes black because they were too poor to buy religious habits. They opened hostels and provided a refuge where women could learn domestic skills in a bid to stay off the streets. It was said that Elizabeth Prout endured the hardships of slum life with 'unshakable faith'. She died just 13 years after her arrival in Manchester in January, 1864.

Nearly 800 prostitutes were believed to be operating in Manchester at the time of Annie Chapman's death in 1894, even though police had shut down 236 brothels. In a strange quirk of fate, Annie shared her name with another prostitute who was found dead in 1888 in another alleyway 250 miles away in Whitechapel – a victim of Jack the Ripper.

The gruesome murders attributed to the Ripper made the seedy underworld of London's East End notorious, but even churchmen accustomed to the wicked ways of Whitechapel were shocked when they travelled to Angel Meadow to save the souls of the slum's prostitutes. The Reverend Mercer, the vicar of St Michael's Church, wrote:

A band of rescue workers from London who worked for a time in Angel Meadow told me that they had found a more vicious state of affairs than prevailed in even the worst parts of Whitechapel. For in London, they said, it is chiefly women who gather together other women in houses of ill-fame, whereas in Angel Meadow, it is frequently young men who hold girls in their power, and who pass idle, dissolute lives on the earnings of their poor slaves.

Women sold sex for exactly the same reasons in London and Manchester. Many thousands travelled to cities from country villages in search of work, only to find themselves without a job. Others were seduced by men who had promised them a better life. Servants were vulnerable to being sexually exploited by their masters or, after losing their job, might turn to prostitution after finding themselves on the street. Alfred Alsop, a Christian missionary who investigated prostitution in Manchester claimed many young women were seduced under a promise of marriage and others were decoyed away by promises of good living and fine clothes.

Flash Mary was a typical example. She earned her nickname from the expensive ring she regularly pawned to pay for drink. Seduced by the bright lights of Manchester, she had become a prostitute despite being brought up by respectable Catholic parents in rural Derbyshire. Alsop wrote of her:

Being remarkably good looking, her attractions became a snare. She fell from virtue's path – the giddy height to which she had ascended was too much. As one dazed, she fell headlong into the black waters of guilt, and, character gone, hopes blighted, prospects ruined, gave herself up to be carried by the stream. Mary, desperate in her deeds, nine times was locked up and imprisoned, serving in all four years of prison life, several times in the hospital, clothes gone, friends gone, a marked character by the police, thus she was bound, fettered and enslaved under the bondage of Satan.

Alsop's story perhaps says more about how middle-class Victorians viewed prostitution than it does about how women really lived. Many women, who earned less than men, found that selling sex was their only way of earning a steady income and avoiding the workhouse. Others worked as prostitutes for years, then married and turned to other trades.

Annie Chapman, unlike Flash Mary, was born within spitting distance of Manchester. She was 5ft 2in, with red hair, blue-grey eyes and freckles. She was brought up a Catholic by her mother, Ann, who ran a pub in Salford, and had become addicted to drink by just 17. She was jailed 24 times between 1872 and 1879 and endured repeated stretches of hard labour. For a while, Chapman managed to hold down a job at a flax mill, but at night she began roaming the streets and selling her body to pay for drink. She drifted between lodging houses and ended up living on the streets of Angel Meadow.

Victorian newspaper readers believed mill girls were the most promiscuous because they worked so closely with the men. Journalist Angus Reach dispelled this myth when he visited the Meadow to interview a mill owner who kept an unusual log book – a register of seduction. Leafing through the crisp pages, Reach found that the 'guilty parties' never belonged to the same factory and the seducers and their prey always met outside the workplace. Reach wrote: 'There appears to be no doubt that prostitution is rare among mill girls.' Reach also found that three times more domestic servants than mill girls were doing time in Strangeways for prostitution.

Court lists from 1882 show that prostitutes, classed as 'incorrigible rogues', often held down a variety of jobs in addition to working the streets at night. Margaret Holland, 29, who worked as a laundress, had 18 convictions for prostitution, although her face was badly scarred from an abscess and she had lost all her front teeth. Eliza Moores, 38, a hawker with 71 previous convictions, was jailed for 12 months with hard labour after she was caught on the streets again.

One prostitute, Elizabeth Kelly, had just finished a month-long jail term when she was re-arrested. She swore at the police officer, Constable Welsh, and resisted so violently that he struggled to get her to the police station. In the cells, she smashed up the food pots. She pulled down a coffee stall as she was marched to court the following morning. In the dock, she rushed at Welsh and struck him in the throat, tore his collar and tried to scratch his face. The magistrate jailed her for six months to see if it would 'break her temper'.

Living conditions in Angel Meadow made it easy for women to turn to prostitution. Visitors discovered that the slum was full of 'hotbeds of depravity, overflowing with victims'. In Gibraltar, one investigator found dozens of men and women sleeping on the clay earth and broken flag floors of charnel houses with the 'foetid Irk rushing in through broken, paper-patched windows'. He said: 'Scores pass the wretched night, littered like human pigs upon shavings or chaff, and almost all without cover to their persons, the sexes indiscriminately huddled together and all sense of delicacy and decency banished from the scene.'

The lodging houses of Angel Street and Charter Street were also considered breeding grounds for vice. A journalist who visited one in 1870 was shocked to find the inmates sleeping naked: 'That decency and morality can be maintained among promiscuous bedfellows is beyond hope. Those who had not retired for the night were crowded into the two kitchens – the men all thieves, the women all prostitutes – almost as nude as though they were in evening dress in the most fashionable society.'

Landlords created the furnished room system to make extra money from prostitution, constructing wooden pens or cubicles between beds to make them more private for the prostitutes and their punters. John Williams, who ran the Grapes beer house, built so many of these pens upstairs in an attic that they formed a rambling network of passages. He then rented them out to prostitutes as 'furnished apartments'. A reporter from the *Manchester Guardian* who clambered into Williams' attic, was shocked to find that Williams had knocked through into the attics of neighbouring houses – including Cabbage Ann's den next door – so that he could extend his 'vile trade'.

The journalist wrote: 'It is registered under the police and a more wretched den of debauchery it would hardly be possible to find.' The Reverend John Jowitt Wilson, an Angel Meadow vicar, received death threats after he brought the evils of the furnished room system to the notice of Manchester Corporation.

Pimps opened brothels in Angel Meadow as a way of escaping police notice. They took over blocks of houses and furnished each room with an old bed, a table and a chair, and then rented out the rooms by day and night. Alfred Alsop said these rooms were kept so clean that corrupt police officers could easily turn a blind eye to their true use: 'Things kept in order, and a clean front, is the method adopted to throw off suspicion, so that should anything be said to the authorities, they cannot see anything amiss – or rather won't.'

One of the slum's few madams, Ann Campbell, was jailed in 1877 for running two 'houses of ill fame' in Mellor's Court, off Charter Street. Three women who lived in the court were each fined £10 for similar offences. It was more common for male pimps to run brothels, from which it was hard for women to escape. The prostitutes put their lives on the line each night to provide these men with a living. Alsop wrote: 'They keep their men in food and money. The same men becoming tyrants to the miserable victims of sin, who, after years of lustfulness, become diseased, and cannot in consequence of a ruined constitution, continue their wickedness, and are often driven off to end their wretched lives in the river or with the razor.'

Annie Chapman was just 20 when she tried to take her own life. At 1am on 10 August 1875, two police officers found her slumped on the pavement surrounded by broken glass from the shop windows she had smashed in a drunken rage. She had to be carried to the police cells on a stretcher. Once there, she pretended to be in a fit and struck one of the officers, Constable Swindlehurst, over the head with her clog. Just five minutes after the cell door was slammed shut, he heard a strange noise and went to investigate. He found Chapman lying on her back, her face blackened, with a piece of string tied tightly around her neck. He cut the string, but at about 1.40am she tried to hang herself again with her garter. Swindlehurst sat on a chair and kept watch over her until dawn. She was jailed for six months with hard labour.

Many prostitutes in Angel Meadow used drugs, as well as alcohol, to help them cope with life on the street. Their drug of choice was laudanum, which many began taking as a treatment for rheumatism – a symptom of syphilis. The drug was cheaper and more stimulating than alcohol. Druggists in Charter Street reported seeing prostitutes downing ounces of laudanum as soon as it was handed to them over the counter. The serious addicts turned to raw opium, which they chewed or swallowed whole instead of smoking.

Angus Reach, who investigated sales of laudanum, was told by one druggist that his opium customers included many middle-aged prostitutes: "They take it when they get low and melancholy. Three of them came together into my shop last night for opium to relieve pains in their limbs. These women swallow the drug in great quantities." Another druggist in Angel Meadow provided a special service for the slum's prostitutes. He was skilled at applying make-up or 'enamelling' ladies' faces. He also claimed the potions he sold over the counter could overcome any malady – tempting for the many prostitutes who contracted diseases as a result of their trade. The lack of medical help meant they had little hope of relieving their symptoms. One continued to work while suffering from a sexually transmitted infection for nine years.

Alfred Alsop said that the slum's prostitutes often spent their afternoons sitting on lodging house steps or leaning half naked out of windows. As darkness fell, they dressed in scanty clothing, painted their faces and perfumed their unwashed hair with oil and dust. Later they could be seen waiting for business in brothel doorways with a 'half maddened stare' or staggering along Charter Street with drunken men they had picked up from the pubs.

Alsop found that prostitutes were used by men of all descriptions: 'married and single, young and aged, poor and healthy' – from the office boy to the 'polished clerk'. One night he found two young married women weeping bitterly at 5am opposite a notorious brothel waiting for their husbands, who had already escaped through the back door. On another night he came across three men in a filthy alley who had spent the night 'in sin and drunkenness'.

In the shadow of Long Millgate stood a pub packed with labourers, who were spending their hard-earned money on prostitutes. A visiting journalist from the *Manchester Evening News* was captivated by a red-faced woman in a glaring red shawl, who was playing a tambourine. Outside in the pouring rain, he found two women in a 'hopeless struggle' to pull out each other's hair. Alsop saw one drunken prostitute goading a soldier into giving her his uniform, which she then put on and began dancing, singing, and shouting wildly.

Men visiting brothels often became victims of crime because pimps knew they would be unwilling to give evidence in court. One victim, Tommy Cooper, was in a brothel with two prostitutes named Mary Ann Lockraine and Mary Arrowsmith for more than an hour before five or six men rushed into the room and kicked over his chair. Lockraine, 23, and Arrowsmith, 17, sat quietly as the thugs stole four gold sovereigns and some silver from Cooper's trousers and appeared sympathetic when he told them afterwards: "The rascals missed my watch." Lockraine then slipped out and returned with three other men, who posed as police officers and asked Cooper to step outside before robbing him a second time.

Annie Chapman had connections to some of the most dangerous men in Angel Meadow. In 1887, she was called to give evidence in the defence of the scuttler Owen Callaghan. He was on trial for the manslaughter of Joseph Brady, who he stabbed to death with a large kitchen knife following a drunken row. Chapman, who was lodging with Callaghan's mother, told the court, perhaps foolishly, that Callaghan had failed to return home on the night of the murder.

The Reverend Mercer believed the only remedy for the 'awful evil' of prostitution was to ensure that women, who were paid less than men, were given fairer wages. He felt it was also important to foster a 'chivalrous spirit' among men. Rescuers from the Manchester Refuge, a few minutes' walk from Angel Meadow, dedicated their lives to saving teenage girls from the evils of prostitution.

One New Year's Eve, missionaries from the refuge found a 15-year-old girl named Agnes, who lived in the Meadow's lower reaches. They recounted her story in a mission magazine: 'Our readers will understand all that is involved in that to a good looking girl of her age. Without father, but with a debased drunken mother, the miserable dwelling was a resort of the lowest and roughest of the neighbourhood.' Agnes was said to be 'on the very verge of ruin' as that night her mother was drinking with a group of boys who had supped several quarts of ale and were shouting and swearing.

Just before midnight, Agnes was sent out to buy another gallon of beer. When she returned home, her mother threw a broken plate at her in a drunken frenzy, hitting her head and leaving an ugly wound. Agnes escaped and found shelter in the refuge, where missionaries put her on a ship bound for Canada, where she was adopted.

Back in Angel Meadow, a police surgeon named Dearden was examining the body of the prostitute Annie Chapman. He washed some blood from her face but found no injuries apart from a small cut on her head, which had been caused by an old piece of tin found next to her body. He discovered during a post-mortem that Chapman had not been murdered by a punter but had died from a fatty heart and pneumonia.

The sorry tale soon emerged. Neighbours in Back Style Street told how Chapman had been living in the privy for some time. They had tried to help by giving her scraps of leftover food, but she had finally succumbed to ill-health. One newspaper journalist wrote: 'She had no home and had several times slept in the entry, which is little better than a hovel, where her body was found. The remains had been shockingly gnawed by rats.'

A juror at the inquest was so upset by Chapman's death that he stood up in front of the coroner and declared that alleyways like the one that became her tomb should be sealed to prevent people from living in them. The coroner told him: "The class of people to whom the deceased belonged will not go into the workhouse, and it was better that she should sleep in an entry than in the open air."

Chapter 21

Scuttlers

Joseph Wood and Michael Hignett had every right to feel safe as they stood talking in the late evening haze of Ludgate Street, deep in Angel Meadow. As members of the slum's fearless band of street fighters or 'scuttlers', they believed no member of a rival gang would be brave or stupid enough to come looking for them in the warren of streets that marked their turf.

Wood, 18, worked as a parcel carrier at Victoria Station. He was also the leader of Angel Meadow's scuttling gang, feared across Manchester and Salford. Hignett was one of his most trusted lieutenants. Their headquarters was a 'blood house' in Welsh's Court, just yards from where they were standing.

It was 9.15pm on 2 June 1892 – the day after a terrific thunderstorm. A rumour was circulating that a man in Manchester had been struck by lightning and killed, leaving a widow and several children. Houses in Angel Meadow had been battered by giant hailstones. Now squally winds had settled into a summer breeze – the calm after the storm.

Wood had been the gang's leader for more than a year after staging a *coup d'état* against their former captain Anthony Gibson. At 10.45pm on St Valentine's Day 1891, Gibson was heading home when Wood emerged from the shadows and rushed at him with a knife. Gibson dodged the blade, but Wood's second-in-command, Oswald Evison, came from behind and stabbed him between the shoulders. He buried the knife so deeply into Gibson's back that it took four attempts to pull it out. Evison, an 18-year-old labourer who carried parcels with Wood at the station, shouted to Gibson from the dock as he was jailed for 12 months: "I'll swing for you when I come out." Wood was cleared after claiming he had taken no part in the attack.

Wood and Hignett were still talking when ten men stepped around the corner from Nicholas Street and stood facing them, bringing the conversation to an abrupt halt. They were John Kelly, John Dean, brothers Richard and Alexander Pearson, and six other members of a rival gang, the Bengal Tigers. The Meadow gang and the Tigers had been in a tit-for-tat street war since May, when Wood was chased into a grocer's shop at knifepoint by Alexander Pearson.

The Tigers formed a line blocking the end of the street. Richard Pearson finally broke the silence when, pointing a stubby finger at Wood, he shouted: "Claim him… and cut him up." Kelly slid an iron poker down his sleeve and charged forward, hitting Wood across the head and smashing him against a wall. Dean struck Wood with a short wooden staff like those used by the police and Alexander Pearson then lunged at him with a baton. Richard Pearson completed the onslaught: he drew a knife and stabbed Wood in the head. Hignett, whose thoughts of self-preservation outweighed his loyalty to Wood, darted into a nearby shop with Dean in hot pursuit.

Wood staggered to his feet and bravely fought his way out of the street. He then began running towards Goulden Street police station. But the Tigers had set a trap – a second unit of the gang was lying in ambush near the station. Armed with knives, they chased blood-soaked Wood back to Angel Meadow, where he finally stumbled across two police officers who took him to the infirmary. His scalp had been slashed and his skull was dented. He was in hospital for more than a week following the attack – the latest in a long list of scuttling outrages.

Police arrested Alexander Pearson and John Kelly, who were both labourers. John Dean, who worked as a galvaniser, went on the run and was caught nine miles away, hiding at his brother's house. Alexander Pearson was a partner in crime of Henry Burgess, the slum's most dangerous man. Pearson's brother Richard had been jailed for two months in 1884 after he and 20 other lads attacked a youth named Robert Lawson with sticks, belts and stones. Pearson knocked Lawson unconscious with the handle of a clasp knife. John Dean had been involved in a separate attack on a boy whose face was slashed from the top of his head to his ear.

Wood told a jury at their trial that he had no interest in street fighting and felt no animosity towards the Tigers. The judge said the attack was the most brutal he had seen for some time. He warned that street fighting or 'scuttling' was rife in Manchester: "It is remarkable that, while all other crimes have decreased, this particular one is now on the increase." Alexander Pearson, Dean and Kelly were jailed for five years, but Richard Pearson escaped justice.

Scuttling first hit the streets of Manchester in the mid-1860s as a shocking new mutation of the Irish faction fights that had already broken so many skulls in Angel Meadow. An article in *Odds and Ends* magazine, published in 1864, revealed that the term 'scuttling' described the way scuttlers ran from combat, rather than how they fought: 'When boys of one street take offence at boys of another street, they often fall to fighting in a body. This is called a "scuttle". There is an English word "scuttle", meaning a short run, a quick pace, and as many run away rather quickly from such combats, we are inclined to think that this is a reasonable derivation.'

Scuttling first made headlines in Manchester as the Franco-Prussian War raged in continental Europe in 1870. Late that year, two groups of boys formed battle lines on opposite sides of Rochdale Road and began pelting each other with stones. Police Superintendent Charles Godby reported that the combatants were Catholics and Protestants. Mimicking the war, the Catholics took the side of the French, while the Protestants became the Prussians. The *Manchester Evening News* wrote: 'The superintendent did not think it proceeded from any feelings of religious animosity, but solely from a love of mischief, and what the boys considered "fun". Great damage had been caused to property in the neighbourhood, and several persons had their head broken.'

By October 1871, Godby was reporting that the 'nuisance' of scuttling had become 'quite intolerable'. By then, more than 480 boys had been convicted. More than 20 'respectably dressed' boys, aged 12 to 16, appeared together at the City Police Court charged with throwing stones. The judge, Charles Rickards, regretted he had no power to whip them. He fined them 40 shillings each and warned that they would be jailed if they failed to pay. The boys' mothers caused a scene in court as they rushed to hand over their money.

On Christmas Day that year, the Sharp Street Ragged School in Angel Meadow held a festive breakfast for its scholars. The master Mr Croughton read out the school's annual report, noting that the average number of scholars had fallen to 244 that summer. He said: "The average is rather less than that of the previous year, owing in a great measure to the dangerous pastime which prevailed in Angel Meadow throughout last winter, and is called scuttling. This consists of wholesale stone-throwing and cudgelling. Broken heads and cut faces were the natural consequences of this game, and unfortunately the bruises were not confined to the combatants." He believed the 'game' had frightened away a number of girls and infants. The Charter Street Ragged School also reported a drop in summer attendance from 383 to 292.

Scuttling quickly shook off its schoolboy innocence. Each area of Manchester and Salford soon had its own gang and the *Manchester Courier* reported that teenagers aged 14 to 18 were quitting good jobs to roam the streets. The boys found they could earn a living wage of between 12 and 15 shillings a week by labouring or parcel carrying at Victoria Station, while older scuttlers favoured market portering. Both jobs required little skill and allowed them to stay on the street.

A journalist from the *Manchester Evening News* came face to face with a scuttler in an Angel Meadow lodging house:

He was a good specimen of his kind: clear, sharp face, with marks of manhood before youth had passed away, closely cropped hair, almost hidden by a tight-fitting cap that showed his ears with uncommon effectiveness, and a wisp of dirty white handkerchief tied loosely round his throat. He rose once to light his pipe and I could see the gleam of his brass-tipped clogs as he shuffled to the fire.

Scuttlers wore tight-fitting punchers' caps, loose jackets and white, black or brightly coloured silk scarves. They also adopted the flared trousers known as 'bells' or 'narrow-go-wides' worn by sailors. If a scuttler went for a job, he would borrow other clothes, as no employer in Manchester would take on a scuttler. However, these 'strong daredevils' were welcomed with open arms by regimental recruiting officers and some reportedly made excellent soldiers in the 'thin red line' of the British Army. Scuttler outfits were completed by narrow-toed, brass-tipped clogs and broad leather belts with brass buckles usually worn by navvies, which scuttler captains decorated using pins and soldiers' buttons. As a final touch, scuttlers plastered their hair across their foreheads with great care. Scuttler girls also wore distinctive uniforms of black and grey shawls, short skirts, pink stockings and clogs. They did their hair in a knot with a low fringe. The girls used their clogs as weapons during street fights. One detective said: "The girls have a regular whoop and the boys a peculiar whistle that calls them together." Many male scuttlers had girls' initials tattooed on their arms and it was not uncommon for them to be inked with the names of a dozen girls.

Scuttler girls also had the names of their men tattooed on their arms. When 16-year-old Billy Willan was sentenced to hang for the murder of a rival, his sweetheart Hannah Robin had herself inked with a tattoo that read: 'In loving remembrance of William Willan.' It proved to be a premature gesture, as Willan was later reprieved.

Such hero worship came at a price and the girls, no matter how tough in their own right, were under constant threat of attack from those they adored. In 1895, two scuttlers named Charles Jones and WJ Walker dragged their girlfriends along Rochdale Road by their hair and threw them down and began kicking them. The girls screamed and the police officers who rushed to the spot were so outraged that they struck the scuttlers with their staffs. Jones and Walker claimed they were only 'wishing the girls goodnight'. They were fined 21 shillings.

Scuttlers' weapons included clasp knives, pokers, scrap iron, sticks and stones. A journalist named Alexander Devine kept a collection of these munitions, which also featured old cutlasses and stone bottle tops which served as sling shots. The scuttlers' favourite weapons were their thick leather belts. In the heat of battle, they wrapped the belts around their fists and used the heavy brass buckles to smash skulls.

As night fell, scuttlers gathered in gangs up to 40-strong at a favoured street corner in their district and sallied forth into the darkness looking for a fight. To provoke a scuttle, a gang member would make an incursion into enemy territory. He would be insulted and knocked down if caught, but this was a challenge to the whole gang and reprisals would swiftly follow. The arrival of a strange lad at a 'blood house', a beer house or lodging house patronised by the gang, would also spark a scuttle. Two scuttler girls, bored of hanging around the same street corner, would sometimes head off to an enemy district on a quest for adventure. Members of a rival gang would make sexual advances and the girls would return to their turf 'terribly offended' and then urge their gang to defend their honour.

The injuries scuttlers inflicted were often horrific. According to a senior surgeon at Manchester Royal Infirmary, scarcely a day passed without a scuttler being treated for severe wounds. In July 1873, Lawrence Coleman was going up an alley near St Michael's Church when he was attacked by a thug named James Murphy and a gang of 50 scuttlers. Murphy slashed at Coleman's eye with the blade and smashed him over the head with a brick.

On 28 March 1888, a near fatal attack took place outside Smithfield Market. Thomas Toole, a labourer who lived in a lodging house in Angel Street, was passing beneath the huge stone bull's head over the entrance to the meat market when he was set upon by 10 rivals in a targeted attack. As the naphtha lights on the market were slowly being extinguished, part of Toole's skull was driven into his brain by a blow from a heavy belt buckle. His chief attacker, 16-year-old market porter Thomas Hughes, was then stabbed in the back by a thug named Thomas Cunningham. Police rushed Toole to the infirmary, fearing he would die. A judge said later it was a 'marvel' that he recovered.

Scuttling had now become an epidemic in Manchester's slums. At midnight one Saturday in November 1890, the police were called to Holland Street near Angel Meadow following reports that 600 'roughs' were taking part in a pitched battle with belts and knives. The officers heard cries of "Murder!" as they ran to the scene and were forced to draw their batons. But the scuttlers drove them back and they had to send for reinforcements. Just three 'rough looking fellows' were arrested and the officers had to fight their way back to Goulden Street because the crowd was so hostile.

A month later on 11 December, a gang of 14 teenage scuttlers from the Meadow launched an invasion of Salford armed with knives, pokers and belts. They chased a man named Preston to the home of his associate Edward Barry and then began beating on the door, shouting their war cry, "The Meadow!" When bricks crashed through the window, Barry stormed outside.

A scuttler named Edward White felled Barry, striking him on the head with a poker. James Martin, a labourer from the Meadow, struck a policeman who came to arrest them. When White, Martin and two other teenagers were found guilty of malicious wounding, the presiding magistrate warned that scuttlers would 'find the law too strong for them.'

Journalists claimed prison posed no deterrent to scuttlers and jail-time only added to their cult status. A missionary who offered help to convicts as they left Strangeways told how scuttlers were met at the prison door by crowds of lads and girls, who hailed them as heroes. Alexander Devine felt the only remedy was to give them a flogging, as at heart the scuttler was a coward. Detective Caminada agreed: 'The howl of the cowardly scuttler as the lash descended upon his shoulders would strike terror into the hearts of his associates and do more to free the streets of this pestilence than all the warnings and sentences of the bench.'

In 1890, a deputation of Manchester MPs and magistrates including the Lord Mayor Sir John Mark travelled to London for crisis talks with Home Secretary Henry Matthews. They told him that the magistrates' sentencing guidelines had failed to put down the scuttling epidemic and gangs were now ordering shopkeepers to pay them protection money. They wanted to give scuttlers a good flogging.

Matthews still had his hands full with the fallout from the Jack the Ripper murders in the East End and dismissed them, saying the House of Commons was 'extremely averse' to flogging. Sir Robert Rawlinson MP later wrote to the *Manchester Times* protesting that flogging was 'degrading, repulsive and abominable'. 'Let the Lancashire mayors and magistrates employ sufficient police to maintain order, and cease thinking about brutal and brutalising flogging,' he protested. If Rawlinson had dared to visit Angel Meadow, he would have seen how insulting his comments were to the city's embattled police force.

In October, 1891, a scuttler named James Gallagher was charged with attacking a police constable named McDermott in Style Street. McDermott was marching a prisoner to the police station one Saturday night when Gallagher, who was known as the Red King because of his 'remarkably sandy-coloured hair', gave him a 'terrible blow' on the head with an iron bar. McDermott was knocked unconscious and was carried into a beer house by some men who came to his aid. He was laid up in hospital for three weeks.

When Gallagher was arrested, he said: "I did it on account of my pals, and now they are laughing at me." He was jailed for six months with hard labour.

Five months later, another 'rough looking' scuttler named George Cooper kicked a police officer in the legs and bit another's hand while he was being arrested. It took four officers to drag him to the station. Cooper, who had already had several convictions for scuttling, was jailed for three months.

The worst attack of all took place on a Saturday night in May, 1894. Constable Stanilous Brierley was on duty in plain clothes in Sharp Street when he was spotted and attacked by five thugs, including Thomas Mulroy, 23, and his sister Jane. The group began kicking and punching Brierley until he was unconscious. Jane Mulroy, 17, then threw a china teacup at the officer's head.

Brierley was picked up by a hawker who found him slumped against a hoarding. Brierley somehow staggered to his feet and chased Mulroy into an alley near St Michael's Church, where a yob named Edward Riley was waiting. Riley tripped Brierley, who fell to the ground. Mulroy then kicked Brierley so hard with his brass-tipped clog that the officer's eye was scooped clean out of his face. Riley, 19, then knelt on Brierley's chest to remove his watch and chain.

Brierley was carried to the infirmary on a stretcher and was still in hospital when the case went to court. Thomas Mulroy was jailed for nine months and Jane Mulroy for two weeks. Riley was acquitted because of a lack of evidence, even though the magistrates were shown the result of the gang's handiwork: Brierley's squashed and lifeless eye.

Police officers began fighting fire with fire. Henry Burgess, who in the hot summer of 1893 had turned Thomas Matthews into a human fireball, was the most feared of all Manchester's scuttlers. At 11pm on 27 July 1894, just over a year after Matthews' death, he shouted without provocation to a police officer named William Corns in Angel Street that 'his days were numbered' and that he would be 'put out' that very night. Burgess disappeared and then sneaked up on Corns armed with a 'formidable' knife and a poker. He told Corns: "Your time has come. I am going to settle you." Corns took a swing at Burgess with his staff, but missed. Burgess hit Corns with the poker and ran off.

Corns called for reinforcements and together the officers went in search of Burgess. They found him crouching in ambush in an alley off Old Mount Street at 12.30am. He had removed his heavy clogs so that he could run through the streets in silence. Burgess jumped up and hit Corns again with the poker, but this time Corns had a better aim. He smashed Burgess on the head with his staff and arrested him following a struggle.

Police described Burgess as one of the worst thugs in Manchester, while newspaper reports called him 'a desperate character'. By then, he had been convicted of manslaughter, burglary, police assaults and scuttling. He was jailed for six months with hard labour for this latest outrage. Robert Armitage, the chairman of the bench, said a longer criminal record had never been read out in his courtroom. He added: "It is the intention of the bench to show the lawless characters of Angel Meadow that their punishment for offences would not only be heavy but speedy." He told Corns he had 'nobly done his duty' and was an 'honour to the force'.

Just two months later, Corns was involved in another fracas in Angel Meadow. At 7pm on 5 September, he and a second officer were asked to turn James Heaton and two other men out of a lodging house in Crown Street. Heaton picked up a piece of iron and struck Corns on the head with a crashing blow. Bleeding heavily, Corns arrested Heaton after a struggle in which his hand was shattered with the iron bar. Corns and his colleague faced a battle to get the trio to the police station as a 'very bad character' named Eunice Birtwell made a 'desperate' rescue attempt. Heaton who had already served two terms of six months for scuttling and police assault, was jailed for another six months.

The Meadow's scuttlers would all end up behind bars as magistrates imposed a crackdown. In February 1896, Joseph Wood, now 22, was working as a hawker. He and other members of the gang went through the streets looking for two brothers, John and Peter Durkin. A fight broke out and John Durkin was stabbed in the face with a clasp knife, while his brother was stabbed in the neck. Wood was jailed for 18 months.

Wood's arch enemy Anthony Gibson and the thugs Henry Burgess and Thomas Cunningham also ended up in the dock charged with stabbing a hawker named Joseph Metcalf. Burgess, Cunningham and Gibson ran towards Metcalf and a man named Michael Callighan armed with pocket knives after spotting them in a street near the Meadow. Cunningham shouted: "Go for them." Metcalf and Callighan began to flee, but Metcalf fell. Burgess, Cunningham and Gibson stabbed him repeatedly.

Chapter 22

Saviours

It was a cold, wet night when the two brothers arrived at the boys' refuge in Strangeways, across the Irk from Angel Meadow. The youngest, aged nine, was weak and starving. The eldest was a tall and haggard 16-year-old with wild eyes and his hair plastered into a thick mop pointing five inches above his head. "I've come to see if you'll take my little brother," he told the two inspectors who met them at the door. They noticed immediately that the two 'street arabs' were covered in lice.

"Where have you been sleeping, my poor lads?" one of the inspectors asked. They had been living in the back yard of one of the worst lodging houses in Charter Street. Their father was dead and their mother was serving her fifth prison sentence for fencing stolen goods. Tears rolled down the eldest boy's blackened face. "We'll not only take your little brother," the inspector said. "We'll take you as well." Every stitch of their clothing had to be burned and their hair was closely cropped that night. "Thank you, sir," was all the boys could offer in return.

The next morning, the two inspectors decided to investigate their story. They went to the house the boys had made their home. As they knocked on the door, a terrifying scream from within made them shrink in fear. They retreated to the street corner, where they were relieved to see a policeman. "Do you know No. 11?" one of the inspectors asked breathlessly. "We've been to the door, but dare not venture in." The policeman's answer was sharp: "You'd better not, Sir. You'll find none but thieves there."

But the next night, the inspectors returned and managed to get a quiet word with the landlady. Although at first she denied knowing the boys, she finally confirmed that their mother was in prison and led the men through the house to the stinking yard where the boys had been sleeping. One of the inspectors later wrote:

In the yard at the back of this wretched house these two lads had been sleeping in such a condition that the wonder was they were alive. The mother was in for nine months and her term expired the first week in

May. We felt that the only hope for the lads was that they should be placed out of her reach before then.

Life was all but impossible for many of Angel Meadow's children. Those without a home slipped between lodging houses or slept anywhere they could find. A few flagstones warmed by a baker's oven represented luxury for those sleeping on the streets. Two boys died one December night after crawling into a brick kiln – they were still asleep when the workmen arrived in the morning and fired up the kilns.

Many of these street arabs were pressed by their parents into selling matches or flowers, while others trained themselves in the art of 'breach buzzing' or picking pockets. One worker who visited Angel Meadow revealed: 'As you pass along our streets you see groups of idle vagrants from about 16 to 18. From these our criminal ranks are being daily fed. It is already too late. Their characters are stamped. They will spend a few more years in our streets and then one by one they will drop into the workhouse or the gaol.'

A band of Christian missionaries stepped into Angel Meadow in 1853, led by a man named James Rutter. They aimed to rescue feral children from poverty and crime – and save their souls from hell. The group planned to 'civilise' the slum and 'excavate the heathen' by offering charity and education. They created a school for the slum's 'uncivilised and thoroughly ignorant lads' within an empty tenement building.

But the heathens fought against this attempt to civilise them. They threw stones through the school's windows, dumped dead cats and dogs on the doorstep and made teaching night classes impossible with their 'discordant noises' in the street. It took the missionaries five years to win over hearts and minds in the slum. One later wrote: 'The men resolved not to be angry. They entered the dwellings of the most determined of their disturbers and gradually succeeded in converting the stoutest opponents into the warmest supporters.'

The institution was known as the Sharp Street Ragged School. It was a single room of 13 yards by 6 yards, in which up to 400 children soon gathered for classes each week. The missionaries pressed boys into selling newspapers and formed a parcel-carrying brigade at Victoria Station to keep them out of trouble. They claimed the school did have a 'civilising effect' on the neighbourhood, but admitted they had many 'narrow escapes' as they walked through the slum beneath a hail of stones. 'In those days it was scarcely safe to walk along the streets to the school without protection,' one missionary said. James Ward, one of school's first teachers, wrote:

In 1855 when I entered Sharp Street Ragged School there were no windows or window frames, but a coarse canvas nailed over to keep out the cold. Our scholars did not come to us. We had to go out to fetch them, aiming always for the lowest and poorest we could find. Our next effort was to find employment for boys who otherwise would have been trained as pickpockets.

The teachers arrived one Sunday evening to find a pale and sickly boy aged nine dressed in 'miserable clothes' hugging his little brother, who looked a 'picture of death'. They recalled in a report aimed at likely benefactors: 'His arms were placed around the child as though he would shield him from all ill. We shall never forget the sight we saw that night.' They taught the children to sing hymns at Sunday school in return for coffee and cake, and handed out more than 19,000 dinners in one year.

But conditions in the Sharp Street building were so bad that 18 teachers felt compelled to leave in 1860. They set up a new school in Nelson Street, off Charter Street, at the foot of Angel Meadow, naming it the Angel Meadow Ragged School. (Sharp Street would also be resurrected in a new building in 1869.) The Angel Meadow Ragged School stood in an abandoned workroom which had recently been used as a dancing saloon for 'immoral and degrading purposes'. It was a former meeting house of thieves, a rendezvous of prostitutes and a 'free and easy'. One of their first annual reports stated: 'The very Sunday night before we entered into possession it was used as a dancing saloon, and for some weeks, our services were carried on with flimsy and gaudy decorations still decking its walls.'

The teachers began canvassing the slum for fresh scholars, who they taught basic skills such as reading, spelling and arithmetic. Their Sunday school soon drew more than 350 boys and girls, but attendances slipped in the summer when long evenings and scuttling proved 'too tempting' for the boys. Around 70 infants were also taught in a cramped cottage next to the school. At Whit Week, the scholars were taken to a park on the outskirts of the city, where they feasted on currant bread and coffee.

Soon the school needed more teachers. At a meeting on 6 April 1861, new master Thomas Johnson was given a three month trial. He would later become the school's best known superintendent. The increase from 18 to 24 teachers meant the school could also offer lessons to the children's parents. The idea was simple. 'If we can reclaim the parents, and make them honest, sober, and industrious,' the teachers said in one of their reports, 'we do much towards removing the evil influences exercised upon our children at their too often miserable homes.'

Around 12 mothers and 16 fathers began trooping through the school's doors each week. The men gathered in a narrow space at the top of the school for lessons in history and book-keeping. The mothers occupied a corner of the schoolroom, where the children fought constantly for their attention. The men had access to a newsroom, where they could read daily newspapers. The women formed a sewing class and were soon making around 150 garments a year, including petticoats, pinafores and shirts.

As well as educating the slum dwellers, the teachers also tried to provide moral guidance, setting up a temperance society after seeing 'the evil effects of drink and the dram-shop'. Nearly 150 people took the pledge, some perhaps tempted by the Saturday night magic lantern displays the teachers provided as an alternative to the dancing saloons.

Suddenly the school was booming. Nearly 40 men were attending classes. Donations from local garment firms of cast-off clothing and clogs from local shoemakers allowed them to help clothe the children. The teachers felt confident enough to try to form a cricket club and to set up a library with 400 books including volumes on theology, history and biography. The poor of Angel Meadow were also given access to a savings bank – the first time they had ever saved. They deposited more than £10 in the first year and withdrew half of it again to buy food and clothing. By 1867, they were making 1,289 deposits totalling £66. One boy withdrew five shillings to buy his parents their Christmas dinner.

The teachers were presently surprised by the attitude of the adults towards the school. A woman who ran a brothel in Charter Street was induced to give up prostitution and earn a living washing clothes instead. When one teetotaller pointed out one of his classmates as a drunken gambling addict, the whole class confronted the drunkard and made him take the temperance pledge. His wife later called the teacher to her house and pointed to a bundle of new clothes lying on the table. "There's teetotalism," she said.

The children who attended the school also began behaving better. A young thief returned to school after his jail term and vowed to lead a better life. Two others were saved from prison thanks to their teachers, who begged magistrates to give them a second chance. But one boy who fought to support a drunken mother was found by teachers lying sick on the bare floor of his home after all the furniture had been sold. The teachers provided him with a straw bed and then sent him to the workhouse hospital until he was fit enough to return to school.

The scholars soon outgrew their dingy schoolroom and the teachers campaigned for funds for a new building, which was erected in Charter Street in 1866. The new Charter Street Ragged School had three storeys and was one of the largest buildings in Angel Meadow. Infants had the lower floor, juniors occupied the middle and parents and senior children the upper floor. The building had room for 600 scholars, but every Sunday in winter an average of 2,000 men, women, and children passed through the doors.

The teachers also set up a hostel for working girls, where they could rent a bedroom for a small fee, and a nursery for infants of working mothers. The aim was to keep young girls from falling into prostitution in the lodging houses and to stop those with young children from leaving them uncared for while they went to work. The inhabitants of the home had use of a laundry and a large sitting room overlooking the Old Burying Ground. The home was opened on a warm July day by the Duchess of Sutherland – Angel Meadow's first Royal visitor.

Inspectors from the children's refuge in Strangeways also helped hundreds of children from Angel Meadow by providing them with food, shelter and a way of making a living by selling newspapers or shining shoes. They found a five-year-old orphan named Lucy living on a pile of sawdust below the stairs in a lodging house occupied by 480 men. She had been left there six weeks earlier by her father, who had never returned, and had been surviving on scraps of food thrown to her by the men. One inspector said:

> As I stood in the lodging house, two men came in. One of them held a couple of haddocks in his hand and, cutting the raw heads off with his pocket knife, he threw them to Lucy, who seized them like a little wolf, and ran under the stairs to eat them. The pale face, hungry and pinched, has only one story to tell, and unless she is rescued at once, death will snatch her away.

A few hours later, Lucy was crying in the bath at the refuge. The rags that covered her body had been eating into sores and the dirt was so ingrained in her skin that she screamed in pain as a nursemaid scrubbed her clean. A few days later, the inspector reported that she was 'quite merry'.

The refuge set up its own shoeblack brigade at Victoria Station. The work instilled discipline and allowed the boys, who wore red tunics, to remain in their natural habitat of the streets. Some of these boys found their way into the army and fought in the Boer War, at battles including the Modder River, Kroonstad and Magersfontein. Others were sent to the refuge's training ships, the *Indefatigable* and the *Warspite*, to prepare for a career in the Royal Navy.

Refuge inspectors sent the worst cases to work on farms in Canada. One 'wild' girl of 15 who was brought up in the Meadow's lodging houses was said to be 'on the verge of ruin'. The inspectors hatched a plan to separate her from her mother and send her to Ontario – a move that would be considered kidnap today. One boy wrote back from Canada saying he had managed to buy his own 40-acre farm – a larger plot of land than Angel Meadow's 30 squalid acres. He told the refuge staff: 'I have a team of horses and three cows, and I will have my first crop this summer. I often think if you've forgotten the time I blew my shoeblack box to pieces with a fire-cracker. I remember it as if it was today. I'm above shoe-blacking now, thank God.'

Inspectors claimed to have overseen a huge fall in the number of boys arrested for juvenile delinquency from 1,063 in 1870 to 602 in 1879 – the lowest figure on record. But the Charter Street Ragged School was facing a decline in attendances because of the rising scuttling epidemic and the teachers worried they were not doing enough. Their annual report noted: 'We find vice and crime surrounding us on every hand. Misery, want, wretchedness and destitution are found in our streets in fearful abundance and we almost despair.'

They stepped up their game and by 1881 had succeeded in closing 20 beer houses in the slum. They also built a gym to try to divert young boys away from scuttling and it soon had 100 members. Inspectors from the children's refuge bought the Victory pub in Angel Street in 1881 and turned it into a coffee house and hostel, known as the Boys' Rest. At one end of the building the words 'To seek and to save that which is lost' were inscribed in large copperplate letters.

By 1887, the hostel's beds had been occupied an estimated 27,800 times and the boys had eaten 50,000 meals. A lad who found himself homeless in Angel Meadow could find a clean bed, a bath and a warm meal at the Rest for a few coppers. 'He will thus be saved,' one observer noted, 'from herding with the depraved of both sexes in the common lodging houses.'

Attendance picked up again at Charter Street and by 1887 the school was teaching more than 1,000 scholars, handing out 3,300 meals and clothing 300 children and adults. In one year they also found jobs for 20 former pupils. Charter Street was rebuilt and extended in 1892 at a cost of £7,500, with more accommodation added for working girls. In 1895, some cottages were bought to complete the extension. Thomas Johnson was appointed the new superintendent.

Johnson found a novel way of improving the health of the slum's children – by taking them to the seaside. On 12 August 1893, teachers visited the homes of excited children handing out train tickets. Johnson later remembered: 'On the morning of the trip, every street, court and alley had its representatives, some barefooted and scantily clad. One could see their parents had done their

best to turn them out as well as possible. All were clean and happiness seemed
to be depicted upon every countenance.'

The children cheered and waved handkerchiefs as they rode at speed
through open country on the way to the coast, out-pacing another train
travelling in the same direction. At Lytham they marched on to the beach
and had breakfast and spent the morning riding donkeys and bathing. In
the afternoon they held races, where the boys won shirts, mufflers and
scarves, and the girls won underclothes and pinafores. Johnson wrote: 'It
was a great pleasure to see these little ones of the slums and poor homes of
Angel Meadow for the first time in their life gazing upon God's beautiful
sea.' Over the coming years, Johnson took nearly 25,000 slum children to
Lytham.

During the foul winter of 1901, the school provided more than 66,000
breakfasts and suppers to children and their parents. Around 4,000 people
were passing through the school each week – the newcomers in a 'deplorable'
state, with flimsy clothing and broken shoes. More than 1,400 boys and girls
had breakfast at the school on Christmas morning and were given presents of
dolls, toys and clogs.

By then, the teachers were able to walk safely through the streets. The report
of the nearby Sharp Street Ragged School said:

> It must be no slight satisfaction to James Rutter and his colleagues, the
> founders, to witness the change that has taken place. In those days it
> was scarcely safe to walk along the streets leading to the school without
> protection. At the present time any male or female teacher may proceed
> alone, night or day, without the slightest fear of molestation, and with
> the certainty of being treated with silent respect by any inhabitants of
> the neighbourhood they may happen to meet.

Perhaps the crowning example of the rescuers' work was a 'bull-headed youth
with a short neck, grotesque attire and defiant look', who was taken to the
Strangeways refuge by a missionary. It was a cold day in early spring and a
cheerful fire gave a comfortable glow to the room. His hard look disappeared
and he seemed to relax as the inspectors jotted down his name. The boy had
worked in a mill and ended up in Charter Street when the machines fell silent
during a strike. He had no money for a lodging house bed and slipped down
an alleyway into a yard, where the lodging house deputy found him curled up
asleep. She sent him off, threatening to have him arrested.

The boy was at the refuge for only a few hours when he got into a fight with
another lad. He ended up being sent to the *Warspite* for naval training and-

became 'every inch' a sailor – eventually rising to the rank of petty officer. One day sailing home from Turkey with a broken arm, he leaped overboard and rescued a drowning shipmate. He won a bronze medal and a certificate from the Royal Humane Society for his bravery.

The boy later told a refuge inspector in a letter: 'I only did my duty sir, but I am right proud of this 'ere medal. I shall want that certificate, Sir, for I have a place to hang it, now I've got a home of my own.'

Chapter 23

Forlorn Hope

The thousands of souls who called Angel Meadow home were still fighting a daily struggle for survival when the Victorian age came to an abrupt end in 1901. The death of Queen Victoria drew a curtain on an era that had seen Manchester become the powerhouse of the Industrial Revolution. But even as the Queen's state funeral was taking place at St George's Chapel in Windsor, families were continuing to live in horrifying conditions in Angel Meadow. The area had missed out on the city's growth in prosperity and remained Britain's most savage slum.

A journalist from the *Manchester Guardian*, who entered Angel Meadow that same year, wrote: 'At present, life in Angel Meadow is dark beyond words and in the near background even the casual visitor soon learns that there is yet a deeper gloom.'

One story above all illustrated the enduring horrors of the slum. On a Sunday afternoon in September 1900, James McKenna, 52, walked calmly out of Kane's lodging house and headed down the hill of Angel Street to a barber shop owned by Burdett Hackett on the corner of Ashley Lane and Long Millgate. McKenna picked up Hackett's razor and drew the blade across his own throat – slashing it open in front of shocked customers.

McKenna spent a week recovering in the infirmary, before he was hauled before magistrates and charged with attempting suicide. McKenna, an unemployed tailor, said he was 'low spirited' because he had been out of work in the slum for several months. Magistrates offered him the only assistance they could: they remanded him in the workhouse for two weeks.

The Reverend John Mercer, the rector of St Michael's Church, told the city's leaders in a speech at the turn of the century that living conditions in Angel Meadow were growing increasingly desperate: "A journey of exploration reveals many strange sights and sounds and smells – long lines of dreary streets, branching off into mazes of narrow, sunless courts and alleys, and a depressing air of poverty, neglect, and dilapidation pervading all." One house the Reverend entered during a pastoral visit was a typical 'crusted specimen of dilapidation'. It was infested with rats that scurried up from the sewers and carried away food left beside a sick woman who was too weak to fend them off.

He called for 'guerrilla warfare' against the insanitary conditions. "Something should be done and done quickly," he warned.

One of Angel Meadow's oldest buildings, Arkwright's Mill, had been destroyed by fire in 1854 and rebuilt in 1888. The mill's old reservoir had been filled with earth and sealed over, and the building – known to slum dwellers as the Old Factory – was eventually sold in 1892 to Laben Baxendale, who owned an ironmongery and steelworks on Miller Street.

Angel Meadow and neighbouring Red Bank were now home to factories and foundries making paper, gas-engines, umbrellas, hats, shoes and waterproofs, and the smell was appalling. The gasworks continued to add its sour taint to the damp atmosphere and, on a hot summer day, the stench from the once-dusky River Irk was said to be 'almost unbearable'.

A huge tobacco factory now also loomed large over the slum's skyline, lending a sickly sweetness to the toxic air. The factory was built by the Co-operative Wholesale Society on Ludgate Hill in 1898 and produced cigarettes and cigars from leaves imported from Borneo, Sumatra, Turkey, Brazil and Cuba. The tobacco had exotic names: Bogie, Nailrod, Pigtail and Shag. Eight people operating machines could produce 3,500 packets of cigarettes an hour, but the most prized workers were the cigar makers, whose nimble fingers could wrap and roll tobacco leaves with the dexterity of classical pianists. The CWS offered no jobs to the slum dwellers, only selecting workers from better parts of the city.

The editor of the CWS magazine, the *Wheatsheaf*, reported to members in 1902: 'The tobacco factory is in it – but not of it. The workers come from other and better class districts.' He added: 'When you go there, you see the women on the doorsteps – unclean, unkempt and undressed. You can study some of the problems of poverty, for this is one of the worst slums in Manchester. Noted in the past as a centre of ruffianism and crime, and the sanctuary of the worst criminals in England, it is now just a squalid, unclean, drunken slum.'

The area's reputation as a criminal underworld was starting to fade. A police crackdown meant Angel Meadow no longer offered a safe harbour for scuttlers, cracksmen and conmen. Mack, the crook who had acted as a guide for journalists to the slum's thieving dens, had begun to look back wistfully at days when thieves were 'put up as nice as could be' in the lodging houses:

Some went to Patsey Reardon's, but he's dead, and his old woman is doing time for taking 300 watches from the guns. One-armed Kitty and Cabbage Ann are still here, but it's a hot shop now. All the old 'uns are gone away, and everything's changed for the bad. Now we have to go outside, anywhere where we can get a place, for we should get hauled up sharp if we went to old quarters.

A journalist who went looking for the slum's criminals behind the grim stone walls and iron bars of Strangeways found them in the newly-painted prison chapel listening to the Sunday sermon. Scuttlers with close-cropped hair were sitting on benches in grey suits marked with broad arrows, among 'bullet-headed' burglars and wife-beaters with 'villainous scowls'. A man charged with murder sat bolt upright, his eyes fixed on the minister, while another knelt with his head in his hands. Warders watched over them with huge bunches of keys dangling from their thick leather belts – the criminals finally cowed by the police crackdown.

Jerome Caminada had finally caught up with his arch-enemy Bob Horridge after he shot and wounded two police officers during a failed robbery. Caminada disguised himself as a labourer and chased Horridge to Liverpool, where he spotted him crossing a street near the docks. Caminada wrestled Horridge to the ground and rammed a revolver into his mouth – warning him he would pull the trigger if he tried to escape. Horridge was jailed for life for attempted murder and died in prison.

The law also caught up with the scuttler and flame-thrower Henry Burgess, who at 35 had more than 40 convictions to his name. In February 1906, Burgess attacked his woman Mary Ellen Burns with a shovel in a lodging house in Red Bank. She lost an eye and suffered a severe head wound. Burgess spent six months in Strangeways for the crime, but it took another two years before the authorities finally shipped him 300 miles away to Dartmoor, one of the country's toughest and remotest prisons, after he was caught trying to steal a copper roller from a wagon on the railway viaduct.

Angel Meadow had also changed for the better in other ways. The Charter Street Ragged School had been repainted in the best lead paint that money could buy and received important visitors including Queen Mary and Winston Churchill, who had breakfast with 1,000 men and women as they sang: "I have never been in a place like this before."

Manchester Corporation had finally shut down the slum's lethal cellars and they were now home only to rats. Engineers began to demolish some of the worst houses and courts. Even the Old Burying Ground had also been 'improved' and children now played on a hard carpet of black flagstones laid over the bare earth to stop it being used as a venue for fighting. It became known as St Michael's Flags.

The Reverend John Mercer, who had played a key role in paving the burial ground, left Angel Meadow in 1902 to become Bishop of Tasmania, where he became an outspoken social reformer and a keen bushwalker. He told parishioners at St Michael's he was going to a 'most beautiful country – a land of luscious fruit, giant trees and beautiful flowers'. St Michael's, he said, had now become 'practically unknown' in the 'fashionable world'. To him, it was 'a gaunt tower rising from the midst of the squalid streets – a vision when seen hurrying northwards by rail'.

Following his departure, the old church that had watched over the slum since its earliest days, fell into disuse and was left on the verge of destruction. It became known to churchmen across the city as 'Manchester's forlorn hope'. The next rector, John Jowitt Wilson had no need for the keys when he finally arrived. The door had no handle and stood gaping. Inside, he found a cat and her kittens living in the organ. The church's walls were filthy and had gone undecorated for 20 years.

Wilson remained optimistic, even though his Sunday collections barely reached 10 shillings after the men of the parish left for France during the First World War. He built a new vestry, opened the tower room for daily prayers and launched a Sunday school in Irk Street. He wrote in his parish newsletter: 'The church has exercised a quiet influence of late in the neighbourhood, which has been noticeable even to the police.' But he warned that the parish faced a 'tremendous battle with evil' and added: 'We cannot spiritually relax a muscle in this strenuous fight.'

Wilson launched an appeal to raise £1,000 for a new organ, a peace garden and electric lights to replace the ancient gas fittings. He hoped to erect a four-dial clock on the bell tower, which he believed would be 'a great convenience' to the slum's inmates and to passengers travelling on the railway. For five years he went around Smithfield Market carrying an iron bucket making collections and it was mainly due to the market workers that the church stayed open a few more years. But Wilson's efforts to secure the future of St Michael's ultimately came to nothing and he died a worn-out man in 1928. Within four years the church would be demolished.

One morning soon after Wilson's death, a group of men armed with notebooks walked across Manchester and stepped into the Angel Meadow. They were members of the Manchester and Salford Better Housing Council on a mission to survey the slum and decide its fate. As they walked the streets, they noticed the dark shadows beneath the railway viaduct, which had been widened in the 1890s. They saw the dim lights of the Charter Street Ragged School, nine pubs and the rows of lodging houses in Angel Street. Houses had been pulled down in the middle of terraced rows, leaving gaps 'like broken teeth'. They wrote in their report: 'The only playground in the area is that by St Michael's Church, marked in green on maps, but actually paved with blackened flags. No blade of grass exists in the whole area.'

The streets off Rochdale Road were overshadowed by factories and warehouses. The investigators found 580 families living in 400 homes in Angel Meadow and Red Bank – the oldest dating back to 1643. One woman told them the old houses looked like 'withered trees'. The inspectors wrote: 'The whole area is unfit for habitation in its present condition, and provides a glaring example of the evils of a mixed industrial and residential district.'

Only four out of 400 houses in the area had baths. Two baths were in converted pubs and a third stood in the middle of a living room. Although the earth closets had been replaced with water closets and the ash-pits by dustbins, one in five houses had no washboiler and hardly any had sinks. Tenants told the investigators they could get no repairs done. Their walls were damp, the plaster was falling away from the ceilings and their doors were so warped they no longer closed. Rats and black beetles scurried about in the darkness, but some tenants were afraid to complain to their landlords in case they were evicted. The worst case of overcrowding the inspectors saw was a family of nine living in a single room.

One house was infested with beetles and the windows were jammed shut. In another the kitchen floor was sinking and the windows would not close, while a third contained an uninhabitable room with gaping holes in the ceiling and floor. Another house had so many bugs upstairs and rats downstairs that the woman and child living there were frightened to be left alone.

One family lived on the upper floor of an old warehouse, where the wind and rain blew in through a door once used for lowering sacks of grain. The couple's baby had pneumonia. Families living nearby in a converted pub shared just one toilet and a sink in a passageway. One woman, who had scrawled the word 'stolen' on her bed sheet to stop it from being stolen, said her family refused to visit her in Angel Meadow.

The investigators concluded: 'There can be few more depressing experiences than spending an afternoon wandering about these dismal houses with their dark passages and squalid rooms, except to live in them. No wonder that some find getting drunk to be the shortest way out of Manchester.'

But the most shocking discovery of all was that two in five people – 207 out of 519 families – told the investigators that they wanted to stay in Angel Meadow. Many of them were traders who needed to be near Smithfield Market.

The investigators made a 'special recommendation' that Angel Meadow be demolished under the 1930 Slum Clearance Act. Members of Manchester Corporation's Public Health Committee later toured Angel Meadow and declared that every remaining house was unfit for habitation and dangerous to public health. More than 1,260 people were to be rehoused.

On 20 April, 1932, just months after their report was published, a plot of land off Style Street went for sale at auction. It contained 625 yards of 'prime building land' and a tumbledown building, St Michael's Church. The congregation had held their final service on Whit Sunday, 1930. The few remaining parishioners stood outside for a long time afterwards and then shook hands and went their separate ways. The auction catalogue specified one condition: that the new owners demolish the church and fence off the site to keep out troublemakers. The church's 'fine bell', forged in 1848, was excluded from the sale.

The bidding went poorly. When it reached only £400, the auctioneers announced that they were withdrawing the sale. St Michael's stood empty and abandoned until 1935, when demolition men finally began tearing it to the ground. Newspapers printed a picture of a lone workman standing in the nave, surrounded by a pile of broken timber and rubble.

Three nights before Christmas 1940, the Nazi bombers came to complete the job. Manchester's air raid sirens began their blood–curdling scream just after 7pm on 22 December. Radar stations along the coast had already detected the shadow of hundreds of Luftwaffe aircraft swarming inland. Soon the heavy drone of the the bombers could be heard in the distance, growing ever nearer until the 'crump' of the first bombs and the bursts of anti–aircraft guns lit up the night sky. More planes came in waves, dropping hundreds of tons of high explosives, firebombs and landmines on the city.

Flames towered above Angel Meadow in the darkness. Bombs crashed into the old merchants' houses in New Mount Street and blasted holes in the former thieving dens along the length of Angel Street. Arkwright's Mill became an inferno during two nights of bombing that killed more than 680 people across the city. After 150 years of suffering, it took just a few minutes to turn Angel Meadow, Victorian Britain's most savage slum, into a burning hell fire.

Epilogue: Ghosts

On a bright, hot day in August, 2011, a young man wearing a black sweater and grey jogging bottoms was hauled into the glass dock at Manchester Magistrates' Court by two security guards. He was one of the 110 people arrested during some of the worst rioting ever seen in Britain. Manchester, London and other cities had erupted in spontaneous riots that summer as police battled to regain control of the streets. Thousands of rioters, including some as young as nine and ten, had thrown firebombs at shop windows as looters made off with designer clothes, electrical goods, alcohol and mobile phones.

The youth in the dock put his forehead to the glass and scanned the room for his parents and then sat down heavily when he saw they were not in the room. They had failed to make the journey to court from their housing estate on the edge of the city. All the boy could see at the back of the court was a crowd of journalists.

The reporters had flown in like moths when the fires started and now hoped to get a glimpse of one of the rioters who had been tearing up the Manchester's streets. They included correspondents from Paris and Frankfurt – a rare sight in a court whose petty cases would usually fail to make even a sentence in their titles.

A reporter from French newspaper *Le Monde* whispered a question into the ear of one of the local journalists as the boy's address was read out by the clerk: "Is that a poor area?" When her report hit the streets of Paris the next next day, it gave readers a vivid account of the boy's 'pale complexion' and 'big droopy eyes'.

Manchester, it seems, still at times holds the power to shock and fascinate international observers in the same way it enticed social reformers such as Friedrich Engels and Alexis de Tocqueville more than 150 years ago. But Manchester has changed beyond all recognition since it was the 'shock city' of the nineteenth century. Angel Meadow, Victorian Britain's most savage slum, is no more.

In the decades after the Blitz, some families continued to scrape a living in the Meadow until clearances in the 1960s swept away the remaining houses and pushed them out to council estates beyond the city centre. Only a few battered warehouses remained as streets once throbbing with life became a silent and empty backwater. The back-to-back houses were flattened into car parks and only their cellars remained, sealed shut beneath the ground like tombs and forgotten until archaeologists finally peeled open their concrete lids in a search for clues about the past.

Today, however, Angel Meadow is quietly becoming a sought-after area for the second time in its history. The old tobacco factory has been turned into luxury flats and the Old Burying Ground – still hiding thousands of bodies – has become an award-winning park. The area's two remaining pubs, the Angel and the Marble Arch, now sell fine food and real ale.

In the heart of the old slum, the Co-operative's towering headquarters of metal and glass now dominates the skyline, while a new ring road, the first change in the road layout since the early 1800s, carries cars at speed along Angel Street. The railway viaduct now takes office workers home to the suburbs in sleek, yellow trams.

But if you sit for long enough on a bench in the Old Burying Ground on a winter's afternoon and peer across at the black upper windows of the Charter Street Ragged School, something happens. The ghosts of the past start tugging at your sleeve – begging you to listen to their story.

Glossary of Angel Meadow Slang

Ale and portering: Supplementing work by thieving.

Bags: Trousers.

Barrow run: Fined £5 at court.

Begging ken: Lodging house frequented by beggars.

Bells: Flared trousers worn by scuttlers.

Bereavement lurker: Conman pretending to be a widower.

Big Fulley: The assize court.

Black Maria: Prison van.

Blind Pad: Beggar pretending to be blind.

Bloaters: Sausages.

Bloodhouse: Beer house used by a scuttling gang as their headquarters.

Blues: The police.

Breach-buzzing: Pickpocketing.

Boozing ken: Beer house.

Bushell and peck: Neck.

Charles Brady: A hat.

Charley Prescott: A waistcoat.

Caser: Five shillings.

Chivy: To knife.

Clem: To stab.

Cornerman: Thief who hangs around street corners.

Country flats: Country folk new to the city and unaccustomed to its ways.

Cracksmen: Burglars.

Crib: A house or a bed.

Cripple dodge: Beggar pretending to be disabled.

Crocus: A quack doctor.

Cross crib: A den of thieves.

Crossmen: Thieves.

Deaner: A shilling.

Daisy roots: Boots.

Darbles: Handcuffs.

Dhudeen: A clay pipe with a short stump, from the Irish dúidin.

Dimmick: A forged coin.

Doing the boat: Transported to Australia.

Doing a half-stretch: Six months in prison.

Doing a drag: Three months in prison.

Doing stir: Serving a prison sentence.

Dossy: A woman.

Downright: A beggar.

Drawing the badger: Badger baiting.

Dry land shark: Conman posing as a sailor selling 'smuggled' goods.

Dukes: Fists.

Dutch doll: A woman.

Eye me float: A coat.

Fawneys: Rings.

Feather: A night's lodgings, as in a feather pillow.

Fencing: Receiving or handling stolen goods.

Fit dodge: Conman pretending to have a fit in the street.

Flemsy: A £5 note.

Fly: A successful thief, never caught.

Fountain: A kettle.

German: A foreigner of any nationality.

Glim: A candle.

Gravel-rash: A graze caused by being dragged on the floor in a fight.

Guns: Pickpockets.

Highland frisky: Whisky.

Hooks: Pickpockets.

Irish: To steal.

Jaw: To punch a man in the face.

Jacketing: Stripping a robbery victim of his coat.

Jenny: A watch.

Jimmy Skinner: Dinner.

Jugg: Prison.

Ken: A house.

Kettles: Watches.

Legs: Low thieves.

Land Navy: Beggars posing as sailors.

Linen lifter: A thief who steals washing from clothes lines.

Little Fulley: The sessions court.

Long-tailed: A £10 note or higher.

Lurk: A begging con.

Lurker: A conman.

Lushed: Drunk.

Maks: Liquor.

Man and Wife: A knife.

Masher: A well-dressed person.

Megsmen: Swindlers dressing in fine clothes to trick victims.

Mill: To fight.

Moucher: A conman.

Mullicrush: To fight.

Mugger up: A cheat.

Narrow-go-wides: Flared trousers worn by scuttlers.

Nine moon: Nine months in prison.

Nogue: To punish.

Nose warmer: The stub of a clay pipe smoked like a cigarette.

On a ticket: Freed early from prison under police supervision.

On the cross: Thieves at work.

Packing: Food.

Padding Ken: Lodging house frequented by tramps.

Peach: A police informant.

Pecking: Eating.

Peepers: Eyes.

Peg it: To run.

Phizog: Face.

Pitch the crack: To leave off begging after being spotted by the police.

Prig: A thief.

Pro: A boxer.

Public: A pub.

Puller up: Conman who stops victims in the street.

Purr: To kick.

Purring: Soliciting by prostitutes.

Round my houses: Trousers.

Scratching: Whipped with a cat-o-nine-tails.

Screeve: A chalk artist who draws pictures on the pavement as a way of begging.

Screwed: Garrotted.

Scuttle: A gang fight, a short run.

Scuttler: A street fighter.

Shake-down: A rough bed made up on the floor in a lodging house.

Shallow cove: A member of the 'land navy'.

Shanks pony: To walk.

Sham sailor: Conman posing as a wounded seaman.

Sharp: A cheat

Shipwrecked sailor: Conman posing as a sailor.

Slop: A policeman.

Smashed: Arrested.

Smugged: Arrested.

Snaps: Handcuffs.

Snide: A forged coin.

Snout: Tobacco.

Snowdropper: A thief who steals washing from clothes lines.

Stand pad: Conman who stands in silence and does not speak to the victim.

Stiff: A letter.

Sundial: A photograph.

Swell: A gentleman, a potential crime victim.

Swell ken: A gentleman's house.

Thirty blow: Thirty shillings.

Tickle sleeper: A light sleeper in a lodging house, not easily robbed.

Tommy Roller: A shirt collar.

Toke: Bread.

Twirls: Housebreaking tools.

Whacker: A friend.

Bibliography

Aikin, John: *A Description of the Country from Thirty to Forty Miles Round Manchester* (John Stockdale, 1793).

Alsop, Alfred: *Ten Years in the Slums* (John Heywood, 1879).

Aston, Joseph: *A Picture of Manchester* (W P Aston, 1816).

Bamford, Samuel: *Passages in the Life of a Radical* (Simpkin, Marshall and Co, 1844).

Banks, Isabella: *The Manchester Man* (Hurst and Blackett, 1876).

Bertenshaw, Mary: *Sunrise to Sunset: An Autobiography* (Printwise Publications, 1994).

Buckley, Angela: *The Real Sherlock Holmes: The Hidden Story of Jerome Caminada* (Pen and Sword, 2014).

Bush, Michael: *The Casualties of Peterloo* (Carnegie Publishing, 2005).

Busteed, Mervyn and Hodgson, Rob: *Angel Meadow, Irish Migration and Settlement in Early-Nineteenth Century Manchester* (Irish Geography, 1994).

Caminada, Jerome: *Twenty-Five Years of Detective Life, Volume I* (John Heywood, 1895).

Caminada, Jerome: *Twenty-Five Years of Detective Life, Volume II* (John Heywood, 1901).

Davies, Andrew: *Gangs of Manchester: The Story of the Scuttlers* (Milo, 2009).

Dickens, Charles: *Hard Times* (Bradbury and Evans, 1854).

Engels, Friedrich: *The Condition of the Working Class in England in 1844* (George, Allen and Unwin, 1892).

Gadsby, J: *A Memoir of the Late William Gadsby* (Groombridge, 1844).

Gaskell, Elizabeth: *Mary Barton* (Chapman and Hall, 1848).

Gaskell, Peter: *The Moral and Physical Condition of the Manufacturing Population* (John Parker, 1836).

Gaulter, Henry: *The Origin and Progress of Malignant Cholera in Manchester* (Longman and Rees, 1833).

Hamer, Edna: *Elizabeth Prout: A Religious Life for Industrial England* (Gracewing, 2011).

Hayton, Sandra: 'The Archetypal Irish Cellar Dweller', *Manchester Regional History Review*, Volume 12, (1998).

Hopkins, Billy: *Tommy's World* (Headline, 2009).

Jones, William Kenneth: *Different Times: A View of life in Inner City Manchester During the First Three Decades of the 20th Century* (Bright Pen, 2006).

Love, Benjamin: *Manchester As It Is* (Love and Barton, 1849).

Lynch, Malcolm: *The Kid from Angel Meadow* (Constable and Co, 1989).

Marr, T: *Housing Conditions in Manchester and Salford* (Sherratt and Hughes, 1904).

Marsden, John: *Forgotten Fields: Looking for Manchester's Old Burial Grounds* (Crown Quarto, 2014).

Mercer, Rev J E: *The Conditions of Life in Angel Meadow* (Manchester Statistical Society, 1897).

Ogden, James: *A Description of Manchester by a Native of the Town in 1783* (John Heywood, 1860).

O'Neill, Joseph: *Crime City: Manchester's Victorian Underworld* (Milo, 2008).

O'Neill, Joseph: *The Manchester Martyrs* (Mercier Press, 2012).

O'Neill, Joseph: *The Secret World of the Victorian Lodging House* (Pen & Sword, 2014).

Phillips Kay-Shuttleworth, Sir James: *The Moral and Physical Condition of the Working Classes Employed in the Cotton Manufacture in Manchester* (James Ridgeway, 1832).

Potts, Bob: *The Old Pubs of Rochdale Road and District* (Neil Richardson, 1985).

Philip, Eric: *Angel Meadow and Red Bank* (Manchester and Salford Better Housing Council, 1931).

Reach, Angus Bethune; Aspin, Chris, editor: *A Cotton Fibre Halo: Manchester and the Textile Districts in 1849* (Royds Press, 2007).

Redfern, Benjamin: 'A Journey from Withy Grove to New Town' (*Odds and Ends Magazine*, 1867).

Renshaw, G: *Criminal Manchester* (Reprinted from the *Manchester Evening News*, 1874).

Roberts, Jacqueline: *Working Class Housing in 19th Century Manchester* (Neil Richardson, 1983).

Shaw, William: *Manchester Old and New* (Cassell and Company, 1894).

Slugg, J T: *Reminiscences of Manchester Fifty Years Ago* (Simpkin, Marshall and Co, 1881).

Stanhope-Brown, James: *Angels from the Meadow* (Christine Pothecary, 1991).

Swindells, T: *Manchester Streets and Manchester Men* (J.E. Cornish, 1908).

Waugh, Edwin: *Sketches of Lancashire Life* (Whittaker and Co, 1855).

Research Notes

Historians in Manchester are blessed with a wealth of archives and I have made good use of them while researching this book. Manchester Archives and Local Studies houses a large collection of material on Angel Meadow, including the records of St Michael's Church, the Old Burying Ground and the Charter Street Ragged School.

Grim details of living conditions in the Victorian slum can also be found in reports of the Manchester and Salford Sanitary Association, the Manchester Corporation letter books, the records of the Manchester Watch Committee and the minutes of Victorian Manchester's brilliantly-named Nuisance Committee.

Benjamin Redfern's fascinating article about Angel Meadow in *Odds and Ends* magazine and the Reverend John Mercer's speech about living conditions in the slum can also be found in the archives at Central Library. The archives hold the Manchester prison records, which are available on-line, via Findmypast.co.uk. They provide intriguing descriptions of Angel Meadow criminals, including their scars, missing teeth and tattoos. Central Library is also home to the Together Trust's archive, which documents the work of the children's refuge in Strangeways and includes vivid details of visits to Angel Meadow by refuge workers and churchmen as they sought to help families in the slum.

The excellent Working Class Movement Library in Salford is a welcoming and useful resource for researching Friedrich Engels and Victorian living and working conditions. It holds a copy of the Manchester and Salford Better Housing Council Survey of Angel Meadow from 1931, which explains why the slum had to be pulled down. The Greater Manchester Police Museum, housed in a former Victorian police station in Newton Street, is home to an astonishing collection of original photo books depicting Manchester's most notorious Victorian criminals and other useful documents detailing Victorian police work.

The National Co-operative Archive, in Hanover Street, also has some interesting records, including the *Wheatsheaf* magazine, which contains descriptions of the CWS Tobacco Factory and the Co-operative Printing Society in Angel Meadow. Chetham's Library, in Long Millgate, and the

Salford Diocesan Archives, in Grosvenor Square, Chorlton-on-Medlock, are home to collections of rare manuscripts and documents which also offer useful insights into life in the slum.

During my research, I have also made use of old newspapers in the British Newspaper Archive – a goldmine of information for researchers and family historians. The on-line archive gives a chilling insight into crimes committed in the slum, plus interesting details about living conditions and even weather reports. The *Guardian* newspaper also has a useful on-line archive. Two of the very best descriptions of Angel Meadow were made by Victorian journalists from the *Manchester Evening News* and the *Manchester Guardian*, who risked all to bring the slum to the world's attention.

Acknowledgements

This book could not have been written without the help of a large number of people. I would especially like to thank the staff at Manchester Archives and Local Studies, who patiently helped me search for records – even to the extent of retrieving them from salt mines in Cheshire, while Manchester Central Library was being refurbished. Jane Parr was a great help in sourcing images for the book.

I would also like to thank Duncan Broady at the Greater Manchester Police Museum, one of my favourite archives. The staff at Chetham's Library, the National Co-operative Archive and the Working Class Movement Library were a huge help, as were Father David Lannon and Lawrence Gregory at the Salford Diocesan Archives, who tracked down some unusual records.

Liz Sykes at the Together Trust kindly allowed me to view the charity's archives. I would also like to thank Howard Walker for allowing me to use some of his photographs in publicising the book.

Ruth Hood and David Donnelly helped me to step back in time with a tour of the Charter Street Ragged School. I am grateful to Peter Hill, who gave me a tour of the Rochdale Road Baptist Chapel. I would also like to thank Ian Miller and Chris Wild from Oxford Archaeology North for allowing me to visit their archaeological digs in Charter Street. Their discovery of my ancestor's home inspired this book.

I am also indebted to the people who sent me information about Angel Meadow, including Geoff Thwaite, who sent me a copy of his research into Arkwright's Mill. Geoffrey Ireland informed me about his wife's ancestor Frederick Wilde and Catherine Wain told me the story of her ancestor Henry Bailey. I am grateful to James Stanhope-Brown for his advice early in the project and to Angela Buckley for her unstinting advice and support. I would also like to thank David Coogan, who first told me the story of the cholera riot around 20 years ago.

Jen Newby, formerly of Pen and Sword, saw something in my original idea and helped me turn my dream of writing a book into a reality, and also gave good counsel while editing the book. I would also like to thank Eloise Hansen at Pen and Sword for her advice and support.

My dad, John, and my father-in-law, Graham, both read drafts of the book and made helpful suggestions.

Most of all, I would like to thank my late mum, Sue, and my dad, John, for bringing me up right and teaching me the importance of family. My dad's stories about growing up in Manchester have given me a great passion for my home city and its history. My biggest thanks go to my wife, Lindsay, and my son, Thomas, who have put up with me during many months of writing and research and have kept me going to the final chapter. This book is dedicated to them.

Index